A HIGHLANDER OF THE NINETY-THIRD.

By H.R.H. Princess Louise, Duchess of Argyll.

THE MUSTER-ROLL OF ANGUS.

SOUTH AFRICAN WAR
1899-1900.

𝔄 𝔑ecord and a 𝔗ribute.

PUBLISHED UNDER THE DIRECTION OF AGNES LINDSAY-CARNEGIE AND
JANE C. C. MACDONALD.

EDITED BY J. B. SALMOND.

The Naval & Military Press Ltd

Published by

The Naval & Military Press Ltd
Unit 10 Ridgewood Industrial Park,
Uckfield, East Sussex,
TN22 5QE England

Tel: +44 (0) 1825 749494
Fax: +44 (0) 1825 765701

www.naval-military-press.com
www.nmarchive.com

In reprinting in facsimile from the original, any imperfections are inevitably reproduced and the quality may fall short of modern type and cartographic standards.

DEDICATION.

Angus to Her Soldier Sons.

To you, my gallant Sons, who have served your Queen and Country in South Africa, in pride and love I dedicate this volume. More precious than the spoils of war, devoted to the service of the Lord when kings went forth to battle long ago, are the offerings of flesh and blood which I have given in you, my valiant children. Lamenting that the cause of liberty and justice must thus be fought in your blood, I yet am proud that when the trumpet-call of Duty sounded, you answered with eagerness and joy. Yours it was not to ask the reason of the fray, but just to play the soldier's part, to do or die.

I am watching at the window with throbbing heart, and crying through the lattice—"Why are the chariots so long in coming? Why tarry the wheels of the chariots?" But, considering how honour doth become you, and pleased that you seek danger where you are like to find fame, I say with Volumnia to every Virgilia who weeps at her sewing—"Had I a dozen sons, each in my love alike and none less dear than thine and my good Marcius, I had rather had eleven die nobly for their country than one voluptuously surfeit out of action."

If your heads may be covered by loving, watchful spirits coming from afar to brood and hover over them, there is none without his helmet in the battle hour. But shelter you do not ask who know that

> "Cowards die many times before their death;
> The valiant never taste of death but once."

I commend you to the care and keeping of Him who, marching to victory by paths which are wet with the blood of millions of His creatures, is yet quick to mark the sparrow's fall.

This Muster-Roll I lay at your feet; but when its letters are illegible and the occasion which gave it birth has been forgotten, your names will still be found upon that other and immortal Muster-Roll of noble hearts who have bled beneath the standard with motto, "Dulce et decorum est pro patria mori."

PREFACE.

"THE MUSTER-ROLL OF ANGUS" is the realization of a patriotic idea which first discovered itself in the minds of Mrs Lindsay-Carnegie of Spynie and Boysack, and Miss Jane C. C. Macdonald, Windmill House, Arbroath. Once discovered, the idea soon developed into a scheme for the publication of a volume in which might be preserved the names and portraits of Men of Angus who had fought in the South African War, or rendered other service at the Front during the conflict. The scheme was not inspired by any provincial egotism; the Promoters had no thought that the services of Men of Angus in the British Forces were more worthy of commemoration than those rendered by men of the Lothians or the Border. They desired simply to do for their own shire-family what they hoped would be done in other counties and communities throughout the United Kingdom and the Colonies—each following its own plan in honouring its valiant sons.

The community of Angus greeted "The Muster-Roll" proposal with unanimity and enthusiasm. Amongst all classes the effort to record the names and commemorate the services of those who, in Angus's name, had answered the call for men to fight for Queen and country, had the heartiest approval. Sons and daughters of Angus, both at home and abroad, and many relatives and other friends along with them, were prompt, whole-hearted, and practical in their benediction; Angus became quick with the sense of kinship and approbation of her children's valour. With what intrepidity her sons have proved themselves worthy of commemoration many an honorable wound, and many a lonely grave, upon which, with silent eyes, the Southern stars look down, may tell. However imperfectly "The Muster-Roll" may fulfil its purpose, Angus has good reason to be proud of the memories the volume is intended to enshrine.

To sons and daughters of Angus upon whom has been bestowed the gift of expression in literature, music, or the graphic arts, of the patriotic feelings which have filled all British hearts concerning our soldiers during the progress of the war, an appeal was made for contributions to the volume. These, it was hoped, would be taken as giving expression to Augus's tribute to the brave sons whom she had given to aid the Empire in its hour of danger. The volume shows how cordial was the response to this appeal.

PREFACE—Continued.

The thanks of the Promoters are, in the first place, due to H.R.H. Princess Louise, Duchess of Argyll, for graciously contributing the portrait of a Highlander of the old 93rd Regiment—now Princess Louise's Argyll and Sutherland Highlanders.

To Angus writers, artists, and composers—(their names will be found recorded elsewhere in the volume)—sincere thanks are due. Their generous enthusiasm so filled the sails of the Promoters' enterprise that from the hour of leaving port a safe and happy voyage-end was assured.

Mr Henry T. Wyse, art master, Arbroath High School, supervised, with characteristic care and good taste, the decorative work in the portrait pages of the volume. The cover of the volume was designed by Mr Wyse, and, with one exception, the decorative designs and borders are Mr Wyse's own or his pupils' work. Misses J. K. Chapel (pp 96 and 146), Helen Chapel (pp 151 and 154), J. A. Bisset (p 142), Marguerite R. Bennet (p 152), Ida Leslie (p 153); Messrs P. K. Hanton (p 141), Charles Fowler (p 149), Albert Bisset (p 150), Roy Leslie (p 155), and Charles Paterson (p 158)—all pupils of Mr Wyse—and Miss C. E. Dickson (p 144) contributed decorative borders. The Promoters desire to have recorded here their thanks to all these artists, and also their great indebtedness to Mr Wyse for service at once distinguished in its artistic excellence, and most generous in its extent, patience, and kindliness.

To the Dowager-Countess of Airlie for liberty to reproduce a crayon sketch of her son, Captain the Hon. Lyulph Ogilvy; to the Earl of Southesk who generously permitted and bore the expense of the reproduction of Jameson's portrait of the Marquis of Montrose; to the Countess of Strathmore who graciously provided a photograph of the fine portrait of Claverhouse in Glamis Castle; and to Mr Low, Montrose, for an excellent water-colour drawing of the Colours of the Angus Fencibles, thanks are also due.

The collection of the portraits and information regarding Angus soldiers included in "The Muster-Roll" would have been impossible without the aid of friends. Colonel William Smith, V.D., J.P., Dundee, with characteristic tact and generosity, looked after Dundee and district. He took great pains to make the Dundee list as complete as possible; and he gathered names of soldiers and subscribers with zeal which made him an invaluable "recruiting officer." To him and to his daughter, Miss Smith, Secretary of the Dundee Branch of the Soldiers' and Sailors' Families Association, "The Muster-Roll" is greatly indebted. Mr Geo. S. Nicolson, of the *Forfar Herald;* Mr James Balfour, of the *Montrose Standard;* Mr D. S. Edwards, of the *Brechin Advertiser*, along with his son, Mr David Edwards, and Sergeant-Instructor Brown, Brechin; Rev. Mr Troup, Broughty Ferry; Mrs G. W. Baxter, Ashcliff, Dundee, Mrs Wilkie, Ardmore, Kirriemuir; and Lieutenant D. W. Fairweather, Arbroath—all these friends gave most valuable aid in the ingathering of information and portraits.

PREFACE—Continued.

In nearly every case the portraits of Officers, Non-Commissioned Officers, and Rank and File have been provided by the nearest relatives of the soldiers, with authority for their publication. In all cases where application has been made to photographers, copies of portraits and permission to reproduce them have been generously given. The thanks of the Promoters are specially due to Messrs Valentine, Watt & Son, and Robertson, Dundee; Messrs W. H. Geddes & Son and Mr and Mrs Anckorn, Arbroath; Mr John Carr, Montrose; Mr W. Mayor, Forfar; the London Stereoscopic Company (for portrait of H. H. Prince Christian Victor); Mr C. E. Corke, Sevenoaks, London; and to the proprietors of the *Pall Mall Magazine*, *Black and White*, the *Illustrated London News*, the *Lady's Pictorial*, and the *Piper o' Dundee*. In the case of a large number of soldiers no portrait was obtainable. In justice to the photo-etchers and the printers it may also be mentioned that a great many of the photographs were so decayed and faulty that reproduction of a good portrait from them was an impossibility.

In acknowledging the multitudinous kindnesses which have attended the promotion of the volume, the services of some generous friends may have been overlooked. To all who have in any way assisted, the Promoters desire that their sincere thanks should be communicated.

The liberality of a number of friends interested in "The Muster-Roll" has enabled the Promoters to provide a copy for the home of every Angus soldier mentioned in the volume. This is a result of their labours which has brought to the Promoters exceeding pleasure. Their supreme hope is that in the homes of Angus soldiers "The Muster-Roll" may keep alive many brave memories, and nourish the valorous love of home and kindred which is one of the best guarantees of freedom, strength, and unity throughout our Queen's vast dominions.

The half-tone blocks in the volume have been produced in the engraving establishment of Messrs John Swain & Son, Ltd, Farringdon Street, London.

In the discharge of his duties the Editor has been aided liberally by many artists, journalists, and other friends. For them he must make one more call upon the "exchequer of the poor" and send them "evermore thanks."

J. B. Salmond

PROMOTERS' NOTE.

Besides all his editorial duties, Mr Salmond kindly undertook to express the thanks of the Promoters to all those who, in varying degrees, have assisted to make "The Muster-Roll of Angus" a success. Of his own services, however, it has naturally been impossible for Mr Salmond to speak, although it is mainly to these services that the success of "The Muster-Roll" is due. From the moment that the idea of "The Muster-Roll" was conceived, until the completion of the volume, Mr Salmond, with patriotic ardour and unwearying assiduity, worked to bring the book into its present form; and the Promoters are well aware that the number and value of the artistic and literary contributions contained in its pages are in no small measure due to his personal influence.

A good cause is always safe in Mr Salmond's hands, and all who see "The Muster-Roll" will assuredly recognise the ability and zeal with which he has rounded off and finished up the book which he so generously undertook to edit. For the sake of those men who went forth to represent Angus in South Africa, and of those at home who watch and wait to do them honour, Mr Salmond willingly and ungrudgingly gave unnumbered days of anxious thought and of unremitting toil. No words are strong enough to express our personal indebtedness for his services; but it is to the gratitude of all who claim kinship with Angus, and are in sympathy with the spirit of "The Muster-Roll" that we would commend our Editor.

Agnes Lindsay Carnegie.

J. C. C. Macdonald.

CONTENTS.

DEDICATION. By Rev. W. J. Nichol Service	5
PREFACE	7
PROMOTERS' NOTE	11
A GREEK SOLDIER'S GRAVE. By A. S. Murray, LL.D., F.S.A.	19
THE DYING SOLDIER. By the Earl of Southesk, K.T.	23
LETTER FROM THE RIGHT HON. JOHN MORLEY, M.P.	30
SOLDIER AND STOIC. By R. Neish	32
THE MUSTER-ROLL OF ANGUS. By Professor Jebb, M.P.	37
DECEMBER, 1899. By Lady Arabella Romilly	42
BRAVE SONS OF ANGUS. Words by J. B. Salmond. Music by Ed. Mason, Mus. Bac.	44
THE BOYS OF THE OLD BRIGADE. By J. M. M'Bain, F.S.A. Scot.	47
OUT ON THE VELDT. By W Allan, M.P.	55
ON GUARD. By Flora Annie Steel	57
SONS AND BROTHERS. Words by Agnes Lindsay-Carnegie. Music by David Stephen	66
GOOD-BYE. By Rev. James Murray	70
FOUR ANGUS WARRIORS. By A. H. Millar, F.S.A. Scot.	73
A CUP OF COLD WATER. By Hon. Mrs Greenhill-Gardyne	87
PROMOTED. By Fergus Mackenzie	89
SOME CASTLES AND MANSIONS OF ANGUS. By George Hay, F.S.A. Scot.	79
THEY TOLD ME YOU WERE DEAD. By H. D. Lowry	111
SERGEANT MAJOR BURNS OF THE 93RD. By J. B. Salmond	113
THE ANGUS MUSTER-ROLL MARCH. By Hon. Mrs F. J. Bruce	126
NOTES ON OFFICERS, COLONIALS, VOLUNTEERS, &c.,	189
LIST OF NON-COMMISSIONED OFFICERS AND RANK AND FILE	205
LIST OF SUBSCRIBERS	227

PORTRAITS AND ILLUSTRATIONS.

"A Highlander of the Ninety-Third." By H.R.H. Princess Louise, Duchess of Argyll ... *Frontispiece*

"A Highlander" By J. W. Herald ... 22

"Dawn after the Battle." By Max Cowper ... 31

"In Memoriam." By James Greig, R.B.A. ... 41

"Highlanders' Charge at Cæsar's Camp." By Melton Prior ... 54

"At 'The Patriotic.'" By S. H. Sime, R.B.A. ... 64

Portraits of Montrose and Claverhouse. Design by J. Eadie Reid ... 72

Portraits of Admirals Duncan and Northesk. Design by J. Eadie Reid ... 78

Colours of the Angus Fencibles ... 85

"A Peaceful Dutch Subject." By A. S. Edward, R.B.A. ... 86

Portrait of H.H. Prince Christian Victor, G.C.B. ... 96

Castles and Mansions of Angus. Illustrations—Aldbar, Anniston, Baldovan, Cortachy, Ethie, Finavon, Glamis, Kinblethmont, Kinnaird, Panmure, ... 97

"Mars and Venus." By Cynicus ... 110

"Hussars." By J. W. Herald ... 112

"At Home and Abroad." By Louisa Macdonald, M.A. Lond. ... 124

"Castlesea Bay." By Helen B. Mill ... 132

Portraits of Officers, Troopers, &c., in Regular, Colonial, and Volunteer Forces ... 135

Portrait of the Earl of Airlie ... 137

Portraits of Non-Commissioned Officers and Rank and File ... 162

THE
MUSTER-ROLL OF ANGUS.

CONTRIBUTIONS BY AUTHORS AND ARTISTS.

THE MUSTER-ROLL OF ANGUS.

A GREEK SOLDIER'S GRAVE.

By A. S. Murray, LL.D., F.S.A., British Museum.

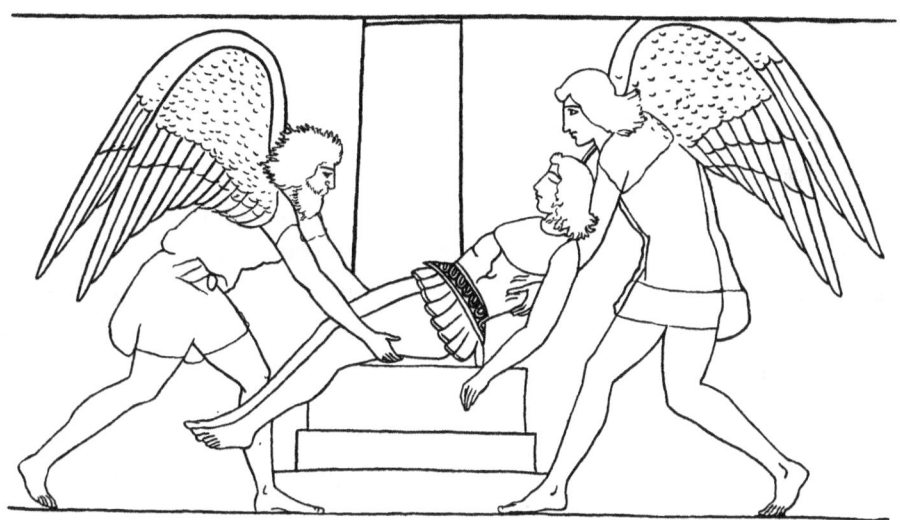

From an Athenian Vase in the British Museum—About 450 B.C.

The Æther received their souls, earth their bodies. . . . They put their lives in the balance against their country's glory.—*Epitaph on the Athenians who fell at Potidæa, B.C. 432 (in the British Museum.)*

THE old Greeks were continually fighting; their poets and historians found inspiration in the theme of war. In their art there is more of deadly conflict than of anything else. Their artists, when they chose, could represent a battle-scene as full of horror and confusion as the most modern picture. Witness the fine mosaic of Pompeii in the museum of Naples, where the army of Alexander the Great crashes into the ranks of the Persian King, Darius. The strange thing is that the artists seldom chose this realistic line. Indeed, they went on painting and sculpturing with unrivalled genius vast groups of gods fighting with giants, or Greeks against Trojans, finding in these mythical or legendary scenes of times long past, subjects in which they might well be excused for not introducing the harrowing details of actual war, for the good reason that no details were to be had. Many of the best of the Greek works of art are of this kind, and as a rule they are now regarded with indifference, so far as their meaning is concerned, or the story they tell, while the artistically far inferior battle-scene of Alexander against Darius strikes the spectator with horror.

Yet it was not from indifference that the greatest of the Greek artists chose to avoid the confusion and turmoil which they knew to be incidental to actual war. Had that been their spirit the public would have resented it soon enough. Nor was it from want of skill. The explanation must be sought elsewhere; and possibly the drawing here given from one of our vases may help us. A young man has fallen in war, and, like so many others, then as now, was buried on the field of battle. His friends at home needed no picture of the dreadful reality to deepen their grief. They would rather listen to some great orator like Pericles, who would tell them how "the whole country was the grave of those who fell in war." There was no consolation for them in art, except by means of imagery, such as that of our vase, where the two winged gods, Death and Sleep, carry the young man's body away to his home, and lower it beside an imaginary tomb prepared for him. The painter knew how Homer had described Death and Sleep carrying off the body of Sarpedon from the field of Troy to his home in Lycia to be buried in a grave, with a tombstone over him, "for such is the guerdon of those who die;" and we in our time find almost the same imagery in the famous words of John Bright during the Crimean War:—"The angel of Death has been abroad throughout the land; you may almost hear the beating of his wings." Let us therefore, in remembering the dead who have fallen in this war, think of them in the kindly Greek manner as being carried to their long home by winged beings as in our picture—Death, grim and bearded with streaming hair; Sleep, youthful and gentle.

In our calamities of war we look to our religion for consolation, and doubtless the Greeks did the same in a less degree. But they were far more dependent on their poets and artists than we are for the interpretation of the mysteries of life and death. They did not want from their artists accurate pictures of what took place—the barest description was enough for that. What they longed for was that their emotions—saddened as they were by the actual facts of war—should be raised to a higher level by means of imagery. To my mind, it was that deep and ever true impulse of the human heart which led the Greeks to seek consolation in times of war from the old myths and legends.

Once the idea of Winged Beings carrying off the dead from the battlefield had taken firm hold of the Greek imagination, it was easy for poets to vary it, and to invent a new legend, in which, instead of Death and Sleep, we have Boreas, the blustering North Wind, and Zephyros, the soft West Wind, carrying the body of Memnon from the plain of Troy, where he fell, to his distant home in Central Africa. In early Christian art under the Roman Empire, the old Greek idea is again modified, and takes the form of two angels bearing the body of an Emperor to the skies to be received by a divine assembly waiting for him. That is what we see on an ivory diptych in the British Museum of the year 476 A.D. The two angels are clearly our old friends, Death and Sleep.

Another idea of the Greeks was: Charon in his boat waiting among the reeds of Acheron to ferry the shades of the departed to the farther shore. In a picture by the greatest of the fresco-painters, Charon was figured as an old man at the oars, the water muddy, and the fish in it more like shadows than alive; and doubtless this was a source of inspiration to the minor artists whose occupation it was to paint vases for the dead, to be placed in the tombs. But on one of the paintings of this kind which we possess in the British Museum, the aged ferryman is standing in the stern of the boat and beckoning to a girl, who seems to hesitate, beside the reeds. It is only seldom that we find a scene of actual sorrow, such as the anguish of a mother over her dead child. Yet, to our notions, pictures of that nature would perhaps have been more appropriate on vases intended to be placed in or on tombs.

Here and there among the remains of Greek sculpture of the best age we find a monument in honour of someone who had fallen in battle, representing him engaged in combat. An instance familiar to those who have visited Athens is a tombstone still standing in the ancient cemetery in memory of a young man who had been slain in a cavalry charge at Corinth, B.C. 494. He is figured in the act of striking down one of the enemy. It is only from the inscription that we learn of his own death during the engagement. How he fell was doubtless well known to his relatives. But that is not indicated in any way by the artist. Indeed, without the inscription no one would suppose the sculpture to be other than a legendary group, like so many of the battle-scenes which fortunately still survive from the great age of Greek art.

A S Murray

A HIGHLANDER. BY J. W. HERALD

THE DYING SOLDIER.

By the Earl of Southesk, K.T.

A SOLDIER lay at the foot of a stone,
   In a pitiful plight was he,
For a rifle bullet had found a bone
   And smashed the pan of his knee.

So there on the hard, rough ground he lay,
   Nor stirred to better his ill,
For the enemy lurked not far away
   And their bullets kept him still.

Low down in a trench they crouched concealed;
   For, although they had held their ground,
The murderous guns from our batteries pealed,
   And shells came dropping round.

He lifted his head,—then bullets sped
   That ruffled his helmet's crown,
While some, from the rocks that around him spread,
   Brought battered fragments down.

And one keen bullet went straight to its mark
   Through his sound leg, barely seen;
So he drew himself close, and lay quiet and stark
   In the bounds of his narrow screen.

From the rise of the morn till the sunset's hour
   No help and no comfort came,
And the fangs of cramp, with a growing power,
   Were gnawing his limbs and frame.

The morning's mist had been dank and chill;
   But when sunshine burst the haze
It glowed like a furnace all over the hill
   And parched him in its blaze.

For a while he knew of nothing but pain,
   Or, fainting, respite found ;
Of a sudden his thoughts were his own again,
   Though they whirled in a mazy round.

One laugh he laughed, and he moaned one moan,
   Then quiet as death he lay,
And he thought that his body was turning to stone,—
   And then he tried to pray.

"Have mercy, O Lord!"—He could thus begin,
   But no words beyond these would come ;
For so long had he revelled in reckless sin
   That his inner soul was dumb.

Again he tried, and again and again ;
   Then he raved in dark despair,
"Lost, lost for ever: my prayers are vain,
   God has no heart to care."

The sun went away, and down dropped night,
   And nought could be seen or heard,
Save where distant camp-fires shed their light,
   And where wounded groaned or stirred ;

Or when ghostly grey figures, slim as breath,
   Crept round in a corpse-light clear—
The spirits of some who had fallen in death,
   Whose bodies were scattered near.

But the wounded man was so crushed by pain
   That his soul had no room for dread ;
Though thoughts without number revolved in his brain
   All else was torpid and dead.

Then again once more he betook him to prayer.
   Though he found not the ease he sought,
He was raised from the dungeon of blank despair,
   And he talked with himself in thought.

"I'm an outcast," thought he, "as I know full well,
   With no hold on a life-giving faith ;
I was born to the world an apprentice of hell,
   Under bond to the devil and death,

"How oft said my father—'This Scripture is true—
  Until saving faith comes in,
There is nothing, my lad, we can purpose or do
  That is not tainted with sin.

"'A man may strive proudly to merit God's love,
  And be honest and rightly behaved;
But unless, through free grace, he is born from above,
  He has not a chance to be saved.'

"Then it's useless to try, and a trouble to sham,
  Said I—and I went to the bad.
Oh! to think what I might be, and know what I am—
  This thinking is driving me mad!

"And now in the darkness I linger in pain,
  And I live with my thoughts alone;—
Yet not quite lonely, for now and again
  I can hear the wounded groan.

"But oh! to be home—and to breathe once more
  Sweet airs from the heather in blow,
And to see the old manse, and the yews at the door,
  And the glint of the river below;

"And the pleasant fir woods on the banks above,
  Where the yellow broom grows high;
Where I met with my lass and we plighted our love—
  Alas, what a traitor was I!

"Could she look on me now, she would come to my side,
  And her gentle tears would fall.
Would she think of her wrongs, or remember her pride?
  She would pity, and pardon me all.

"O mother, O mother, my heart is sore.
  What worlds would I give but to know
I should see you again, and should listen once more
  To your voice so soft and low.

"What though my life be evil and black,
  Though all should banish your child,
You never would drive your darling back—
  Blest mother, sweet and mild!

"But, what of my father, that stern old man—
  Could I dare to brave his sight?
In the pulpit how harshly I've heard him ban
  Bold haters of God's light,

"And have seen the hard smile that his features wore
  When he mocked mere fools that sin.
Grim as he is, if I stood at the door
  I know he would let me in.

"He would mutter a text from the 'Prodigal Son,'
  To repress the kind words from his heart;
He would not embrace me, whatever was done,
  But he would not say—'Depart.'

"And sweet mother—how well I can picture her face,
  Her tears of compassion and love.
Oh, why on this earth should we meet with such grace,
  And with nought but damnation above!"

He sighed. Then a voice in his soul did say—
  'Should your father be deaf to your prayer,
If, wasted and weary, you sought him some day,
  And prayed for forgiveness and care;

'Should your mother but turn from you, bitter and dry,
  As you there imploring her stood,—
Would men, would the angels, would God on high
  Declare such dealings good?'

"Good?—Yes, very good—on the devil's plan;
  But would Christians reckon it right
If you drove from your door a poor penitent man
  To perish in the night?

"And if wrought by a father to ruin his son,
  What a hateful deed it would be."
Then a light through his spirit appeared to run—
  "I was blind—now I see, I see!

"Oh, how could I think that God most great,
  Whom the heights and the depths obey,
Is less good than the men that His hands create,
  Frail creatures of a day!"

And at once he saw, as the truest of things—
    Deny it those who would—
That the God from whose being all goodness springs
    Must be Himself all-good.

Then over his soul came a calm so deep
    That he ceased to remember his pain,
In the arms of the angels he seemed to sleep,
    And in quiet bliss remain.

And, as if in a dream, to himself he said—
    "Oh, thus 'twould be sweet to stay;
But, as soon as my body is cold and dead,
    They will bear my soul away.

"They will bear me to realms where all is bright,
    Far over the arch of the sky,
And set me in face of the throne of light
    Where God doth reign on high.

"I will stand like a man, in that radiance clear,
    As a Scottish soldier should;
Not crouch like a coward—I never must fear,
    For I know that God is good.

"I will say to the Lord—for His might is so great
    He will pity my might so small—
'Have mercy, O Lord, when Thou fixest my state,
    As Thou art Father of all.

"'O, Father, most holy, though still Thy son,
    It is meet that I now should go,
For evil wrought and for good undone,
    To anguish, toils, and woe.

"'But I ask Thee—I ask in that Saviour's name
    Who on man's earth has stood,
Who bore, for love of us, pain and shame,
    And taught us Thou art good—

"'Consign me not to an evil place,
    To dwell with Thine outcast foes,—
I ask it, Lord, from Thy boundless grace—
    Let me not dwell with those.

"'Grant me some place, where through my pains,
  I may learn to serve Thee well—
Far, far from heaven, where glory reigns,
  But far, O Lord, from hell.

"'I could not live where the angels stay,
  For my soul is black and scored;
But I hate the fiends that have wrecked my way,
  And Thee I love, O Lord.'"

. . . .

Cold, cold was the night, and, as hours went on,
  The fires of his life burnt low:
His heart ceased beating, all sense was gone,
  His soul was free to go.

No more could he think about earthly things,
  But his spirit still could pray.
Then angels sought him, on gentle wings,
  And led his soul away.

. . . . . .

Bright rises morn, and the voices of war
  Break loud on the mountain's marge,
The rifles rattle, the cannon roar,
  The Gordons head the charge.

With steel they carried that trench on the hill;
  And, in searching the front of the place,
They came on their comrade, pale, rigid, and chill,
  God's sunshine on his face.

THE GALLANT GORDONS.

FORTH to the front the Gordons go,
Filled with joy, to seek the foe;
Marching lightly on with gay and easy swing,
While the pibrochs float above their van like eagles on the wing.

On to the hill the Gordons go,
Fired with joy, to find the foe ;
Up through the rocks, nor stop to draw a breath,
Though the bullets yell around their heads and strew the ground with death.

Into the trench the Gordons go,
Mad with joy, to meet the foe ;
Drive them out with steel, and smash them hand to hand—
'Tis the only trick the treacherous knaves can never understand.

'Bydand, bydand,' the Gordons stay,
To hold the hill at the close of day.
Many have been wounded, and many have been slain,
But their glory shall be 'bydand' bright, while Scotland doth remain.

Note.—'Bydand'—the Gordon motto—is the old Scottish form of the word *Biding*—waiting, abiding, enduring.

LETTER FROM RIGHT HON. JOHN MORLEY, M.P.

57 ELM PARK GARDENS,
SOUTH KENSINGTON, S.W.

Feb. 6. 1900.

Dear Mr. Salmond,

I sincerely hope the "Muster-Roll of Angus" will be as successful as its purpose deserves. Whatever view may be taken of the policy of the war, it is impossible to think of the men to whom the volume is intended to be a tribute, without admiration for their intrepidity and valour, and pity for the hearts and the homes that this scourge of war has made desolate.

Yours most truly,
John Morley.

DAWN AFTER THE BATTLE—THE ROLL-CALL. BY MAX COWPER

SOLDIER AND STOIC.

By R. Neish.

There was a curious contrast between those who were leaving and those who were left.

The soldiers were in great spirits, their hearts beating high with hope and anticipation; but the women, although they made valiant efforts to appear gay and cheery, had some difficulty, now that the moment of parting had actually come, in keeping back their tears. Even the men's faces grew momentarily grave and anxious as they exchanged a last greeting, or murmured a farewell word; but they soon grew cheerful and eager again, and it seemed as though all the bitterness of the sorrow fell, as it ever does, on those who were left.

There was, however, one striking exception to this rule, for an old General stood positively beaming as he bade a last good-bye to his only son. "You're in luck's way, my boy," he said heartily, "in luck's way; and I only wish I were going with you."

"I wish you were, sir," replied his son as heartily. "Remember me to all the boys at Redford when you go north to Angus. Tell them I'll be back hale and hearty for the Twelfth! Good-bye, dad!"

"Right you are—good-bye, and good luck to you," called the General; and with another warm hand-clasp—a little closer perhaps this time—they separated.

. . . .

A few hours later the stately transport, the "Bristol Castle," was slowly gliding seawards, and General Ogilvy was speeding back to town.

He sat in a corner of the railway carriage, staring aimlessly out of the window, his eyes still soft with love and pride, but his lips set in a grim determination to suppress a strange sinking at his heart.

A melancholy-faced man, seated opposite to him, leant forward and said deferentially to the old soldier—"It is a sad thing to lose one's son, sir."

He spoke with a deprecating smile, for the General did not look either genial or inclined to talk.

"Lose him—why should you lose him?" asked General Ogilvy, turning irately towards him.

"One never knows," answered the melancholy man; "and one instinctively fears the worst in these days."

"I don't know why one should fear the worst in these days more than in any other days," said the General, stiffly.

"He is my only son," replied his companion slowly.

"My only son has gone too, sir," said the General almost fiercely, "and my only regret is that I haven't half-a-dozen of 'em to send." Here he glanced half-contemptuously at the melancholy-faced man. "And as to snivelling about it, why, d—n it, sir, we'll leave that to the women."

"Ah! my dear sir; you take a soldier's view. I am not a soldier, and I cannot lay claim to the qualities of the stoic. I am only a lonely, idle man, and my son is everything to me."

"Is he?" replied the General unsympathetically. "Well, I'm happy to say that my son is everything to his Queen and to his country."

. . . .

General Ogilvy had left his club, and was being driven rapidly down Piccadilly homewards, when suddenly the hoarse cry of the newspaper-vendor resounded on every side of him. "H'orful disaster to the British — great slaughter—eleven guns lost—great disaster!"

The General set his mouth grimly, and put his cane up through the little door. "Paper," he said, laconically; and the driver pulled up with a jerk at the corner of the street. "Here you are, sir; *H'Echo, Sun, Evening News, Star,* sir?"

"Anything you like, confound you," said the General; and snatching the first paper handy, threw the boy a shilling. He opened the *Evening News* with a hand that shook in spite of his stern self-control, and looked eagerly down the list of killed and wounded. Seeing him so absorbed, the newspaper boy, taking his chance, looked up at the driver and said with ready wit —"Right you are, cabby," and turned to secure another customer.

The cabman drove on, and the General continued to pore over his paper. "Not even a scratch," he muttered at last, and breathed more freely; and then, with sudden recollection, put his cane through the little door again,

"Here, where the devil are you driving to?" he spluttered, angrily. "Where's my change?"

The cabman, aghast at having been so easily taken in, rapidly pursued the small boy, and came up to him as he was demanding twopence from a luckless old lady for a halfpenny paper.

"Here, you scoundrel," cried the General angrily, "where's my change? I've a good mind to give you in charge."

"Beg parding, sir. It was the cabby's fault, sir. Tried to foller you, sir; but couldn't catch him up. Thank you, sir;" and the boy ruefully handed up his ill-gotten gains.

The cabman dropped a volley of curses, and raised his whip threateningly, but the boy ran off. "A head for emergencies, that boy; he'd make a good soldier," muttered the General, and became absorbed in his paper again.

. . . .

A month later, General Ogilvy sat in his study, grim and defiant, grimly facing life and possible disappointment, and defying a curious instinct of coming sorrow. As he sat there, a man, calling lustily in the street below, paused under his window. "Great—British—Victory! Capture of the——" A passing vehicle drowned the last sentence. "Great British Victory—3 Orficers wounded —Casualty List—Death of Major Ogilvy—Great British Victory!" The General sat rigidly grasping the arm of his chair. Perhaps, perhaps, he had not caught the name correctly; besides there might easily be two or even three Ogilvys. He would have rung the bell, but a sharp pain in his side that had greatly troubled him lately prevented his moving. Suddenly the door opened, and the old housekeeper, who had been with him for many years, stumbled rather than walked into the room.

"Sir," she stammered, piteously, "the Major—Master Jack!" and the paper dropped from her trembling hand to the General's feet.

. . . .

On the following morning General Ogilvy came slowly downstairs. The pain in his side had been insistent during the whole of the long night, and his step tottered slightly as he crossed the hall. He opened the library door and steadied himself for a moment against a chair — his son's favourite armchair. The blinds were down, and the room was dimly lit by one electric light. He looked vaguely round, and then, pulling himself together, rang the bell sharply.

The butler came in and stood waiting in the doorway. "Who pulled these blinds down?" asked the General, pointing towards the window as he spoke.

The man stared at him.

"Why don't you answer?" he asked, angrily. "Who put these blinds down, and what for—eh?"

The man looked at him in amazement, not unmixed with anxiety. "Sir, the—the Major!" he stammered, and became abruptly silent. He could not conceive that his master had forgotten his son's death. Surely the trouble had unhinged his mind, he thought; and took a hasty step forward.

"Well, and what of the Major?" said the General drawing himself stiffly erect, and only laying his hand involuntarily on his left side for a moment as he did so. "What of the Major, Barnes? Do you think we are going to mourn for him. Hasn't he died a glorious death, and aren't we proud of him —eh? Haven't we heard him say a hundred times, when he fired his little gun in the woods at Redford, and drilled the gardener's children on the lawn, that he would be a brave soldier—eh? Wasn't he a brave boy, Barnes? and hasn't he died as a brave man—worthy of Angus and of the Ogilvys—eh? We are proud—proud, I tell you. You can go and pull up the blinds everywhere, for there shall be no whining in this house—go, go——" He moved his hand peremptorily. The man hurriedly withdrew, and had barely left the room before General Ogilvy sank with a wholly irrepressible moan of pain into his son's favourite chair.

. . . .

"Great British Victory—List of yesterday's casualties—Great Victory——" The hoarse cries rang up and down the long empty street, for it was late in the evening.

"He's been looking very queer all day," said the butler, as he stood for a moment in the doorway of the housekeeper's room; "and he hardly touched his dinner, although he took everything I offered him—for he's a 'ero, that's what he is; or, if he ain't, the Lord Almighty alone knows what a 'ero is."

"Go down and see if he wants anything now," said the housekeeper anxiously; "I don't like the look of him at all."

The butler went downstairs and softly opened the library door.

The General was sitting in his son's chair by the fire, and did not move as the man came in.

"Great British Victory—Great Bri—tish——"

"Is there anything I can get you before I lock up, sir?" It was an unusual request.

The General shook his head impatiently. "What is—it they—are—saying?" he asked, slowly. "I can't quite make out what they are saying."

The voices came nearer, rang out less huskily—"Great British Victory! Great——"

"Ah, I hear now," muttered the General and smiled faintly. "Another victory isn't it, Barnes?"

The butler, alarmed at the ghastliness of his face, hurriedly crossed the room and bent over his chair.

"Sir," he cried, anxiously, "what is it? Are you feeling ill?"

He looked eagerly into the ashen, smiling face, and, bending closer, cried tremblingly, "What is it, sir—what is it?"

There was no answer!

R. Leish.

"THE MUSTER-ROLL OF ANGUS."

By Professor Jebb, M.P.

Χαίρετε, κυδαλίμου μεγαλήτορα θρέμματα γαίας,
εὐπολέμων πατέρων ἔκγονοι εὐπόλεμοι,
τῶν ἀγαθὴ πέμψαι κουροτρόφος εὔχεται Ἄγγος
χιλιάδ' ἐν δεινῷ καρτερόθυμον Ἄρει.
5 πολλὰ μὲν ὑμετέρους ποτ' ἀριστεύσαντας ἐπεῖδεν
ἔν τε πόλει προγόνους ἔν τε μάχαις Βορέας·
νῦν δ' ἀρετάς, στροφάδων Ἄρκτου κατέναντι κελεύθων,
ὑμετέρας Σταυρὸς[1] δέρκεται ἀστερόεις.
ἐν Λιβύης πεδίοισι, λόφους τ' ἀνὰ παιπαλόεντας,
10 πὰρ ποταμῶν τ' ὄχθας στείχετε δυσμενέων·
οὔτε ταλαιπωρεῖν ὀκνεῖτ', οὔτ' ἀγλαὸν ἥβην,
ἢν καλέσῃ δαίμων, ἐν προμάχοισι λιπεῖν.

πολλάκι δ' ἐν μέσσοις, οἶμαι, καμάτοισιν Ἄρηος,
εἴθ' ὁπότ' ἐν Λιβυκῷ κῶμά τιν' εἷλε πέδῳ,
15 Μνημοσύνη μαλακαῖσι παρηγορίαισιν ὀνείρων
πατρίδος αἰχμητῇ φάσμα βόρειον ἄγει·
Γράμπιά τις δοκέει λεύσσειν χιόν' ἄκρ' ἐπέχουσαν,
ἢ παρὰ Βρωθόξου[2] καλὰ ῥέεθρ' ἴμεναι·
ἔνθα πολύλλιστον Βασιλεὺς πάρος εἵσατο νηόν,
20 κεῖνος, ὃς οὔνομ' ὁμῶς κῆρ τε λέοντος ἔχεν[3],
καὶ Θωμᾷ δόμον ἤγνισ', ὃν αἰδοίοις παρὰ βωμοῖς
ὤλεσε δυσσεβέος πεῖρα συνωμοσίας,
σῆμα δ' ἐκεῖ κατέθηκεν ἀρήϊον[4] εἰν ἀδύτοισι,
δαιμόνιον θνητοῖς τοῖς μετέπειτα τέρας,
25 μνῆμ' ἁγίου φωτός, τὸν ἐν ἀγχιάλοισιν Ἰώνη
θρέψε μυχοῖς θέλκτρον πραΰ περικτιόνων·
κεῖν' ἐπίσημον ἔχων ἱερὸς λόχος[5] ἤρατο νίκην,
σᾶν, Βάννοξε, ῥοᾶν ἐγγύθι μαρνάμενος.
ἔννεπε δ' ὡς νηόνδε ποτ' ἠγερέθοντο ἄνακτες[6],
30 ἄνθος ἀρηϊφίλων, Μοῦσα, Καληδονίων,
ἐν δὲ πρόμοις Βασιλεὺς νικηφόρος ἡγεμονεύων
Ἀρχιερεῖ Ῥώμης πέμψε τοιούσδε λόγους·

"μήποθ', ἕως ἂν ἔχωσι πνοάς, ξείνοιο τυράννου
ἴσθι Καληδονίους ῥήματι πεισομένους·
35 οὐ κράτος, οὐ πλοῦτος πολὺ φίλτατον ἀνδράσι κεδνοῖς,
ἀλλὰ βίου κορυφὰ παντὸς ἐλευθερία."

νῦν δὲ καὶ ἐν Λιβυκαῖς πόλεμον συνάγουσιν ἀρούραις
εἴνεκ' ἐλευθερίας ἄμμι σύνοιδε Θέμις·
Ἄγγε, νέον δὲ σέθεν λάμπει κλέος ἶσα παλαιῷ·
40 δεῖξε γὰρ ἐξ οἵων σὸν γένος οἷον ἔφυ.
πρωτογόνων τίς, ὅσους τε τρέφεις, οὐκ ὤπασε οἴκων[7]
τάγμασιν εὐάνδροις υἷας ἀερσιμάχους,
τὸν μὲν ἐν ἱππευταῖς μεμαῶθ', ἕτερον δ' ἅμα πεζοῖς,
τὸν δ' ἐνὶ ναυάρχοις πατρίδι θρέπτρα τίνειν;
45 ὧν τινας εἶχεν ἔσω κλεινὴ πόλις[8], ἔνθαπερ ἐσθλοῖς
δηρὸν ἀμυνομένοις ἐσθλὸς ἄρηξε λεώς.

Νηϊάδες κρήναισι φίλαι τὰς ἔλλαχεν Ἄγγος,
ὕμμι γάρ, ὦ νύμφαι, καὶ τὰ παλαιὰ μέλει,
ἀλλὰ τιν' ἔσθ' ὑδάτων ψιθυρίσματα, τῶν ἀΐουσαι
50 μανθάνετε σκοτίαν αἶσαν ἐφημερίων,
ἄλλο τι νῦν ὑμοῖσιν ἐν οὔασι νάματα φωνεῖ,
ἢ παρ' ὁδοὺς πατέρων ὡς ῥέεν ἡμετέρων,
εὖτε Καληδονίας Βαννόξιον εἶδε φάλαγγας
ῥεῖθρον ἐπ' Ἀγγλιγενῶν ὀρνυμένας στρατιάν;
55 οὐκέτι νῦν πολέμῳ δίχα τέμνεται αἶα Βρετάννων,
οὐδ' ὁμόροις ἄϋπνου φροντὶς Ἐνυαλίου·
εἷς ἔρος, ἓν δὲ σέβας, μία πᾶσιν ἑκούσιος ὁρμὴ
ξυνὰ μιᾶς φράζει πατρίδος ἔργα τελεῖν·
ἶσα Νότῳ Βορέας τόδε δέρκεται, Ἕσπερος Ἠοῖ·
60 γνῶ δ' ὁ τραφείς τ' οἴκοι ταῦθ', ὅ τ' ἄποικος ὁμῶς·
τιομένη δ', ὡς οὔτις ἐπὶ χθονὶ τίεται ἄλλη,
βουλομένων σὺ νέμεις πᾶν, Βασίλεια, κράτος.

NOTES.—1 The Southern Cross.   2 The Brothock.

3 The Abbey of Aberbrothock was founded by King William the Lion in 1178. It was dedicated to the memory of Thomas à Becket.

4 The consecrated banner ('Breacbennach') of St Columba, which King William gave to the Abbey.

5 The men of the Abbey were marshalled under the banner of Columba at Bannockburn (1314), where their Abbot, Bernard de Linton, fought at the side of King Robert Bruce.

6 In April, 1320, the Scottish Parliament met at the Abbey of Aberbrothock, under the presidency of King Robert, and sent to Pope John XXII. the famous Declaration of Scottish Independence.

7 The houses which have done most to make the history of Angus are well represented at the war: among them are those of Ogilvy, Carnegie, Lindsay, Lyon, and Maule.   8 Ladysmith

"THE MUSTER-ROLL OF ANGUS."

[TRANSLATION.]

HAIL, great-hearted children of a glorious land, valiant offspring of valiant sires, a thousand sons, the pride of Angus, Mother of the Brave, who has sent you forth, steadfast of spirit, in the dread stress of war! Often has the North seen the high deeds of your fathers, in peace or on the stricken field: and now, at the other Pole from the circling paths of the Bear, the Southern Cross beholds your deeds of prowess. Your ways are on the plains of Libya, and over her rugged hills, and by the banks of hostile rivers; ye shrink from no hardship, nor, if Heaven calls, from laying down your strong bright lives in the front of the battle.

But often, I ween, amidst the toils of warfare, or when the soldier has sunk to rest on Libyan soil, Memory brings to him, in the gentle promptings of dreams, a vision of his own Northern Land. He seems to look on the snow-mantled heights of the Grampians, or to move by the fair waters of the Brothock; where an Abbey, goal of many a vow, was founded of old by that King who bore the name and the heart of a Lion; and he dedicated the shrine to Thomas, who perished near the hallowed altar by the onset of an unholy band. And there he laid up a war-banner within the sanctuary, a mystic wonder for men who should come after, a relic of that holy man who lived in the shelter of sea-girt Iona, whose soothing spell was felt by all who dwelt around. That banner waved over the warriors of the Abbey when they conquered in the fight by the Bannock. And tell, O Muse, how the barons, the flower of Scottish chivalry, came together to that Abbey of yore, and their victorious King, presiding among his chieftains, sent a message on this wise to the Pontiff of Rome: "Know that Scotsmen will never yield, while breath is in them, to the behest of a foreign master. Not power, not wealth is dearest to brave men, but freedom, the crown of all that life can give."

And now, it is in Freedom's cause, as Justice is our witness, that we are warring on the Libyan fields. Angus, thy renown shines anew, bright as of old: thy children have shown their mettle and their breed! Where is that house, among all thy noblest, that has not given its sons, kindlers of battle, to the ranks of our heroes—horse, or foot, or leaders of seamen,—eager to do their duty by the land that bare them? Of whom some were within that famous town where brave succour came at last to brave defence.

Naiads who haunt the fountains of Angus,—for ye, O nymphs, are not forgetful of the past,—is there another sound in the whispering of the waters, from which ye darkly learn the fate of mortals, creatures of a day,—is the voice of the streams changed in your ears from the time when they flowed by the paths of our fathers,—when Bannockburn saw Scotland's armed array close in battle with the host of England? No more is Britain rent in twain by strife: the dwellers on the Border live no more in fear of sleepless war. One love, one loyalty, one spontaneous ardour bids all to work for the common welfare of their country. So is it seen from North to South, in the East and in the West: the Mother-land is one in spirit with her sons beyond the seas; and, honoured as no other Lady upon the Earth, our Queen reigns in the hearts of all.

In Memoriam.

TUGELA and the Modder glide
    Red with the heart-blood of the brave,
    And lonely veldt and rough hillside
Are marked with many a grave.
Our lads have fought as heroes fight,
    And died as Scottish men should die,
Their slogan "Liberty and Right,"
    Their hope and trust in Him on high.

The clash of steel, the cannon's boom,
    The shrieks that speak of awful strife,
Fall on the hearts, like sounds of doom,
    Of maiden, mother, and of wife.
For peace their prayers ascend above—
    Not for the peace of victory,
But for the abiding peace of love—
    That Boer and Briton kin may be.   J.G.

"DECEMBER, 1899."

By Lady Arabella Romilly.

WHEN the Angel of Death stands by me
    And asks me, "What have you done
    In this life of labour and trial?"
    I shall answer, "I gave my son—
I gave my flesh to my country,
    I gave myself to the foe;
For I gave the child born of me;
    And do we not reap as we sow?"

My blood has sprinkled God's country—
    God's country as much as this—
For in His eyes every country
    And each mother's son is His.
And the wails of the desolate mothers
    Rise to the foot of His Throne;
For to every mother, God knoweth,
    Hers is an only son!

Arabella Romilly

MUSTER-ROLL SONG.

BRAVE SONS OF ANGUS.

"Your Queen and Country called you,
And with courage as of old
You answered Duty's call, nor reasoned why!"

WORDS BY J. B. SALMOND.
MUSIC BY ED. MASON, MUS. BAC., 2ND V.B.R.H.

BRAVE SONS OF ANGUS.

Words by J. B. Salmond.   Music by Ed. Mason, Mus Bac.

The Muster-Roll of Angus.

BRAVE SONS OF ANGUS.

con - quer or die, boys, With a smile in your eye, boys, That made our hearts thrill, boys, Brave sons of An - gus

VERSES *Espressivo. a Tempo*

1. There were eyes that filled with tears, There were hearts that throbbed with
2. There were some who cried in an-ger, That for nought but greed of
3. Our broth-ers' cry was heard. From be-yond the south-ern
4. When the bat-tle strife is ov-er, May you all come safe-ly

BRAVE SONS OF ANGUS.

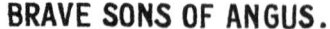

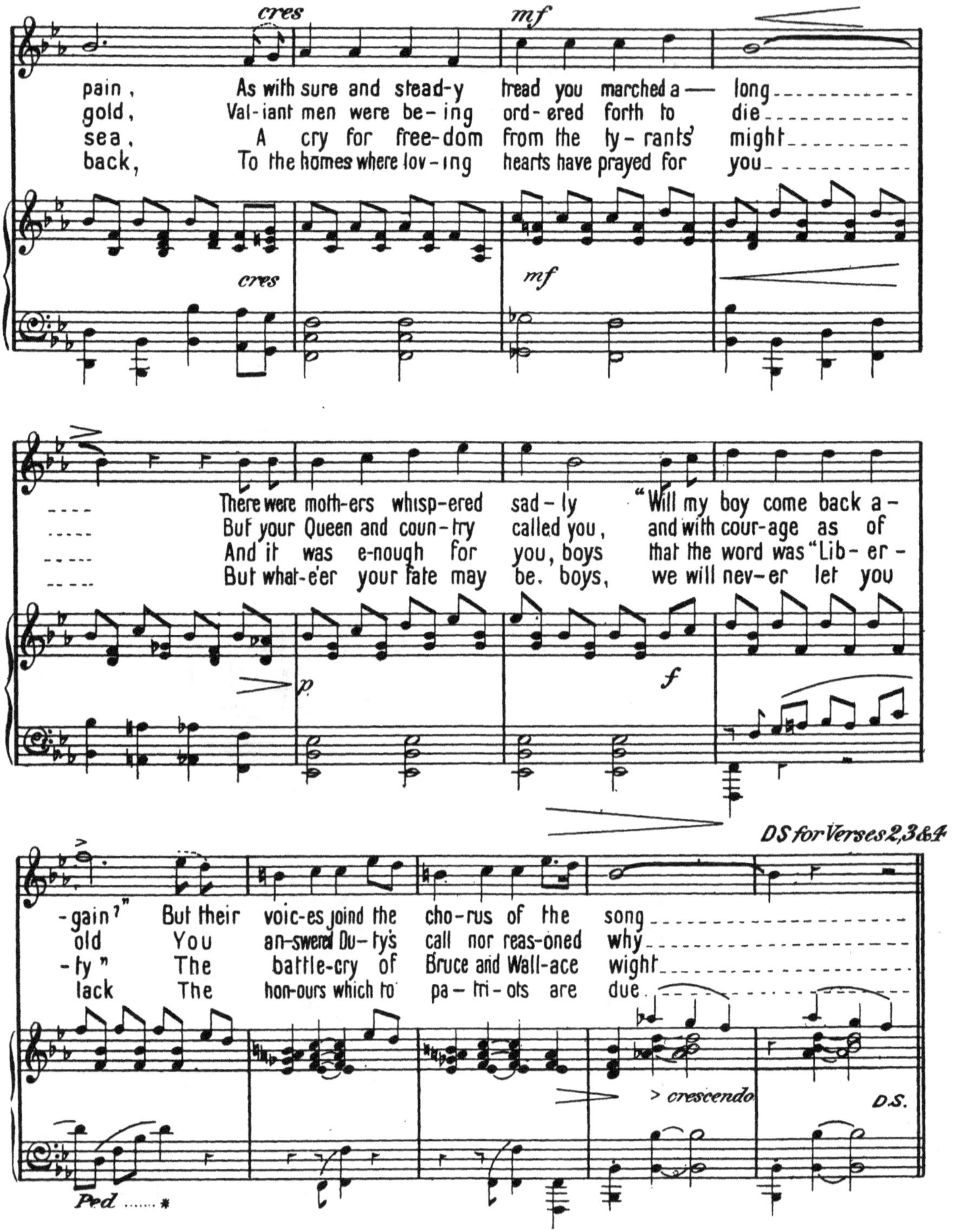
cres
mf
pain, As with sure and stead-y tread you marched a— long
gold, Val-iant men were be-ing ord-ered forth to die
sea, A cry for free-dom from the ty-rants' might
back, To the homes where lov-ing hearts have prayed for you
cres
mf
There were moth-ers whisp-ered sad-ly "Will my boy come back a-
But your Queen and coun-try called you, and with cour-age as of
And it was e-nough for you, boys that the word was "Lib-er-
But what-e'er your fate may be, boys, we will nev-er let you
p
f
DS for Verses 2,3&4
-gain?" But their voic-es joind the cho-rus of the song
old You an-swered Du-ty's call nor reas-oned why
-ty" The battle-cry of Bruce and Wall-ace wight
lack The hon-ours which to pa-tri-ots are due
crescendo
D.S.
Ped ...... *

"THE BOYS OF THE OLD BRIGADE."

The Angus Volunteers of the Napoleonic Period.

By J. M. M'Bain, F.S.A., Scot.

IN the brave old days when King Robert Bruce was making Scotland a nation, in no quarter of the country—as the records of those who answered his call to Bannockburn show—did he find more patriotic support than in Angus. Nor can it ever be forgotten that it was from the memorable Parliament which was held in 1320 in the Regality Chamber of Arbroath Abbey there went forth that famous Declaration of Independence, the reading of which, it was said, made Pope John XXII. tremble. Through the intervening years our Maules, Lindsays, Ogilvys, Carnegies, Ouchterlonys, Duncans, Lyons, and Raits, as well as the rank and file of our fighting men, have done deeds of daring on field and flood. The sons of Angus are as ready to-day as their sires were of old to lay down their lives in defence of the honour of our much-loved Empire.

The "Muster-Roll of Angus" carries the memory back to the stirring times when the aggressive wars of France which followed the Revolution of 1789, threatening the safety of Britain, made her look to her means of national defence. Then, as now, the spirit of patriotism—voiced in 1320 by the Warrior-Abbot of Aberbrothock—which still burns in the bosom of the men of Angus, was manifested in the enthusiasm with which they responded to the call to arms. From every town, village, and district, and from every mansion house and farm-steading in the county, the men of Forfarshire gave ample proof of their loyalty to their King and their devotion to their country. The magistrates and prominent citizens in each of the burghs took the lead in organizing and equipping corps of Volunteers, which were quickly formed into divisional regiments, and so were prepared to present a bold front to any foe who dared to plant his foot on British soil.

Dundee entered into the movement with that vigour which still characterises her citizens. From January, 1797, to July, 1805, the Town Council minutes bear ample evidence of the thoroughness with which that body, as representative of the community, took up the work of organisation. On 31st January, 1797, under the presidency of Provost Riddoch, the Council, after giving expression to their thorough appreciation of the important purposes to be served by the institution of a Corps of Volunteers, unanimously resolved to recommend to the inhabitants of Dundee in the strongest terms to join the Corps. And they further resolved "that the persons who have already entered, or may enter, with the Volunteers in this place, and who are not Freemen, shall be entitled to the freedom of the Burgh during their lives." Dundee was not alone in offering the freedom of the Burgh to the members of the Volunteer Corps; the Town Councils of Arbroath, Brechin, Montrose, and Forfar came to the same resolution; and in those days of close civic government this was no small honour. But not content with the formation of one Corps, the Town Council of Dundee, at a meeting held on the 11th March following, unanimously resolved to make offer to the Government to raise an additional Corps to be called "The Dundee Second Volunteer Corps;" this Corps to consist of three hundred men, to be divided into six companies, and to be commanded by officers to be recommended by the Magistrates and Town Council. Within six weeks thereafter the Provost was in a position to announce that His Majesty had been graciously pleased to accept of the six additional Volunteer Companies offered by the Council. The Council at once set to work to have the requisite number of men enrolled. In this they had considerable success, for the Committee appointed to carry out the Council's resolution was able within a fortnight to report that there had already been two hundred and fifty men enrolled. While the members of the Council were thus active in beating up recruits, they were equally willing to volunteer their own services, and so it came about that the bulk of the first officers of "the Second or Light Infantry Dundee Volunteer Corps"—as it was resolved to designate it— were drawn from amongst the Town Councillors of that time. The nominations made by the Council were submitted through the Lord Lieutenant of the County, and in due course the following officers of the Light Infantry Corps were gazetted, viz.:—Lieut.-Colonel A. Riddoch; Major Wm. Scott; Captains Thomas Webster, Alex. Balfour, J. Allison, J. Strachan, T. Webster, jr., and A. Peddie; Lieutenants John Guild, David Martin, James Edgar, John Crichton, Alex. Blyth, John Souter, William Small, Hen. Blyth, jr., and J. Webster, jr. The officers of the first-formed corps were—Lieut.-Colonel James Mylne; Major Robert Duff;

Captains Sir A. Douglas, Jas. Johnstone, Pat. Stirling, Thomas Bell; Lieutenants Wm. Lindsay, Wm. Pitcairn, James Mitchell, Andrew M'Kenzie, Robert Stirling, Wm. Webster, David Brown, George Blair, and James Keith.

While townsmen of all ranks were willing to give their personal services, the Council were not niggardly with pecuniary help. At a meeting held in February, 1798, they resolved to subscribe £600—"towards the defence of our native country whose very existence as a nation is at present threatened by our determined and inveterate enemies." So the minute runs. Nor were the other towns in the County in loyalty a whit behind their bigger neighbour. While Dundee was busy enrolling members in its two corps, Arbroath was equally active in mustering her loyal sons. A large number of townsmen were speedily enrolled, the officers, as in the case of Dundee, being chiefly drawn from the Town Council. The Arbroath Companies were under command of Provost Balfour with the rank of Major, the other officers being Captains John Colvill, Charles Low, William Mill and John Airth, with Lieutenants William Colville, Grant, Hennip, P. Sturrock, J. Lumgair, with John Nicoll as Adjutant. The Montrose Corps was under command of Lieutenant-Colonel A. Gardiner, with whom were Major A. Lyall, Captains Edward Green, A. Paterson, John Glegg, Lieutenants William Gibson, Alexander Scott, Alexander Thom, John Napier, Robert Webster, Andrew Millar, Robert Walker, and Charles Middleton. The Forfar Companies were officered by Captain William Don, Lieutenants William Adam, Robert Carrick, and Charles Webster, while Brechin had a similar corps under the command of Major Colin Gillies. These, so far as we can make out, were the officers of the Volunteer Corps of Angus as raised in 1797.

These Volunteer Corps, besides being furnished by the Government with clothing and arms, were also paid a shilling for each turn-out. As to their dress, their coats were scarlet, the cloth being of a rather finer texture than that of the soldiers of the line; but for this quality they had to contribute a certain part of their pay. Their cross-belts were well pipe-clayed; their head-gear being the same as that of the line. Their hair was powdered, and down behind hung queues rolled in ribbons of silk with a tuft at the termination.

After considerable negotiations the Peace of Amiens brought a truce to Volunteering; but this was only for a very short time. In 1803 it became known that Napoleon Bonaparte had formed a design to invade Britain, and once again the call to arms resounded throughout the land, and was every-where enthusiastically responded to. It was stated in Parliament on the 9th

December, 1803, that the Volunteer Force of Great Britain at that date numbered 379,943, while the force in Ireland numbered 70,000.

Again the men of Angus flocked to the standard. The Dundee Town Council, on the application of Colonel Riddoch and Colonel Mylne, agreed to pay each of them the sum of £50 in aid of their respective regiments, and at the same time the Magistrates showed their interest in the defensive operations by voting money for similar purposes. Bounties were provided by the Council to induce able-bodied seamen residing in or belonging to the town or parish of Dundee "to enter with Captain Laird, Regulating Officer at Dundee for His Majesty's sloop 'Minorca,' commanded by the Hon. Captain Henry Duncan, son of the late Viscount Duncan, or for any other ship to which Captain Duncan may be appointed."

Arbroath came forward with four companies of sixty men each, under the command of John Colvill, the Town Clerk, as Lieutenant-Colonel, and Provost Mill, banker, as Major. The Brechin men were commanded by Lieutenant-Colonel Molison, the then Provost of the ancient city, and the Forfar contingent by Major Don.

While each corps was busily engaged with its own training, occasional joint drills were held for the practising of battalion movements. Now and then sham fights were engaged in. It may be interesting to recall one of these held at Arbroath, the combatants being the Forfar, Brechin, and Arbroath corps. Colonel Molison, of the Brechin contingent—who, in his younger days, had been a captain of the Royal Marines—having a fine military air, and being minus an arm —lost in a duel—had a rather veteran-like appearance. The opposing forces met on the Arbroath Common. There was neither artillery nor cavalry on the ground. The Forfarians were the proud possessors of two howitzers, but they were either too lumbering to draw or too precious to be trusted so far from the county town. Skirmishing was kept up in vigorous style till the order was given for the Arbroathians to retreat; which, under cover of the Light Company, they did, taking up a position behind a low dyke which then separated the lands of Hospitalfield from the West Common. The Brechiners were ordered to charge, and Colonel Molison, proceeding in advance of his men to reconnoitre, peeped over the dyke, when he was greeted with the contents of an Arbroath musket, which fairly winged him, not of his other arm, but of the one side of his whiskers, thus constituting the only "casuality" of the day. Colonel Molison was grandfather of the late Major-General Smith, who resided for several years at Kelly Castle. Provost Molison afterwards held the post of Lieutenant-Colonel Commandant of the Forfarshire Militia. Indeed, many of the officers who commenced service in an Angus Volunteer regiment, afterwards had commissions in the local militia or in the Angus Fencibles.

While the duties were exacting and sometimes irksome to our civilian-soldiers, previously unaccustomed to the strict routine of a military life, that life was not altogether destitute of amusing incidents. Sir Walter Scott, in the "Antiquary," describes a false alarm at "Fairport," when the Volunteers are beat "to arms," and everything is bustle and excitement; when men of every rank, from the Earl of Glenallan to old Mucklebacket, are seen hurrying to and fro in active preparation to meet the coming enemy. The scene which Sir Walter so exquisitely conjures up was suggested by the following real incident in the experience of the Arbroath Volunteer corps. One evening after they had finished drill, and had been dismissed, some vessels were observed in the offing, which, seen through the fog, appeared to be of much larger dimensions than they were in reality. Taking advantage of this, the officers determined to try the mettle of their men. The drums beat to arms, and the bugles were heard in every street. In an incredibly short space of time the corps was under arms, ready to dare everything in defence of their King and country. The roll was called, and, with the exception of two, all the members of the corps responded to their names. But where were these craven loons? The one, who was a sort of limb of the law—a sheriff-officer or messenger-at-arms—had hid himself underneath his bed. A neighbour wife, whose guidman had gallantly "gone to the front," called on the "shirra officer's" better-half that they might condole with each other on the danger to which their two valiant spouses were at the moment believed to be exposing themselves. While wiping a tear out of her eye with the corner of her apron, she stumbled over the feet of the cowardly carle, who in his fright had forgotten to haul in his lubberly limbs. The other was a weaver in East Abbey Street, who, hearing the call to arms, threw his musket into a draw-well, took to his heels, and, making for the Magungie Woods, there remained till all danger was over. Meantime, the fog clearing away, "the enemy" was found to be two flax-laden vessels on their peaceful passage from Riga to Dundee, which had to wait in the offing till the clouds rolled by.

This was not the only incident in the history of the Angus Volunteers which furnished the novelist with material to "adorn a tale." "Delta," in his "Mansie Waugh," makes Mansie the hero of an amusing adventure. Here too the story, as Dr Moir tells it, is founded on fact, the incident having actually occurred in the case of a Brechin Volunteer while drilling on the Links at Montrose. Colonel Molison had noticed one of his men, Geordie D———, regularly obeying the word "load," but when this was followed by the order "fire" the trigger was never drawn. In this way eight charges found a lodging in the barrel of Geordie's gun. This was more than the Colonel could stand, so raising his voice he fiercely ordered the offender to discharge his musket. This Geordie tremblingly did, causing the barrel to burst, but happily with no worse result than the knocking down of the nervous Volunteer. The Colonel and the other officers rushed up to the fallen figure, expecting to find him mortally wounded, but Geordie, energetically waving his hand to prevent their approach, roared out—"Stand back, sirs, stand back; there's seven as gweed to come yet!"

Besides doing their usual drills, the Volunteers were called out for a continuous military exercise of twenty-one days. During this period they were generally marched to and stationed at some of the neighbouring towns. In Lamb's "Dundee: Its Quaint and Historic Buildings," under the subject "Dudhope Castle," is given a list of all the regiments that occupied it when used as barracks, and on two occasions the Forfarshire Volunteers are recorded as being quartered there:—"Forfarshire Volunteers, 4th Battalion (Dundee), 357 men; Lieutenant-Colonel Riddoch, Major Wm. Scott; entered quarters, 1804, February 22nd; left, 1804, April 25th." "Forfarshire Volunteers, 1st Battalion (Arbroath), 300 men; Lieutenant-Colonel John Colvill; entered quarters, 1804, April 25th; left 1804, May 14th." To do their twenty-one days the Brechin men were quartered at Montrose, and it was on one of these occasions that the amusing incident just narrated occurred. The Forfar men were also sent to Montrose. The writer remembers asking an old Forfar Volunteer who was boasting about his soldiering days whether he had ever seen foreign service, and got for answer—"Oo aye; I was ance at Ferryden!"

The Angus Fencibles, raised by, and under the command of, Major Fraser of Hospitalfield, and locally known as "Fraser's Men," were nearly all Angus men. The regiment comprised four or five companies, and was embodied in 1794-5. The minutes of the Arbroath Town Council, of date 6th August, 1794, bear that John Fraser, Esq., as Deputy-Lieutenant of the County of Forfar, waited on the Council and suggested the enrolment of the inhabitants for the defence of the town, &c. After hearing Mr Fraser, the Council adjourned for two days, and, on meeting again on the 8th of the same month, they resolved that such an enrolment in the present situation of this country may be of service, and they unanimously recommend to the inhabitants to enroll themselves. Of course the immediate cause of this proposed enrolment was the unsettled condition of the country following on the French Revolution; but the appeal thus made ended in the embodiment of the regiment raised in the county under the name of the Angus Fencibles.

This regiment was stationed at Dumfries when Robert Burns died, and a detachment of the Angus Fencibles took part in the funeral obsequies, Major Fraser putting the first shovelful of earth upon the coffin of our national poet.

It is outwith the purpose of this paper to tell the story of the Volunteer force which came into existence amidst so much enthusiasm in 1859; suffice it to say that the same spirit which animated the Angus men of 1797 and 1803 was that which moved the men of 1859 to rally round the throne of our beloved Queen Victoria. To-day the same patiotic spirit lives in the hearts of the men of Angus, and, to a man, they are ready to defend with their lives the honour of country and Queen.

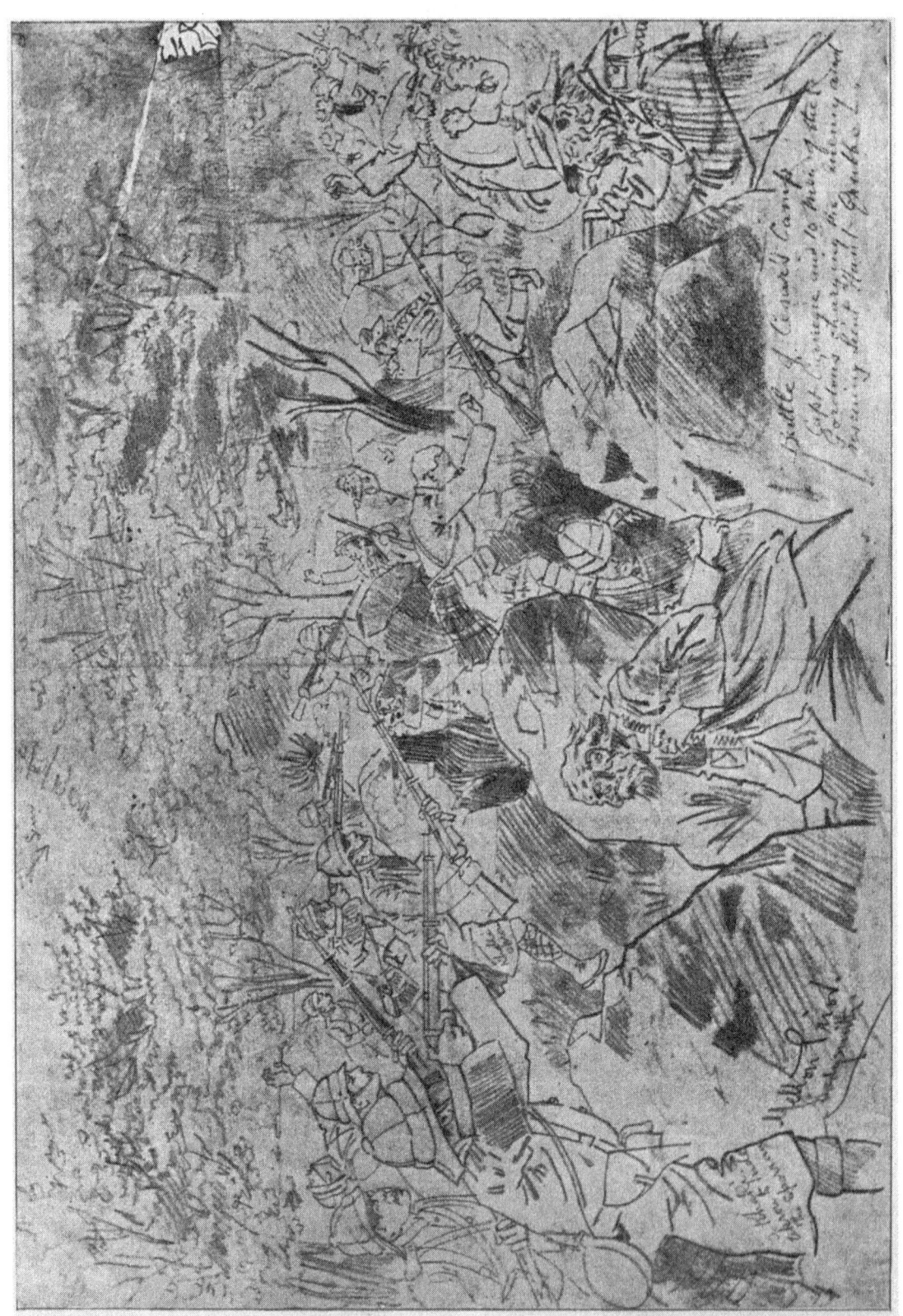

Sketch by Melton Prior, "Illustrated London News" Special Artist.

CAPTAIN HON. ROBERT CARNEGIE CHARGING WITH GORDON HIGHLANDERS AT CAESAR'S CAMP, LADYSMITH

OUT ON THE VELDT.

By William Allan, M.P.

OUT on the veldt Angus Gordon was lying,
    Angus, the pride of the Highland Brigade;
Out on the veldt the young warrior was dying,
Hit! when the tempest of bullets was flying
  From the long trenches the Boers had made;
Back we were driven from hills so defended,
Leaving our comrades behind us untended—
    Out on the veldt.

The dank dews of death over Angus were stealing
  As darkness succeeded the twilight's sad grey,
Vainly he strove, as his senses were reeling,
To staunch the dark wound from whose ruddy revealing
  The fount of his life-blood was ebbing away;
While death's cruel fire was his throbbing heart burning
As he lay in wild agony writhing and turning—
    Out on the veldt.

Ere passed the life-light from his blue eyes for ever,
  A vision of home and the Old Land appeared,
He saw the green hills and the dark purple heather,
He saw a wee cot by the loud-roaring river,
  He saw his fond mother, and once again heard
Her sweet voice of love on his ear gently falling,
"Angus, my Angus!" she seemed to be calling—
    Out on the veldt.

He listened with joy and his bright eyes shone brighter,
  "Mother! I'm coming!" he faintly replied—
The moon looked with pity upon the young fighter,
Whose cheeks 'neath her cold kiss grew paler and whiter,
  As slowly death's fingers his life-bonds untied;
Then marched the brave soul, to the camp field of heaven,
Of Angus whose life for his country was given—
    Out on the veldt.

ON GUARD!

(Founded on Fact.)

BY FLORA ANNIE STEEL.

HIS name was Alexander Kidd, and even B Company of the Black Watch—fond as it was of nicknames—could find none better suited to him than his own; for "sandy" he was, and not even a baby in arms could have been more child-faced, more child-hearted, than this "kid." So they called him either interchangeably; and the boy laughed at both names, as he had laughed at life generally, ever since he had been born in a ploughman's cottage in the Howe o' Strathmore, not far from Glamis. His father, an honest, dour man, of the true type of ploughman who learns silence or short speech behind his team, would say briefly, with a look at the gude-wife, that Sandy was a Souttar, as if that explained everything. Perhaps it did; since if tales be true the "Souters o' Forfar" were not always so douce as their neighbours. Not that Sandy was a bad boy. Far from it; he only laughed more than his brothers and sisters, and cried more, too, when he was a little chap.

Yet when the time came for him to leave the ploughman's cottage and follow the drum, as he had consistently and persistently said he would ever since he could speak, there were neither tears nor smiles. He just stood fair, and tall, and young, in his brand new uniform, and kissed his mother silently. Then he and his father shook hands. It was rather a long hand-shake, so that he had time to say, almost apologetically, "Weel, weel; I must just awa," before No. 34 B Company marched through the little garden patch, keeping time, no doubt, to the unseen drum and fife which had called him all his life.

It was a time of peace, not war, and he was only one of a draft for India; but India was an unknown land full of possibilities for Sandy Kidd, as it has been for so many sons of Angus. For it lives still, in some parts of the country-side, that glamour of the East which, in the old Company days, sent whole families, like the Binnys and the Arbuthnots, to seek the pagoda tree and return, after long years, to tell of having found or lost it; to tell many another marvellous tale which sank into the hearts of another generation.

Perhaps he was not aware of the rule which until very lately was in force, namely, that every soldier going to India should pay the War Office for his coffin in advance; but if he had been, it is doubtful if the knowledge would have checked the young recruit's huge enjoyment of life.

Even the journey by rail from Bombay to Meean Mir, which is surely the most deadly and distressing of experiences—even with the halt at Deolali thrown in—was to him an unending panorama of amusement.

"For Godsake give the Kid a bottle, an' stop its crowin'," said one of the older men who had been to India before, when, in the early dawn, they were roused out of their attempt to sleep by the boy's laugh. He laughed at everything; the crows, the sleeping yellow dogs, the bits of old rail which did duty as bells, the *baboos*; even at himself for being there, an alien, a stranger, and yet one to whom the sons of the soil *salaamed*.

Perhaps it was the perception of this fact which made him noticeably graver by the time his journey was over. Meean Mir itself, however, might have been sufficient to explain the fact; Meean Mir with its circling horizon of risen dust, its centring plain of fallen dust, bare, treeless, broken only by the crumbling bricks of forgotten graves. On the other hand, it may have been the tales which the older men had to tell; tales which inevitably crop up afresh for every young soldier in India. Of the dark days of mutiny, the bright ones of untarnished fidelity to the flag. Jhansi, Cawnpore, Delhi, Meerut, what words were these to conjure withal! Small wonder, indeed, if a soldier-lad's face should pale, his laugh die down, as the memorial spire, red as the Ridge itself, showed above the trees in which the taken city of Delhi hides itself from view.

Then last of all, it *is* sobering for *any* recruit to find himself—without warning—one of an army of twenty-six thousand men gathered together to do honour to Her Majesty on the anniversary of her assuming the title of Empress of India!

It is a big title. Those three days and nights of continuous travelling by rail—for the draft had hurried up so that the regiment might look its best on the great day—had brought *so much* home to the most thoughtless of these boys.

The last day of the old year was just breaking when the draft marched from the station into camp, and on New Year's Day—Proclamation Day—the biggest parade that Meean Mir had seen for many a long year was to be held. Half the Punjab was in to see the show, to join in the festivities of the Viceroy's visit to Lahore. Far as the eye could reach the white tents rose, and all day long guns were firing in salute to the feudatory chiefs as they paid their visits of vassalage to the Viceroy's tent. It was the first time that Alexander Kidd had heard the constant reverberation of distant guns as an accompaniment to all the pomp and panoply of war in a big camp, and the noise of it straightway went to his head; so that instead of making up, as his companions did, for those three nights of snatched sleep, he spent every hour he had of leisure in wandering about, careless of the blinding sun, careless of all things but his curiosity and the growing sense of elation, yet of responsibility, that was coming to his young laughter. Then it was Hogmanay, and when he came back at tattoo, after filling heart and brain with strange new things, all centreing round the English flag which rose in front of the Viceroy's big *durbar* tent, there was "Auld Lang Syne" to be sung, and the toast that is drunk in silence to be given. Sandy, like the kid he was, drank it in milk, for somehow his young healthy taste had not as yet taken to strong drinks. And when more than one veteran, disposing of a "stiff un," shook their heads and warned him that milk was worse than whisky in India, he had his child-like, incredulous laugh for the wisdom. He had drunk nothing else but milk coming up in the train, for it had been a novelty to him to see the great earthen jars of it being hawked about at every station. And he had never felt better in his life! Never! though he had scarcely slept for three nights. Yet he was not sleepy. How could a recruity feel sleepy when he found himself in the smartest company of—naturally—the smartest regiment in the camp? Found himself also put in the front rank by the sergeant because of his marching. Yet who could help marching well when those unseen drums and pipes had been playing "Hieland Laddie" in one's ears ever since one could recollect anything at all? How could a recruity feel sleepy when the men on either side of him told him briefly that if he spoilt the show they'd kill him; when others in the tent were frankly jealous, and talked of d—d youngsters who didn't know what duty was? Under such circumstances, was it not better to sit up and polish everything that could be polished, and then sneak off to a quiet spot and show yourself how you could march to the tune that was singing and buzzing in your head —the tune of Empire which had that refrain of "Hieland Laddie?"

Sandy Kidd's fair baby face was more child-like than ever in its flushed cheeks and limpidly bright eyes, when—before starting for the march past—the sergeant formed his men up. An approving nod sent the lad into a seventh heaven of glory; and after that he was conscious of nothing save himself and the flag that lay somewhere to his left. The older men looked for it, found it ahead, and so saved themselves for those few supreme minutes of actual passing; but Alexander Kidd started as he finished, and finished as he began. The sun —dimmed by the dust of the battalion in front of him—was in his eyes as, with every nerve on the strain, he tried to be a credit to the regiment.

The *feu de joie* took some of the strain from him; but it returned again when, in one long massed line, backed by battalions of dust rising from the feet of twenty-six thousand soldiers, the troops advanced for the salute. He could not help seeing the flag now; it was straight in front of him rising out of glittering uniforms, seen against a queerer background than Sandy Kidd had ever dreamed of. Elephants in cuirasses and frontlets of gold, camels caparisoned in crimson, and carrying wild figures hung with floating tassels; dark faces beneath the sparkle of diamonds, sweet white faces that needed no jewels but their own eyes——

Right, left! right, left! right, left!

Then that sudden stop that made your heart stop beating also; a clatter of arms, a surge of "God Save the Queen," and, above all, the wildest tumult of conceivable sound as a hundred and twenty elephants raised their gilded trunks and trumpeted!

How he managed to get back to tents Sandy scarcely knew. His head ached horribly; he could not touch his food; but he was glad he had not yielded to the impulse to go and lie down, when, later on, the order came for a guard to be sent to the Viceroy's camp. There was to be a big reception in the evening, and extra men would be wanted. The thought of this fresh honour seemed to do his headache good, and as the sun, sinking in the west, ceased to stare at him, even his laughter returned. But it was noisier than usual, and more than one of his companions told him to shut-up and not make a fool of himself. But how could you help playing it, just a little, when, if luck would have it, you might be on guard at the very flag itself; right before the entrance to the *durbar* tent; right in view of everybody who came to do honour to the Representative of the Queen Empress; right in front of every Rajah and Nawab, big or little, reminding them that they were but vassals of Empire!

But luck was against it. The westering of the sun had done Sandy Kidd's head good, but—strangely he thought—darkness made it worse. The chill which comes with the dusk set him shivering; at least so he thought, till one of the older men said to another—

"Eh, mon! what am I aye tellin' ye. The boys they're sendin' us the noo are no' fit for the regiment. See to him—weel eneuch tae look at, but nae staminy—nae staminy ava! Ae blink o' the sun, an' fever an' agy—if it's no' waur"—he added, significantly.

Nevertheless they were kind to the fever-struck boy, and shook down a straw bed for him in the guard tent, and told him how the sun knocked the strongest down for a few hours, and that he might be himself again before morning. If not, it would be time then to go to hospital. They even made him strip to his shirt, and raised a blanket or two somehow, and then piled his clothes over him and more straw; so leaving him in the dark to wrestle, till he sweated, with the fever fiend. But as they went out he heard that grudging voice remark that it was well India had had better stuff in Mutiny time, else the flag might have been in more danger than it was.

True. The fever fiend whispered to Sandy Kidd that he was a failure, and all in the dark alone he reverted to that other childish habit of crying. It was so hard when one meant so differently. So very hard. And yet the tears seemed to cool his brain, to dim the visions of dark faces, women's faces, flags, elephants, and above all, of the red memorial spire above the red Ridge. So, with the faint strains of the National Anthem, played as the Viceroy entered the reception, in his ears he fell asleep.

Yet scarcely asleep; the fever gripped him too hard for that; but he lay unconscious even of dreams, till suddenly they came back to him, and he sat up in the dark trembling—

Where was he? And where was the flag? God in heaven!—he had been on guard! He was on guard still! He was a traitor if he was not!—

He was out of the straw in a second; the next he was out in the night with his rifle—nothing else.

. . . .

Number 35, B Company, had been keeping himself warm in the chill before dawn by walking up and down in front of the sentry-box beneath the flag. But now there was a stir at the entrance to the tent; the sentries there pulled themselves together, as an *aide-de-camp* passed the word out that their Excellencies were leaving; so No. 35 turned back to his box.

"Halt! Who goes there?" rang out a challenge from within it.

At that moment the curtains of the tent door were drawn back in readiness, and, by the light which streamed out, a figure with nothing but a shirt on, yet with a rifle at the present, showed clearly, and No. 35 fell back with great promptitude.

"Who goes there? Halt! or I fire!" came the challenge again.

No. 35 stood rigid as a stone. He did not even dare to call for help. But the light had shown — as it could not fail to show — the strange sight to others at the door of the tent, and there was quick questioning and answer.

"You must get him out somehow," said the *aide-de-camp* hastily. "Her Excellency will be here directly."

The corporal hesitated. "We can shoot him, sir"—he began, thinking of the Kid's face as he had stood for inspection, and doubting if anything else would succeed. Yet he went forward a step or two with soothing words—

"Halt! Who goes there?" came the challenge once more.

"You must rush him from behind. I tell you Her Excellency——" began the *aide* frantically; then paused, for it was too late.

Down the crimson-carpeted anteroom came a man with a star on his breast, and a woman with a sweet kind face. Nothing very grand about them; just an Englishman and an Englishwoman. But she was a soldier's daughter, and she understood.

"Perhaps," she suggested quietly, "if you were to relieve guard?——"

The corporal's face beamed assent, as he saluted. "You've hit it, ma'am," he said, enthusiastically, forgetful of dignities.

So, with the *aide* as officer, a patrol formed up, and marched towards the sentry-box, where Sandy Kidd kept guard over the flag.

"*Guard turn out!*"

"*Who goes there?*"

"*Officer's patrol.*"

"*Give the countersign, officer's patrol.*"

"*Empire.*"

"*Pass, officer's patrol.*"

There was no pause, no hesitation, and the guardian of the Empire stepped further into the light, his bare white limbs showing clear against the chill darkness. He had kept his post. His work was done.

They handed him a greatcoat, saying it was his, and he put it on. So, obediently, he went to hospital; and he stayed there for a week or two. He even smiled when a lady with a kind face, who the nurses told him was Her Excellency, came and brought him a bunch of violets. She reminded him of his mother. Perhaps that was why he seemed to forget all things, even the

Empire, after that, and to be a boy again fishing in the Curbett, laughing at everything.

But the drums and fifes claimed him to the last, though his ears could not hear them playing "The Flowers of the Forest," and though the salute which rang out over the grave of a soldier was the only fire he had ever been under: His only service, save that one "On Guard."

For enteric kills more young soldiers than any war, and will do so, till we choose to fight the wrong that lies at our own doors.

F. G. Eliot

AT "THE PATRIOTIC." BY S. H. SIME, R.B.A.

"SONS & BROTHERS."

A SONG OF EMPIRE.

Words by
AGNES LINDSAY-CARNEGIE.
OF KINBLETHMONT.

Music by
DAVID STEPHEN, DUNDEE.

The Muster-Roll of Angus.

SONS. & BROTHERS.

one though broad seas di-vide us, one in hope, in heart in fame, We are sons of the same great Mo-ther, and guardians of her name, We are heirs of Great Bri-tain's glo-ry of her sway over land and sea We are faith-ful to one a-noth-er in the Em-pire of the free

V.3. Be sure that the war is right-eous which brings to the birth great deeds of

V.4 Oh no-ble sons of Bri-tain who ren-der their strong right hands Oh!

SONS & BROTHERS.

"GOOD-BYE."

By Rev. James Murray.

I HEAR the call—my country's call—
   On Scotsmen shall she call in vain?
   Good-bye, Sweetheart! Sweetheart, goodbye!
For I must sail across the main
   To fight for Queen and Fatherland,
   Away upon a foreign strand.

Behind the Sidlaws sinks the sun
   That flecks with gold our Northern sea;
Before the darkness on us falls
   I, dear, must tear myself from thee—
But naught on earth can break the tie
That binds two hearts. My love, Good-bye!

By Modder's grim and bloody trench,
   By Tugela's swift and drumly wave,
Our Angus men stand side by side
   Among the bravest of the brave,—
Thou wouldst not keep me, though I sigh
Good-bye, Sweetheart! Sweetheart, good-bye!

From Lunan bents to lone Lochlee,
   From silver Esk to queenly Tay,
From many a home in Angus towns
   They march away! they march away!
"For Queen and Country!" Hear their cry—
   Good-bye, Sweetheart! Sweetheart, good-bye!

Dear fatherland! Should one refuse
   The best beloved to shield her name,
Our patriot fathers from their graves
   Would cry him shame; would cry him shame.
Then let me go and cease to sigh
When honour calls. Sweetheart, goodbye!

And when the hard campaign is o'er,
   And gallant troops home proudly come,
Two Angus hearts will fondly beat
   To music of the pipe and drum;
We'll meet, no more to part, or sigh—
Good-bye, Sweetheart! Sweetheart, goodbye!

James Murray

FOUR ANGUS WARRIORS.

By A. H. Millar, F.S.A. Scot.

JAMES GRAHAM, First Marquis of Montrose.

JAMES GRAHAM, "the great Marquis" of Montrose, was, according to Wishart, "Chief of the Grahams, a most ancient and famous family in Scotland." He could trace his descent from William de Graham of Abercorn and Dalkeith, who flourished early in the twelfth century, and was one of the witnesses to the Charter of 1128, whereby David I. founded the Abbey of Holyrood. The first of the Grahams to settle in Forfarshire was William's great-grandson, David de Graham, who obtained the lands of Kinnaber and other property near Montrose, about 1200, from William the Lion. Among his famous descendants were Sir John the Graham, the companion-in-arms of Sir William Wallace; Sir Patrick Graham of Kincardine, who fell at the battle of Dunbar; Sir Patrick, Earl of Strathearn; Malise, Earl of Menteith; Sir William of Kincardine, who obtained the lands of Auld Montrose in 1407, and married the sister of James I., thus becoming ancestor of the Grahams of Claverhouse; Patrick, first Lord Graham (1445); William, first Earl of Montrose (1504), who fell, with his brother George, on Flodden Field; and many others whose names are deeply wrought into the history of Scotland.

James Graham was the only son of John, fourth Earl of Montrose, and of Margaret, daughter of William, first Earl of Gowrie. He was born in 1612, succeeded his father in 1626, when in his fourteenth year, and matriculated at St. Andrews in January 1627. In 1629 he married Magdalen, daughter of the first Earl of Southesk, and spent several years on the Continent, returning to this country in 1634, equipped alike as scholar and soldier, and accounted "one of the most accomplished gentlemen of the age." His reception at the Court of Charles I. was not so appreciative as he expected; and probably disappointment had some share in driving him to take up the cause of the Covenanters. It has been asserted that Montrose was then in favour of giving representation in Parliament to the people; hence his joining in the popular movement against Episcopacy. In November, 1637, he was received at Edinburgh as one of the Presbyterian leaders, and took an active part in imposing the Covenant in the following year. The abolition of Episcopacy by the General Assembly at Glasgow in 1638 had his full approval, and he became the acknowledged head of the party. Consequently when Scotland rose in arms against the King, Montrose was the principal military officer, and successfully led the Covenanters' army to Aberdeen, which he occupied, "imposing the Covenant, at the point of the sword, upon the inhabitants of the town and the surrounding country." After this victorious campaign, Montrose was invited to meet the King at Berwick, and it seems that the eloquence of Charles I. won him over, or at least made him disaffected towards the Covenanters. The result of this conference was the Cumbernauld Bond, dated August, 1640, by which Montrose and several other noblemen practically undertook to restore the King's prerogatives.

The position of Montrose at this time has been thus reasonably described: —When he first went to the Court at Whitehall he found Scotland under the control of the Marquis of Hamilton and Archbishop Laud, and to resist them he joined the Covenanters; but it was soon apparent to him that he had exchanged the tyranny of Hamilton *plus* the King, for the worse tyranny of Argyll *minus* the King, so he finally decided to abandon the Presbyterians and devote his sword to the Royalist cause. Thenceforth the struggle was between Montrose and Argyll, but the details of that long contest cannot here be repeated. Suffice it to say that on 11th June, 1641, Montrose was arrested and imprisoned in Edinburgh Castle, and remained in captivity till the beginning of the following year. He retired to his own house, but continued to plot against both Hamilton and Argyll. Preparations were made to overthrow the Presbyterian party, and to invade Scotland in the King's name. On 16th May, 1644, Montrose was raised in the Peerage to the rank of Marquis, and was constituted Captain-General of the King's Forces in Scotland. At the head of the Royalist army he defeated the Covenanters at Tibbermuir, Alford, and Aberdeen, and achieved two notable victories at Inverlochy and Kilsyth. On 13th September, 1646, he was surprised and defeated by General Leslie, and though he kept up a guerilla warfare in the north for some time, the news of the King's surrender compelled him to desist. He made his escape to the Continent, where he remained till after the execution of Charles I. He then organised an army with which he invaded Scotland, landing at Orkney in March, 1650, and ravaging Caithness and Sutherland. After suffering a severe reverse near Tain, Montrose was forced to flee, and while a fugitive he was betrayed by Macleod of Assynt, captured, taken to Edinburgh, and executed 21st May, 1650, without even the form of a trial. His dismembered body, after having been exposed for some time in the principal Scottish towns, was buried at the foot of the gallows in Edinburgh; but after the Restoration, Charles II. caused his remains to be disinterred, and buried honourably in St Giles Cathedral, Edinburgh.

Montrose's latest biographers—the Rev. A. D. Murdoch and H. F. Morland Simpson, the translators of "The Deeds of Montrose"—write thus regarding him:—"Montrose is a historical paradox; the victorious Covenanting leader of the Bridge of Dee is the champion of the King unto death; the friend of Spottiswoode is a ruling elder in the Glasgow Assembly which excommunicates him." Bishop Wishart, the friend, companion, biographer of Montrose, thus eulogises the hero in the Latin poem which he wrote on the first anniversary of his execution:—"The glorious hero, Montrose, at once the shame and glory of his ungrateful country, her pride and her reproach, Scotland's love and sorrow, ascends to his starry home, Heaven's shining palaces, the stately mansions of the angels beyond the spheres. There beneath his feet beholding the vanities of the perishing world, he has his joyous portion in the honour and love of God."

The most familiar portrait of Montrose is that by Honthorst which is now at Brechin Castle, and which has been frequently reproduced. It is given in Mark Napier's "Memoirs of Montrose," in Taylor's "Pictorial History of Scotland," in Chambers's "Eminent Scotsmen," and in Murdoch and Simpson's "Deeds of Montrose." The portrait of him by George Jamesone of Aberdeen (the "Scottish Vandyck") which is now in the possession of the Earl of Southesk at Kinnaird Castle, is included in "The Muster-Roll of Angus" by the kind permission of Lord Southesk. It shows Montrose in his bridal dress, before his marriage to the daughter of the first Earl of Southesk, and is of interest alike to the historian and to the art-critic.

JOHN GRAHAM OF CLAVERHOUSE. VISCOUNT OF DUNDEE.

FEW men of his rank have caused more controversy among historians than John Graham of Claverhouse. By one party he is hailed as the "lion-hearted warrior," and apostrophised as "Last of Scots, and last of freemen"; by another party he is denounced as "the despot's Champion," and is depicted as a barbarous monster, who warred alike upon unarmed men, defenceless women, and helpless children. Both pictures are distorted and exaggerated, and the truth will be found between these extreme views, though Claverhouse still waits the advent of an impartial biographer. John Graham was descended from Sir William Graham, Lord of Kincardine, who was married to Lady Mary Stewart, daughter of Robert III. The eldest son of this marriage was Sir Robert Graham of Fintry, whose wife was Janet (not Elizabeth) daughter of Sir Richard Lovell of Ballumbie. Of the two sons of Sir Robert, the elder became the founder of the Grahams of Fintry, and the younger was John Graham of Balargus, ancestor of the Grahams of Claverhouse. Sir William Graham of Claverhouse married Lady Jean Carnegie, daughter of the first Earl of Northesk, and his eldest son was John, afterwards Viscount of Dundee. He was born about 1643, and studied at St Andrews University. Having completed his course, he took service in France as a volunteer, and was afterwards a Cornet in the Dutch Guards. In 1674 he saved the life of the Prince of Orange at the battle of Seneff, and was then promised the command of the first Scots Regiment in the Netherlands. But he was twice deceived. Hugh Mackay of Scourie was promoted to a Lieutenant-Colonelcy in 1675, and again in 1677 Mackay was made Colonel in succession to Henry Graham. Insulted by this duplicity, John Graham resigned his commission and returned to Scotland in 1677; and it is worth noting that at Killiecrankie he opposed his old rival Mackay, and fought against the faithless Prince of Orange.

Shortly after his return to Scotland, John Graham was appointed to the command of a troop of cavalry raised for the purpose of enforcing the Episcopalian ritual on Scottish Presbyterians. His severity in accomplishing this task has been frequently condemned, especially by historians on the Whig side. On the other hand, it is maintained that as he held a commission it was his duty to execute the King's commands, and to shorten the Civil War by extreme measures. He received a severe check from the Covenanters at Drumclog, on 1st June, 1679, but three weeks afterwards he avenged his defeat by the victory of Bothwell Brig. His services to the Royalists were acknowledged and rewarded. In 1682 he was made Sheriff of Wigtonshire, and in 1684 he was sworn of the Privy Council, made Colonel of a Royal regiment of horse, and received the lands and Castle of Dudhope and the Constabulary of Dundee, which had fallen to the Crown through the forfeiture of Charles Maitland, Lord Haltoun. In 1688 he held the rank of Major-General, and in that year assumed, with the King's consent, the office of Provost of Dundee. On 12th November, 1688, he was created a Peer of Scotland, with the titles of Lord Graham of Claverhouse and Viscount of Dundee. When the crisis of the

Revolution came he adhered to the cause of James II, and counselled strong resistance. After the flight of the King, Dundee endeavoured to oppose the Revolution Settlement in Scotland; but failing to rouse the Convention of Estates he retired to Dudhope Castle, setting out from that place to enter upon the campaign which was terminated at Killiecrankie, in July, 1689, where the gallant leader fell in the moment of victory. He was ambitious, but he had ability to justify his ambition, and he succeeded in raising himself from the position of a humble Forfarshire laird to the rank of Viscount, with the reputation of being the bravest and most chivalrous military leader of his time. The adverse judgment upon Dundee may be traced back to Wodrow's partisan history, written for the purpose of lauding the Covenanters at the expense of the King and the Episcopalians; but some letters written by Dundee, which were lately discovered by Sir William Fraser, tend to clear him from many of these aspersions. The student of history must chose between the detraction of Dundee's enemies, and the partiality of his friends, as in the lofty tone adopted by James Philip of Almerieclose, Dundee's comrade in arms at the last struggle, in his Latin poem of "The Grameid," the opening passage of which has been thus translated :—" We sing the noble Leader, calling brave men to arms for an exiled King, and himself rushing to meet cruel wounds. We sing the Graham, the great Hero, terrible in the dust of battle, mighty in spirit and in arms. We tell of warlike deeds for times to come."

WILLIAM, SEVENTH EARL OF NORTHESK.

FROM the time when John de Balinhard acquired the lands of Carnegie in 1340, and assumed the designation of John de Carnegie, the family which he founded has given many prominent men to the service of their country, in the Court, the Senate, and the Camp. Walter de Carnegie of Kinnaird was one of the victorious leaders of the Royalist army at the battle of Brechin in 1452. Sir Robert Carnegie of Kinnaird was one of the early Senators of the College of Justice founded by James V. in 1532, having been appointed to that high office in 1547, and frequently serving as an ambassador to England and France. Two of his grandsons were raised to the peerage—David, the elder brother, being created Earl of Southesk, while the younger brother, John, was successively made Baron Lour and Earl of Ethie, the latter titles being exchanged by him in October, 1666, for those of Baron Rosehill of Rosehill and Earl of Northesk. To the latter branch of the Carnegie family belonged the distinguished naval

commander, William, seventh Earl of Northesk. He was the third son of George, sixth Earl of Northesk, and Anne, daughter of the Earl of Leven, and was born on 10th April, 1758, at Leven Lodge, near Edinburgh. He chose his father's profession, and entered the Royal Navy in 1771 when in his eighteenth year, serving first with the Hon. Captain Barrington in the "Albion," and afterwards with Captain Macbride in the "Southampton" frigate. In 1771 he was appointed master of the "Apollo" by Lord Howe, and served on the American station. Thence he was transferred to the "Royal George," and set out with the fleet under Sir John Lockhart Ross in May, 1779, which joined Admiral Rodney at the Spanish Coast; and he was present at the famous action on 9th January, 1780, off Cape Finisterre, when the Spanish convoy, carrying provisions to the force besieging Gibraltar, was captured. He accompanied the prizes to Gibraltar, and assisted in the relief of the garrison. Rodney's fleet encountered the Spanish fleet off Cape St Vincent on 16th January, and made havoc among them, carrying off the admiral, Don Juan de Langara, as a prisoner. On February 13th Carnegie sailed under Rodney from Gibraltar for the West Indies, having a position in the "Sandwich," the admiral's flag-ship. With Rodney he was present at the battle off Martinique on 18th April, 1780, and so heroic was his conduct that the admiral appointed him to the command of the "Blast" fire-ship. On the 7th April, 1782, he was advanced to the rank of post-captain, and took part in the glorious victory by Rodney over De Grasse, off Guadaloupe, on 12th April in that year. He returned to England in the "Enterprise," frigate, and was paid off at the peace of 1783. His eldest brother, David, died without issue on 19th February, 1788, and as the second son had died in infancy, Captain Carnegie succeeded to the courtesy title of Lord Rosehill. On 9th December in that year he was married at Paris to Mary Ricketts, niece of the renowned Admiral John Jervis, Earl of St Vincent. He entered upon active service in 1790, taking command of the "Hermione," frigate.

George, sixth Earl of Northesk, died at Ethie House on 22nd January, 1792, being then the third flag officer in the British Navy, and Lord Rosehill succeeded to the title and estates. In January, 1793, he sailed to the West Indies in the "Beaulieu," frigate, returning with a convoy in the "Andromeda." He was appointed to the command of the "Monmouth," 64 guns, in 1796, and joined the North Sea fleet under Admiral Duncan. The mutiny at the Nore had affected some of the seamen in Admiral Duncan's fleet, and some of the ships had to be sent back to England lest the lawless spirit manifested should spread throughout the fleet. The "Monmouth" was one of the vessels thus returned; and when the vessel came to the Nore, a number of the mutineers on the "Sandwich," led by Richard Parker, boarded the "Monmouth," and appealed to Lord Northesk to lay their claims before the Admiralty, as they considered him "the seaman's friend." He went on board the "Sandwich," and held a conference with the ringleaders. engaging to lay their grievances before the authorities. In Toone's "Chronological Historian" the result is thus briefly narrated:—"1797, June 7; Lord Northesk, captain of the "Monmouth," arrived at the Admiralty from on board the rebel fleet at the Nore, with a petition to the Board, couched in very lofty language; and a letter to His Majesty, in which the mutineers threatened to do something which would astonish the nation if their terms were not complied with." The application had no effect, for the ringleaders were tried by court-martial during the latter half of June, and the foremost of the mutineers, including Parker, were executed. As Lord Northesk did not rejoin the North Sea fleet, he had no share in the glorious victory of Camperdown, which rendered famous the name of his neighbour and old shipmate, Admiral Duncan.

Having resigned the command of the "Monmouth," Lord Northesk was not in active service till 1800, when he was placed in the "Prince," 98 guns, and joined the Channel Fleet under his kinsman, the Earl of St Vincent. In this vessel he remained till the peace of April 1802, and he was unemployed till the declaration of war against France was made on 18th May, 1803. Lord Northesk was then appointed to the command of the "Britannia," 100 guns, and took his place in the Channel Fleet under Admiral Sir William Cornwallis, and this position he retained till May, 1804, when he was promoted to the rank of Rear-Admiral of the White. He made the "Britannia" his flag-ship, and was commissioned to maintain the blockade of Brest during the winter of that year, a task which he successfully accomplished. In October, 1805, Lord Northesk was ordered to join the fleet under Vice-Admiral Collingwood, off Cadiz, and he was thus third in command at the battle of Trafalgar on 21st October. His share in that victory is thus described in "The Carnegies of Southesk":—"The "Britannia," which still bore his flag, broke through the enemy's line astern of their fourteenth ship, pouring in on each side a tremendous and destructive fire, and continued engaging the enemy's ships on both sides of her—frequently two or three of them at a time, with very little intermission, for five hours, when all resistance ceased." About the middle of the action, Admiral Lord Nelson was fatally wounded, and the completion of the conflict thus devolved upon Collingwood and Northesk. Their success was, duly acknowledged. On 26th November the Court of Common Council of the City of London directed that "the thanks of the Court, and the freedom of the city, and a sword of 200 guineas value, be awarded to Vice-Admiral Lord Collingwood, and the freedom of the city and a sword of 100 guineas value be awarded to Rear-Admiral Lord Northesk." In January, 1806, Lord Northesk received the dignity of G.C.B., and both Houses of Parliament passed votes of thanks to him, while a vase, valued at £300, was presented from the Patriotic Fund at Lloyd's. On 2nd August, 1806, the King gave him authority to bear an augmentation of arms introducing the name "Trafalgar" on the shield over the arms of the Carnegies of Northesk, the eagle bearing a naval crown, and the supporters holding banners with the words, "Britannia Victrix."

Lord Northesk was raised to the rank of Vice-Admiral in April, 1808, of Admiral in July, 1814, and of Rear-Admiral of Great Britain in November, 1821. He was appointed Commander-in-Chief of the British Navy at Plymouth in May, 1822, and remained there till 1830. He died in Albemarle Street, London, on 28th May, 1831, in his seventy-third year, and was buried in St Paul's Cathedral, where a brass tablet is erected to his memory, beside the monument of his fellow-warrior, Lord Nelson. Two of Lord Northesk's sons entered the navy. George, Lord Rosehill, his eldest son, born 1791, was drowned at sea in the wreck of the "Blenheim," in February, 1807. Swynfen Thomas Carnegie, Lord Northesk's fourth son, born 1813, rose to the rank of Rear Admiral, was a Companion of the Bath, a Knight of San Fernando of Spain, and had the decoration of the Medjidie of Turkey. He died on 29th November, 1879. The present (tenth) Earl is the great-grandson of Admiral, the Earl of Northesk.

ADAM DUNCAN, VISCOUNT OF CAMPERDOWN.

ADMIRAL DUNCAN is one of the naval heroes whose career reflects glory not only on the county of Angus which gave him birth, but on the nation in whose service he spent his life. Of him it has been justly written by his latest biographer, the Earl of Camperdown (great-grandson of the Admiral) that "he had the honour to be one of the great Sea Commanders whom the perils of Great Britain in the eighteenth century called into existence. Boscawen, Hawke, Keppel, Howe, Rodney, Hood, St. Vincent, Nelson, Collingwood, were of the number." An earlier biographer thus tersely describes his character:—"It would, perhaps, be difficult to find in modern history another man in whom, with so much meekness, modesty, and unaffected dignity of mind, were united so much genuine spirit, so much of the skill and fire of professional genius, such vigorous and active wisdom, such alacrity and ability for great achievements, with such entire indifference to their success, except so far as they might contribute to the good of his country." The student of naval history might say that had not the battle of Trafalgar been consecrated by the death of Nelson, and made thus more impressive for the popular mind, Duncan's victory at Camperdown, against superior numbers, and with the possibility of mutiny among his own men, would stand forth as one of the greatest naval battles recorded in history. And it is interesting to note that two "Men of Angus"—Lord Duncan and Lord Northesk —took part in both of these "glorious victories."

Adam Duncan was the second son of Alexander Duncan of Lundie, who was Provost of Dundee from 1744 to 1747, and had thus the difficult task of ruling the burgh during the Jacobite Rising. His mother was Helen Haldane, daughter of John Haldane of Gleneagles, and he was the third son, having been born in the Provost's Mansion in the Seagate, Dundee, on 1st July, 1731. When about fifteen years of age Adam Duncan entered the Royal Navy as a midshipman under his kinsman Captain Robert Haldane, and served with him on the "Shoreham," frigate, for three years. He exchanged in 1749 to the "Centurion," 50 guns, of which Captain (afterwards Admiral) Keppel was in command, and remained with that ship for six years. The interest taken by Keppel in the young midshipman was so great that to that eminent commander he owed much of his knowledge of seamanship. Under Keppel he served as midshipman, third, second, and first lieutenant, and flag-and post-captain, and even in his later years he was familiarly known as "Keppel's Duncan." For two years the "Centurion" was cruising in the Mediterranean, endeavouring to check the expeditions of the Moorish pirates; and after her return Keppel was appointed Commodore of the North American Station, and Duncan received his grade of Lieutenant on 10th January, 1755, and set out with Keppel in the "Centurion" to convoy the troops under General Braddock to take part in the American War. On his return a year afterwards Keppel removed to the "Torbay," 74 guns, and Duncan joined him on 10th July, 1756, with the rank of Second Lieutenant. For nearly three years Duncan was with the Channel Fleet, employed in the blockade of Brest and other services; but at length in October, 1758, he was sent with the expedition under Keppel to take the island of Goree, near Cape Verd, and there Duncan received a wound in the leg from a musket-ball—the only wound he ever received in the fifty actions in which he was engaged during his life. He obtained the rank of First Lieutenant after this battle, and from this date his promotion was rapid. He was gazetted Commander on 21st September, 1759, and Post Captain on 25th February, 1761, and appointed to the "Valiant," 74 guns, serving under his old friend and patron, Admiral Keppel. When the Admiral set out on his expedition to Belleisle, he made the "Valiant" his flagship, and Duncan honourably distinguished himself in the conflict. From this place the Admiral and his protege set out for the West Indies and remained there till the conclusion of the war with Spain.

Britain was at peace for several years, and Duncan was not actively employed till the renewal of hostilities in 1778, when he was appointed to the command of the "Monarch," and served under Admiral Sir Charles Hardy against the combined French and Spanish fleets. Towards the close of 1779 a powerful flotilla was formed, under the command of Admiral Keppel, and dispatched to the relief of Gibraltar, in which service Captain Duncan again distinguished himself. It was his fortune to return to Gibraltar in 1782 in Admiral Howe's fleet, and he was specially mentioned for his bravery in the conflict that took place at the Straits in October of that year. When the hostilities were terminated in 1783, Duncan exchanged to the "Edgar," 74 guns, one of the Plymouth guard-ships, and here he remained for the usual period of three years. On 14th September, 1783, he was promoted to the rank of Rear-Admiral of the Blue; on 24th September, 1786, he was gazetted Rear-Admiral of the White; on 3rd February, 1793, he became Vice-Admiral of the Blue; on 12th April, 1794, he was raised to the grade of Vice-Admiral of the White; and on 1st June, 1795, he was made Admiral of the Blue. These rapid steps in promotion were not the result of active service, for Duncan had not obtained command in any of the naval engagements between 1786 and 1795, though he had applied for posts on several occasions. At length his opportunity arrived. In April, 1795, he was appointed Commander-in-Chief in the North Sea, and chose the "Venerable," 74 guns, as his flag-ship. With that vessel his name was ever after to be honourably associated. After a cruise in the North Sea he returned with several French and Dutch prizes, and while his fleet lay in Yarmouth Roads there were symptoms of disaffection among his men, the result of the Mutiny at the Nore. By the exercise of discretion, suavity, and his powerful personal attractiveness Admiral Duncan succeeded in quelling the symptoms of rebellion in his own fleet; but it was with a very insecure feeling that he set out again on 28th May, 1797, with orders to blockade the Dutch Fleet in the Texel, for his confidence in the loyalty of his men had been shaken, and his fleet had been reduced. In estimating the importance of the victory at Camperdown, due allowance must be made for the difficulties which the Admiral had to encounter among his own followers.

The orders given to Admiral Duncan in May were that he was to keep the Dutch fleet under Admiral De Winter from leaving the Texel and joining the French fleet in a projected descent upon Ireland. Though Duncan's fleet was so inferior in numbers at the first that he did not dare to risk an encounter, he managed to blockade the Texel for more than eighteen weeks. He had to return to Yarmouth to refit, and De Winter took the opportunity of Duncan's absence to venture out to sea. When Duncan returned in October to a point opposite the coast between Egmont and Camperdown, he found the Dutch fleet in the open. By a daring and risky movement Duncan formed his line of battle so as to place the principal Dutch ships between himself and the shore, while he sent a portion of his fleet to leeward, so as to prevent the enemy receiving support from the land. On 11th October the battle of Camperdown was fought, with much bravery on both sides, and resulted in a great victory for Duncan, who took as his prisoners the three Dutch commanders—Admiral De Winter, Vice-Admiral Reyntjes, and Rear-Admiral Meuses. The plan which the French Directorate had conceived, of throwing a French and Dutch Army of Invasion into Ireland—which, with the Channel Fleet demoralised by mutiny, might have been easily accomplished—was thoroughly destroyed, and Britannia had once more justified her claim to rule the waves. The importance of the victory was enthusiastically acknowledged. On 17th October, 1797, the Admiral was created Viscount Duncan of Camperdown and Baron Duncan of Lundie. The freedom of the city of London was conferred upon him, together with a sword valued at 200 guineas; he received the thanks of both Houses of Parliament, and the Crown bestowed upon him a pension of £2000 per annum, to be continued to himself and the two next holders of the title; and Dundee, Glasgow, and Dublin placed his name on their Rolls of eminent burgesses, and gave him suitable memorial presentations. A special thanksgiving service was held in St Paul's Cathedral, London, on 19th December, at which the King and the Royal Family were present, Admiral Duncan carrying in the procession the flag of the Dutch Admiral which he had taken at Camperdown. The Admiral's portrait was painted for the Dundee Town Council, and a service of plate was presented to him. The old name of the estate of Lundie was changed to Camperdown, and in Glasgow and Edinburgh there were convivial clubs founded having the designation of "Camperdown." On 14th February, 1799, Lord Duncan was raised to the rank of Admiral of the White, and he retained his position as Commander-in-Chief in the North Sea until the spring of 1800, when he retired into private life. In July, 1804, he went to London to offer his services to the Admiralty. He was then in indifferent health, and had suffered from recent family bereavement, which had broken down his spirit. On his way home from London he was taken ill suddenly, and died at Cornhill, near Coldstream, on 4th August, 1804, being then in his seventy-third year. His body was brought to the churchyard of Lundie, and interred there, where a simple slab briefly records the dates of the birth and death of a great naval hero. A splendid monument to his memory, with a life-size marble figure of the Admiral, stands in St Paul's Cathedral, a testimonial from a grateful nation; but the modest inscription on the humble panel in Lundie kirkyard, which was partly devised by himself, is more typical of that earnest, sincere, whole-hearted Scottish patriot, Admiral Viscount Duncan of Camperdown.

A. H. Millar.

COLOURS OF THE ANGUS FENCIBLES

A PEACEFUL DUTCH SUBJECT.   BY A. S. EDWARD, R.B.A.

"A CUP OF COLD WATER."

By the Hon. Mrs Greenhill-Gardyne.

A LITTLE lad of tender years,
   Of worn and feeble frame—
  For him the lamp of life burns low,
   No oil to feed the flame.
He lies within the shadow-land,
   His course is well-nigh o'er;
No more for him shall daisies bloom,
   Nor laverocks sing and soar.

But high the spirit thrills with life!
   His mind is active still;
His busy fancy wakes the power
   Of kindling heart and will;
His being is athirst to hear
   Of daring deeds afar;
His thoughts by day, his dreams by night,
   Are centred in the war.

He sees the tents in scattered lines
   Spread o'er the dusty veldt;
He sees the burning light of heaven,
   In purple distance melt;
He hears the martial bugle-call,
   The rolling of the drum,
The tramp and swing of marching bands
   As to and fro they come.

Ah, more than this his vision shows!
   From rocky mountains steep
Flashes the deadly rifle-fire,
   The screaming shrapnel sweep;
Unshaken is the swift advance,
   Steady the bold attack—
Only—a line of fallen men
   Has marked that onward track,

"Think you, might I rise up once more,
  Once more be well and strong,
That to the war I might go forth,
  As I so greatly long"?
"My child," his kindly friend replied,
  "How could your wish come true?
How could you be a soldier brave,
  A little lad like you?"

"I could not be a soldier brave,
  A soldier of the Queen;
I could not join the desp'rate charge—
  My strength is small and mean.
Yet, maybe, I could give some help;
  How gladly, if I might,
A drink of water I would bring
  To those who fall in fight!"

Spirit of War, stern monitor!
  Though awful is thy face,
Yet sometimes in thine aspect grave
  A milder glance we trace.
When at thy touch sweet Pity fills
  The heart of Innocence,
We know true insight is vouchsafed
  Unto that purer sense.

For ever amid storm and strife
  The lines of Progress grow;
The truest peace-makers are they
  Who fearless meet the foe.
The ardour of self-sacrifice
  Shall lighten every toil,
And fairest flowers of Love shall spring
  From that blood-watered soil.

PROMOTED!

By Fergus Mackenzie.

THEY were a small company of the Queen's servants resting under the eaves of "The High Roof of the World," with the great shoulders of the Hindoo Koosh towering above them into the night. The sound of a stream rushing down the gorge fell upon the wearied soldiers' ears with a cadence softened by the distance. An occasional moan indifferently suppressed, a cry of pain, as one forgetful of his wound tried to turn on the hard bed of earth, let one understand there had been a sharp engagement in the daylight; and now with the battle-fever slowly subsiding, suffering men put in the hours of darkness with what fortitude they might.

Colonel Dempster, who was in command, lay on the earth conversing in a subdued whisper with his faithful ally, Sergeant Chisholm. Both were men of Angus, and both came from the same parish—the one from the battered old Castle whose grey towers rose up among the beeches; the other from the croft with its thatched cottage on the brae head. This night, after the carnage in which blood flowed like water, and many a brave man saw the sun for the last time, their hearts were tender; they longed for the pleasant fields of their native land, for the familiar haunts, and for the faces and voices of old friends.

The two had been boys together, had fought, not side by side, but against each other with a stubborn dourness which had left with each a life-long respect for what the other could do; and when the young officer enrolled the enemy of his school days, he was proud of his company. There was much coming and going between the castle and the croft; and with each letter from abroad, the laird and his lady had a message for Widow Chisholm, while she, too, had news to impart; and the difference in education and station was bridged over by the love of the parents for their soldier sons. It was with a common joy they heard of promotion to the two; and when the one attained his colonelcy and the other his sergeantship, it looked as if the world held little more for the fond parents except to have their sons home again.

"I had a letter from home to-day, Davie, and the old folk have a message for you. Your mother has not been as well as usual, but she is stepping about again. Influenza, they say—with perhaps a touch of old age; eh, Davie? My father has been keeping the house a good deal of late, too," the officer said musing. He knew the years were whitening the hair and giving a stoop to the shoulders of his loved ones at home.

"When this business is ower, are we likely to be sent hame—for I wad sair like to set een on my auld mither again?" the sergeant asked with something of the fretfulness of an unweaned child.

"It is hard to say; for the ways of the War Office are past finding out. But I should like to see the old folk too. I would give something, Davie, for a scone fresh off your mother's griddle and a tumbler of milk. Would they taste as sweet as in the old days?"

"An' I wad fain spend a summer gumpin' for trout i' the Lunan as I did when I was a loon. I can smell the Queen-o'-the-Meadow yet."

"How these poor fellows are groaning! We have escaped without a scratch; how cold it has grown!"

The day had been fiercely hot, the night was as fiercely chill; and that intolerable thirst which seizes the wounded tormented the little company grievously. Some one with a strong Scotch accent groaned half-mournfully, half-mirthfully—

"Hech, sirs, but I am dry. I wad fain gie half-a-hunder o' thae hills for a'e drink o' caller water."

A merry little Gurkha, with a comical attempt at the idiom and accent, retorted—

"Hech, Sandy, but I am dry too"—and somebody laughed. It was well they had heart enough to laugh at their calamities.

The cry for water became more general; and a wounded soldier, springing to his feet in a delirium of fever, staggered stream-ward a few paces, when he sank to the earth groaning:—

"Get me water, or I shall go mad, mad, mad!"

The stream raved through the gorge far below; the banks on both sides were held by the enemy in force, and to attempt to get water from such a source was to court death. Yet the cry was become very bitter, and it wrung Colonel Dempster's heart.

"Davie," he said earnestly, "have you ever felt as Hagar felt when in the wilderness she turned aside that she might not see her child die? What would I not give to get this moaning stopped."

"Men," he cried, moved by a sudden impulse and unable to hear their complaining longer, "I shall fetch you water;" and unbuckling his sword with nervous haste he seized a pitcher; and was only prevented from setting out by the intervention of Sergeant Chisholm.

"Colonel Dempster, ye daurna gae, you canna gae; your safety is the safety o' the company, and their lives hing on your life; let me gang;" and seizing the pitcher from the Colonel's grasp, he shouldered his gun and was ready to start.

"Leave your gun, Davie; everything you can do without, leave. It must be by speed, not by fighting that you can succeed," the Colonel said in a grave, low voice.

"Gin I dinna come back, Colonel, ye can tell my mither—oh—onything; that I hae married an Afridi, an' hae settled doon for gude; but ye'll gie her a look in whan ye get hame, an' ye can say—I—"

Davie Chisholm hesitated. He loved his mother—but he never said so much to himself, much less to another. "Ye can say I was speirin' for her;" and he dashed off into the darkness as lithe and fierce as a tiger. Woe to the Afridi who barred his passage!

In the suspense heightened by the darkness and inactivity, the moments dragged past with leaden feet; and only the rush of the stream or the thunder of a mass of rock hurtling down the mountain side fell upon the ear. The wounded men had ceased to moan; and a cry of dismay arose from the hill-side when down below a sudden clamour and the firing of many muskets broke out.

"Can he get through?" a hundred hearts were asking; and as the minutes slowly piled up into an hour with no sign of the returning soldier, their hopes sickened and died, and the wounded gave way to their moaning again. Colonel Dempster was bitterly regretting this madcap venture, when a sentinel called sharp and distinct—

"Who goes there?"

"Water from the well at Bethlehem's gate," was the quick response; and the soldiers, raising cheer after cheer, crowded about the Sergeant; while those harder hit sat up, waved their hands and made such demonstration as they could.

He was just telling of his adventures when a cry arose for more water; in his haste he had spilled half the pitcherful—and it more precious than gold!

"I'll gang again, lads!" he said readily; "I ken the lie o' the land, an' it'll be an easy job neist time. Besides they saw the first was a false alarm; an' they'll no' stir so speedily anither time."

A second, a third time he threaded his way through a country sown thick with the enemy, through a land shadowing with wings, and those the wings of death; yet in perfect safety, without scratch or bruise, he made his way through a hail of bullets; and many a man as he raised the water to his burning lips whispered—

"God bless Sergeant Chisholm!"

"I shall recommend you for the V.C.; yours is a heroic deed, Chisholm," his officer said proudly.

. . . .

In succeeding months events followed each other in rapid succession. The war on the ridge of the world was brought to an end; and prior to their leaving for the home country, the officers gave a grand Tamasha to certain Kashmir notables. But the feast, which was under Sergeant Chisholm's superintendence, was not a success; the salt was not salt, and certain puddings were thickly dusted over with a condiment which provoked profane language on the part of whoever tasted it. The Sergeant swore it was cinnamon; the feasters swore it would have passed for powdered bath brick, had it not been for its monstrous effect. The War Office, whose ways are past finding out, took no notice of Colonel Dempster's recommendation; and it was the current belief that Sergeant Chisholm had forfeited his V.C. through failing to be as good a caterer as he had proved a soldier.

It was a pleasant thing to get home again, to stroll by the Lunan, and see the kindly faces of old friends; but when dark clouds gathered over South Africa and war was declared, not a man but longed to get into action! Off to the front again with light hearts Colonel Dempster and his men went, thinking little of death and much of hard work and stiff fighting, with the prospect of deserving a V.C. whether they got it or no.

It was the night before Magersfontein, and the Colonel took the precaution of confiding one or two matters to the care of Sergeant Chisholm.

"I have written home, Davie; and if anything happens to me you shall see to the letter and to my parents' getting all information about me they wish. I have made everything right for your mother, in the case of anything happening to you."

The Sergeant said nothing. If a Scotchman speaks when he is moved, it is an infallible sign he is tipsy; and in a gayer tone the Colonel, continued,

"You *may* get a V.C. this time; promotion of some sort, certainly."

"Ay, gin ye dinna set me to the cookin' again, Colonel," the Sergeant said mischievously; "in which case I may be reduced."

Colonel Dempster laughed as he recalled the sad havoc the Sergeant's catering had wrought among the officers and the notables of Kashmir.

"What did you use for salt on that never-to-be-forgotten occasion, Davie?"

"There was naething wrang wi' the saut; *it* was richt eneuch, and was the very best saut to be gotten," David answered doggedly.

"Yet no matter how much one took, it never got any salter!"

"That was hardly my wyte. I got it oot o' a bottle in your ain cupboard, labelled and never opened, so that there cou'd be nae mistak'. It was ca'ed Eno's Fruit Salt; an' gin that werena gude eneuch, tell me whar I was likely to get better?"

Colonel Dempster laughed, and when one would have thought he had done laughing he set off afresh, much to the Sergeant's annoyance.

"And yon u'.arthly powder you sprinkled on the puddings, Davie; what was it? The like has not been tasted since."

"Yon, sir, was intended for grund ceennamon."

"Yes; and what was it?"

"I understood it to be grund ceennamon; I gied it for that, an' meant it to be ta'en for that."

"No doubt; but what was it, Davie?"

"Ye'll be a happier man, Colonel Dempster, gin ye never ken what yon grund ceennamon was; I'll alloo I made a slicht mistak' there, although the saut was a' richt," the Sergeant answered, blushing as he made this tantalising acknowledgment; and his officer had a greater desire to unearth the mystery than ever.

"Well, Davie, since you will not tell, and as I may not be here to-morrow to be told, you will see to the letter. May we get through the day's work with nothing worse than a whole skin; and promotion of some sort for the pair of us. Good night!" the Colonel said, as one says it who may be taking a last farewell.

"Gude nicht, sir; an' whatever befa', may we do oor pairt."

They made ready for an early start; and Colonel Dempster thinking of the unrewarded exploit of his Sergeant felt that had he lived in the days of the

Psalmist he would have ranked among David's three mighty men. But valour had become so common in the British army of late that it might easily be overlooked.

Next day the battle of Magersfontein was fought, and men fell in swathes like grain before the reaper. Far into the hours of darkness the stretcher-bearers carried in the wounded and the dying; and officers and men waited with aching hearts for missing comrades and friends. Colonel Dempster's battalion had suffered severely, and only a battered handful answered the roll-call. Among the missing was Sergeant Chisholm.

The stretcher-bearers crowded up with their pitiful burdens, when the officer's eye caught the stricken face of his friend. In a moment he was by his side, and stooping over the helpless form he asked—

"Are you badly hit, Davie?"

The soldier smiled faintly, and whispered—

"Promoted at last, Colonel!"

"Can I do anything for you?"

"Ye'll no forget my auld mither; it'll be sair on her."

"She shall be provided for, Davie."

"God bless ye!"

Sergeant Chisholm closed his eyes, and the ashen hue of death crept over his lips, while Colonel Dempster knelt by his side holding the nerveless hand. For a moment the dying man opened his eyes and smiled.

"Yon grund ceennamon, Colonel——"

"Don't think about that, Davie," the officer exclaimed as he paused from weariness.

"Was Keating's Insect Poother."

"I do not care though it had been prussic acid, if you had escaped this day," the Colonel said vehemently. Then with bared head and a faltering tongue the strong man committed his friend, whose life-span was limited to moments, to the gracious care of Him who has vanquished death.

Sergeant Chisholm, bravest of the brave, was, through interest with certain Higher Powers, promoted to a grave on the Veldt; and in far-off Scotland two women sat by a peat fire weeping. The old Laird and his "Leddy" had gone to comfort Widow Chisholm with their son's letter, written on that fatal day. Amid her sobs the lady read, "A better man, a truer friend, a more fearless soldier in the hour of danger there was not."

The old Laird stood at the cottage window, erect, stern, with hands clasped behind his back, looking across the woods and the high grounds where the sky line touched. Far beyond the horizon his imagination travelled, till he saw the blood-red fields of Africa; and he prayed, "Oh that the reign of righteousness and love might come, that wars should cease, and peace dwell for evermore."

James Anderson.

PRINCE CHRISTIAN VICTOR, G.C.B.

SOME CASTLES AND MANSIONS OF ANGUS.

By George Hay, F.S.A. Scot.

THE County of Angus is so rich in Castles and Mansions that merely to mention them would be to produce a catalogue of considerable length. Many of the old castles are in ruins, having been wrecked in the tribal or family feuds which were common in Scotland in times less happy than our own. In some instances, however, the ruin was not the work of war, but simply of time, the inconvenient though strong old tower being abandoned when, although every man's house continues to be his castle, it is no longer necessary that he should so build it as to enable it to resist a siege or an armed assault. Some of the older castles of the county, however, such as Glamis, that fine specimen of Scottish baronial architecture, are still inhabited houses, and are amongst the best houses in the kingdom; while, as at Kinnaird, the site of the old castle is occupied by one that is comparatively modern. About them all, and situated as they generally are on sites of natural beauty, there cling the charm of story and romance, often of ballad poetry, and the recollection of deeds which find a place in national history.

Not a few of the old castles cluster about or are in the district of the head town of the shire. Forfar itself, when the Scottish monarchy was somewhat migratory, was in the time of the Alexanders a royal residence; but of the castle in which the kings resided, and from which William the Lion made visits to Arbroath to watch from time to time the erection of his Abbey, nothing remains. Glamis, a few miles west from Forfar, was also a royal residence at an early date, and there is a constant tradition that one of the kings, Malcolm II., was murdered there in 1033. That was fully five hundred years before the erection of the present Castle of Glamis, the date of which is generally given as 1578. Some of the castle is probably older. A bit of it must be older, if we are to accept as authentic the tradition that the worthy who is known in history as the "Tiger" Earl of Crawford, or "Earl Beardie," is in a shut-up room there, along with his boon companions, playing cards, rattling his dice boxes, and drinking his wine, and will continue to drink and gamble till the Day of Judgment. The weird tradition is that this interesting crew had consigned their souls to the Prince of Darkness, and were taken at their word. The well-known story further goes that the whereabout of the hidden chamber is known only to the Earl of Strathmore, his heir, and the factor on the estates, and that this knowledge is transmitted by them to their successors. The present Earl of Strathmore and Kinghorne—an amiable man—does not impress his friends with the notion that he is custodian of a dreadful confidence. His family came into possession of Glamis in the fourteenth century by the marriage of Sir John Lyon with the second daughter of Robert II., the Princess bringing the thanedom of Glamis to her husband as her dowry. The family history of the Lyons is throughout very interesting. The Hon. Malcolm Bowes Lyon, one of the Earl's sons, has gone to the front in the South African War, and in thus serving his country has shown himself worthy of the best of his ancestors.

At Kirriemuir we get to the centre, as it were, of what was once a very extensive barony, over which the ancient Earls of Angus, the immediate successors of the Celtic chiefs of the land, held sway. North from Kirriemuir is Cortachy, the seat of the Earl of Airlie. The Ogilvys, who are descended from the second of the old Earls of Angus, obtained a grant of lands bearing their name from William the Lion. They have been at Cortachy since about the middle of the fourteenth century, and at Airlie, with its "Bonnie Hoose," from a century later. Cortachy is one of the instances of a house of palatial dimensions and character occupying the site of an ancient feudal keep. Its situation, with the river South Esk flowing through its extensive grounds, is very beautiful, as are all its surroundings. In fighting times the Ogilvys were a strong, masterful race, taking a prominent place in the history of Scotland, and active, as they still are, in the business of the shire. It would have been strange if to a family of such antiquity as that of Lord Airlie there did not attach a "ghost." The tradition is that when a member of the family is about to die strange music is heard within the castle—sometimes the wail of the bagpipe, sometimes the shrill sound of the fife and the beating of the drum, accompanied with a sound as of the tramp of soldiers. Having regard to the family history, it might well be the tramp of soldiers. Like many of his ancestors, the present Earl of Airlie is serving his country in war. Scorning a life of ease, with the soft allurements of beautiful Cortachy, he has stuck to his profession, and, having gone through the Modder River battles, is serving under Field-Marshal Lord Roberts in the Boer war, as are also his brother, the Hon. Lyulph Ogilvy, and two of his nephews.

About midway between Cortachy and Kirriemuir is Inverquharity, an old home of the Ogilvys. It dates from the fifteenth century, and is still a strong tower, not greatly damaged by time, but an example of the Angus castles which have been abandoned by their owners owing to their unfitness as dwelling-houses to the requirements of modern life. At its entrance there is still a massive yett, or gate, of grated iron, such as are to be found at the entrance to many baronial houses in Scotland. These yetts were of a defensive character, and could only be erected by royal licence. The licence for the Inverquharity yett was granted by one of the Jameses to Sir Alexander Ogilvy. It was granted "to fortifie his hoose and strenth it." The licence still exists, and is in the possession of Sir Alexander's descendant, Sir Reginald Howard Alexander Ogilvy, Bart. of Inverquharity. It was Sir Alexander Ogilvy who, on 23rd January, 1445, fought in the sanguinary battle of Arbroath with the Lindsays, headed by the Master of Crawford — the "Tiger" Earl — for the office of Justiciar of the Abbey. To those who knew the late Sir John Ogilvy, many years member of Parliament for Dundee, the contrast between that fine type of gentleman and the rough fighting race from which he sprung must have appeared sufficiently remarkable. But in all the wars of Great Britain, and certainly not least so in the war in South Africa, it has been amply demonstrated that the refinements of modern life do not in our country diminish fighting power or patriotic ardour when the necessities of the country call for their exercise. A son of Sir Reginald Ogilvy — Commander Frederick Charles Ashley Ogilvy, of H.M.S. "Terrible" — has served with the Naval Brigade in Natal. He was in the battle of Colenso, and was honourably mentioned in the dispatches of General Sir Redvers Buller. Colenso was his first battle, and his gallantry in it was recognised by his promotion to the rank of Commander. The grandfather of Sir John Ogilvy sold Inverquharity. He had succeeded to Baldovan, near Dundee, which is now the principal residence of the family. The house is beautiful for its situation and the simplicity of its architecture. Baldovan, it may be added, is to many an interesting place-name in connection with the orphanage and asylum which were established there by Commander Ogilvy's grandmother, Lady Jane Ogilvy.

Finavon, or Finhaven, near Forfar, is a great name among the castles of Angus. It was one of the chief homes of the Lindsays, once very powerful in

GLAMIS

CORTACHY

the shire. They also possessed Edzell—which, even in its ruins, shows traces of former magnificence—Invermark, and other strong places. The old castle of Finavon seems to have been more extensive than Edzell. It stood on the Highland border, guarding the passes through the valleys of the Isla, Prosen, and Esk. Only the ruined tower now remains. Finavon was at one time a royal residence. It was the chief home of the "Tiger" Earl, and of his predecessors and successors in the Earldom of Crawford. Within its walls Margaret, daughter of Cardinal Beaton and Marion Ogilvy, was married to David Lindsay, Master, afterwards Earl, of Crawford, and "in such state," as Knox says in his "History of the Reformation," "as if she had been a prince's lawful daughter." There is a "ghost" tradition about Finavon, that of Jock Barefoot, whom the "Tiger" Earl hanged :—

> "Earl Beardie ne'er will dee,
> Nor puir Jock Barefoot be set free,
> As lang's there grows a chestnut tree."

Finavon passed from the "lichtsome Lindsays" in the seventeenth century. It became a possession of the Carnegies. Mr David Greenhill-Gardyne succeeded his cousin, Mr Carnegie Gardyne, in the estate of Finavon, and died in 1867. It was he who built the present mansion. The old place of the Lindsays is connected with the South African war through the service in it of Captain Greenhill-Gardyne of the Gordons, and Walter Greenhill-Gardyne, who enlisted as a trooper in the Imperial Yeomanry.

Panmure, in the Arbroath district of the shire, has for considerably more than six centuries been a possession of the family of Maule, represented by Arthur George Maule Ramsay, born in 1878, and who as fourteenth Earl of Dalhousie succeeded to the titles and estates on the death of his father in 1887. The Maules, a family of French extraction, came into possession of Panmure in 1224 by the marriage of Sir Peter Maule with Christian, daughter and heiress of William de Valoniis, whose father had received a gift of Panmure, with other lands in Angus, from William the Lion. The old Castle of Panmure, the foundations of which can be distinctly traced, occupied a strong position a short distance from the comparatively modern Panmure House. It was occasionally the scene of fierce conflict. Sir Robert Maule, the fifteenth baronet, having opposed the project of marriage between the infant Mary Queen of Scots with Edward VI. of England, Panmure Castle was in 1543 besieged by an English force under the Protector, the Duke of Somerset. Sir Robert Maule was severely wounded, and the castle surrendered. Sir Patrick Maule, the eighteenth baronet, was in 1646 raised to the

KINNAIRD

ETHIE

peerage as Lord Maule of Brechin and Navar and Earl of Panmure. The erection of Panmure House was begun twenty years afterwards, in the time of George, the second Earl. The builders were John Milne, master mason to the king, and, on his death, Alexander Nisbet, who succeeded him in that office. John Ouchterlony, in his "Account of the Shire of Forfar," says of Panmure House, then but recently erected, that "it is thought by many, except Holyruid House, the best house in the kingdome of Scotland." The house has been improved and beautified in modern times. It is associated with the rebellion of 1715, and there is a tradition that the "Old Gate" has never been opened since Earl James, whose estates were forfeited in consequence of the part he took in the rebellion, quitted Panmure to die an exile in France in 1723. From Panmure the Maules have extended over a wide part of Angus. In 1679 they were in possession of Kelly Castle, the old home of the Ouchterlonys. Sir Thomas Maule, brother of Sir William Maule of Panmure, lost his life in 1303 in bravely defending the historical castle of Brechin, of which he was governor, against Edward I.; but it was not till 1634 that the Maules obtained by purchase the lordship of Brechin and Navar. Brechin Castle has long been their chief residence in Forfarshire. Shortly before the Stuart rebellion, Earl James bought the lands of Edzell, Glenesk, and Lethnot, and thus became lord of the old Lindsay castles of Edzell and Invermark. It is said that his object in making this purchase was to strengthen the Jacobite interest in Angus, his support of which proved so disastrous to himself. The estates of the forfeited Earl were bought back by his nephew, who was raised to the Irish peerage by the title of Earl Panmure. This Earl died unmarried. His sister, Jean Maule, had married George, Lord Ramsay. It was through this marriage that the Angus estates of the Maules passed to the Ramsays of Dalhousie. Lord Dalhousie, who represents both the Maules and Ramsays, obtained a second-lieutenancy in the Forfar and Kincardine Militia, and he has recently been gazetted to the Scots Guards. Lieutenant Edward Maule Young of Lincluden, son of the late Major Thomas Young, and grandnephew of Fox, eleventh Earl, and of George, twelfth Earl of Dalhousie, was killed at Karée in the South African War on 29th March, 1900.

In the Arbroath district we have also Ethie Castle, represented in the South African war by the Hon. Ian Carnegie, of H.M.S. "Powerful," who was in the Naval Brigade at Ladysmith, and endured the dangers and privations of the four months' siege. Mr Carnegie is brother of the Earl of Northesk. Ethie Castle has associations with one of the most important figures in Scottish history about the middle of the sixteenth century, Cardinal Beaton. It is said to have been

KINBLETHMONT

ANNISTON

built by him while he held the abbacy of Arbroath. A room in the castle, now used as a store-room, is called "Beaton's Chapel," and his "ghost" was formerly credited with a lingering fondness for the place, as, according to former vulgar belief, the tramp of a foot, popularly known as the Cardinal's *leg*, was heard at night walking up and down the original stone stair which connects the ground floor with the second storey. But it is doubtful if much of Ethie Castle dates further back than the seventeenth century. The house has frequently been altered. Extensive alterations were made in the time of the late earl. In the course of these, what was found to be a built-up cellar was opened, when there was made a discovery of very old wines. Ethie is a mile from the Redhead. Possibly its proximity to the sea has had something to do with many members of the family having entered the navy. The sixth and seventh earls were admirals. The latter served under Lord Nelson, and was third in command at Trafalgar. Mr Ian Carnegie has revived the interest of the family in the naval service of their country.

Also within the Arbroath district of Angus we have the estates — with their mansions—of Kinblethmont and Anniston, both of which have a connection with the war in South Africa and with the present work. The Laird of Anniston is himself a soldier, and a distinguished one. Lieutenant-Colonel Arthur John Rait, C.B., was present at the capture of Bomarsund, in the Baltic, in 1854. Joining the Royal Artillery in 1857, he served in the Rakamundel Field Force in 1859, was in the New Zealand war in 1863-64, and in the Ashanti war, 1873-74, in which he served on the staff of Sir Garnet (now Lord) Wolseley. He raised a force of native artillery. Both in New Zealand and Ashanti Colonel Rait was frequently mentioned in the dispatches of the General commanding. The Queen recognised his services by conferring upon him the Companionship of the Bath after the Ashanti war, and about the same time he received from its Town Council the honorary freedom of the Burgh of Arbroath. Colonel Rait takes an active part in county business. His son, Lieutenant Walter Garnet Rait, is at the front. The Raits have long been settled at Anniston, Inverkeilor. They are a branch of the family of Rait of Hallgreen, in the Mearns.

The Laird of Kinblethmont is Henry Fullarton Lindsay-Carnegie of Spynie and Boysack. He received his commission in the Bengal Engineers, in the East India Company's Forces, shortly before the Mutiny. He served as Lieutenant throughout the Mutiny, and was present at the seige of Delhi. He afterwards joined Lord Clyde as Assistant Field Engineer, and took part in the capture of

PANMURE

FINAVON

Lucknow and subsequent military operations against the native chiefs in Oudh. In an attack upon one of the Oudh strongholds Lieutenant Carnegie was entrusted with the command of a detachment sent to blow up one of the gates. A sudden explosion of the powder wounded him severely, and he was invalided home. His services and courage gained him the special favour of his superior officers. Major Lindsay, nephew of Mr Lindsay-Carnegie, is serving in the South African war. The Lindsay-Carnegies have as one of their ancestors the first Earl of Northesk, and in later times they have been connected by marriage both with the Northesk and the Airlie earls. They are also, as Jervise says in "The Land of the Lindsays," "the only remaining proprietors in Forfarshire lineally descended of the great Earls of Crawford." The first of the Kinblethmont Lindsays was the youngest son of the tenth Earl of Crawford. He was Vice-Chancellor of Scotland in the reign of James VI. Mrs Lindsay-Carnegie is a sister of Colonel Rait. She is well known in Forfarshire for the interest she takes in benevolent institutions.

Captain the Hon. Robert Carnegie, son of the Earl of Southesk, and Lieutenant Romilly, a grandson, are on the "Muster-Roll" of the war. Lord Southesk is the chief of the Carnegies. His Forfarshire seat is Kinnaird Castle, near Brechin. The name "Carnegie" is that of the lands of Carnegie, in the parish of Carmyllie, which in the thirteenth century came into the possession of the progenitors of the Carnegies of Kinnaird, who assumed the title from Carnegie of that ilk. When in 1869 he was created a Peer of Great Britain, Lord Southesk connected the title of his British peerage, Lord Balinhard of Farnell, with the ancient and present residences of his family, Balinhard being in Arbirlot, in the neighbourhood of the lands of Carnegie, and Kinnaird Castle being in the parish of Farnell. Lord Southesk is a K.T. He is a poet of striking originality, an accomplished archæologist, and a highly-cultured man. His sister, the late Lady Charlotte Elliot, wrote one of the finest of modern hymns, worthy to rank with the best of the ancient hymns of the Church—"Just as I am, without one plea." Strong intellect has appeared from generation to generation among the men and women of the Carnegies of Kinnaird. They lost themselves for a time, however, by their loyalty to the Stuarts in 1715. The then Earl was in the battle of Sheriffmuir. His estates were forfeited in consequence, and he died in exile. In 1764, Sir James Carnegie of Pitarrow, on whom the representation of the family had devolved, bought back the estates. The present Earl succeeded to the baronetcy in 1849, and in 1855 he was restored to the forfeited Scottish titles of Earl of Southesk and Lord Carnegie of Kinnaird and Leuchars. Kinnaird, which

BALDOVAN

ALDBAR

occupies the site of an old castle, is a magnificent house of the French chateau type.

Aldbar, also in the Brechin district, is the residence of Patrick Chalmers of Aldbar. The war in South Africa has a personal and special interest there through John Ernest Chalmers and Cecil Wolseley Chalmers being troopers in Colonel Plumer's Rhodesian Horse. Aldbar Castle, which occupies a beautiful situation on the South Esk two miles from Brechin, is an instance of the conversion of an old castle into a modern mansion. The estate has been in the possession of the Chalmers family for about a century and a half. The most eminent member of the family was Patrick Chalmers, who represented the Montrose District of Burghs in Parliament from 1835 to 1842. He was public-spirited, philanthropic, and a man of excellent literary taste. Chalmers edited a number of club books, and was the author of that important contribution to the archæology of Scotland, " The Sculptured Monuments of Angus."

The castles and mansions mentioned here have some connection with the South African war, and it is for that reason they have been selected for notice. What has been said is sufficient to show that the inmates of the castles, as well as of the cottages and town dwellings of the shire, have not been behind in devotion to their country in what has been regarded as a crisis of the Empire.

MARS AND VENUS.   By "CYNICUS."

"THEY TOLD ME YOU WERE DEAD."

By H. D. Lowry.

THEY told me you were dead, dear,
   A hundred years ago;
   For every moment is a year
To the prisoners of woe.
They told me you were dead, dear,
   That I might understand
Why light of sun and moon and stars
   Had left the dismal land.

They told me you were dead, dear,
   And flowers were sweet no more;
God's self could find no gift for me
   In all His wondrous store.
They told me you were dead, dear,
   I could not understand
Why sea and sky and place of dreams
   Were empty as the land.

They tell me you are dead, dear,
   They tell me that I live;
Yet He who holds the keys of death
   Alone hath boons to give.
They told me you were dead, dear,
   A hundred years ago;
For every moment is a year
   To the prisoners of woe.

HUSSARS. BY J. W. HERALD.

SERGEANT-MAJOR BURNS OF THE NINETY-THIRD.

A Sketch in Angus Vernacular.

By J. B. Salmond.

WHAT a chield my man Sandy is! I'm sure I micht juist as weel hae been oot in the Free State sin' we pley'd wi' thae Boer billies; for the state Sandy's keepit me in a' winter has been a doonricht scunner. D'ye ken, I've been nearhand dotrifeed wi' him an' his argey-bargeyin' an' ither ongaens. There's been naething but war in his heid for mair than a sax-month noo. I'll swag, Donal' an' me ha'e haen a hankle to thole; we'll be bley'd when the war's ower, I can tell ye.

Mornin', noon, an' nicht Sandy's been at it. He's generally devourin' the papers afore he has his galaces buttoned; an' i' the middle o' suppin' his porridge he'll gi'e Nathan an' me a lang laberlathan aboot koppies an' ither sik-like fyke-facks an' kyowows, an' the mistaks that Buller an' Roberts, an' a curn mair o' oor generals are makin', that wou'd gar you think that gin Sandy were oot aboot he wou'd go hammerin' roond the Boers like a cooper roond a cuid.

An' I can tell ye Donal' has haen some gey days o't when the British got a lampin' frae the Boers! I'm thinkin' he'll no forget Magersfontein or Nicholson's Nek in a hurry. Sandy thrashed him wi' his cornal whups, an' ruggit at the reinds till Donal' got fair doited; an' he bunged the tatties oot o' the scales into the wives' baskets like's he had tint his rizzen athegither. You never saw a man in sik a pavey!

"Fine mornin', Sandy!" said Leerie Ethart, as he was busy cleanin' the lamp at the corner o' oor street that mornin' the wird cam aboot Spion Kop.

"Ay," says Sandy, glowerin' at him like a warlock; "a fine mornin' for lazy whaups like you scoongin' aboot at hame when you shou'd be awa' fechtin' for your country. Man, if I'd been twenty 'ear younger, I'd hae clappit a saddle on Donal's back, an' aff to ha'e a peelik at the Boers mysel'. You a volunteer! G'wa back to the butter-market an' gi'e in your breeks an' your bayonet! You shou'd be ashamed to be seen gaen aboot!"

Leerie was that taen aback, he near fell aff his ladder. "What are you rampagin' aboot, you cankered wratch," says he. "I ga'e in my name; an' they wou'dna hae me 'cause I was married."

"G'wa! Tyach, man!" says Sandy, as ill-natur'd as a whittret. "You'd nae business bein' married;" an' he ga'e Donal' a wallop that sent him an' the cairt roond the corner like a flash o' lichtnin'.

"What a girnin' vampire that man Bowden is," said Leerie to Swack, oor policeman, as he stood at the corner an' leuch.

"Imphm!" said Swack wi' a smile that garr'd a' his face an' neck turn like a washin'-board wi' lirks. "He's no juist very perjink in his langitch. But, still an' on, the sicht o' Sandy on that ramfeezled sharger o' his micht fleg a fell curn Boers."

It was juist aboot as far the ither wey wi' Sandy that mornin' that noos cam' o' the relief o' Ladysmith. He ga'e Donal' a feed o' corn that micht ha'e gi'en an elephant a teenge; an' at nicht when he was beddin' him he biggit the clean strae up aboot Donal's hurdies till the cratur was fear'd to start till his supper! An', I can tell ye, there was nae jimp wecht that day! The ae scale was gaen doon wi' a doish that nearhand pitched the wechts oot o' the ither. Ye may tak' my wird for't, the profit o' that day's dealin's wasna ill to spend!

Its a mercy the British didna win every mornin', or, it's as fac's ocht, we'd been roupit to the door gin this time. Patriotism is a grand thing, nae doot. There's nane fonder than me o' country an Queen—God bless an' preserve her kind heart for mony a lang day! But when patriotism gangs the len'th o' echt-pound to the half-steen—mercy me, ye ken, there's no' a livin' in't ava. But that's nether here nor there!

Well, then, as I was genna tell ye—but there's aye sae muckle to tell aboot that man o' mine!—juist the neist week Sandy was in the backshop i' the forenicht, wi' the Smith an' twa-r-three mair o' his cronies, busy ootflankin' the Boers amon' the butter-kits, and explainin' hoo he cou'd ha'e timmered them up if he'd been in Buller's place.

"Juist suppose, for instance, that this was a Boer commando" says Sandy, settin' half-a-dizzen butter-kits in a row. "Weel, here's Buller here, an' there's them there. The richt plan is juist to jook roond their flank, alang by the meal-girnel there so to speak, d'ye see, through the nicht; jink up ahint their sentries an' get grips o' them by the thrapple afore they can lat a single peek. Then i' the mornin', there ye are! Ye're in ahint them, an' they've ether to gi'e in or get blotted aff the slate, as Rudyard Kiplin' says. That's the wey I wou'd snod them."

"No' a bad idea, Sandy" says the Smith; "but suppose they mibby jinkit roond your flank when you was jookin' roond their's! That wou'dna be so handy, wou'd it?"

"I'll no' say but that there micht mibby be a possibeelity o' them doin' that," says Sandy, gi'en his heid a claw. "But then's the time to left wheel an' pour in a cross fire at close range, d'ye know, d'ye see? Frontal attacks is fair murder. The only wey to gi'e the Boers a richt paikin' is to get at them through the nicht when they canna see you."

Weel, Sandy was juist in the thick o' a tirr-wirr wi' the Smith aboot what should be dune wi' Cronje, when clash to the wa' gaed the shop-door, an' in floo Ekky Hebbirn wi' the paper. You see, we're Ekky's farrest-awa customer, an' he comes skelpin' ootbye here like a huntit tod frae the station, roarin' his papers a' the road, but never stoppin' to sell a single copy. He's a droll sacket, Ekky!

Sandy's nose was into the heart o' the paper like a terrier efter a foumart; an' there was naething but "imphms" an' "ows" an' "ays" for five minutes. Syne he suddenly gae a jump aff his seat. "Eh?" says he, haudin' the paper at airm's len'th, an' starin' intil't like's he was mesmerised. "What say ye?" says he. "No' possible! Bliss my heart!"

"What's this noo, Sandy?" says the Smith. "Naebody hurt or killed that we ken I howp."

"Bawbie!" cried Sandy like's he'd gotten his fingers nippit. "Come 'ere 'oman, an' hear this! What d'ye think? Roddie Burns has gotten the Victoria Cross—presented by Buller at Ladysmith, for bravery at the battle o' Colenso! Losh keeps, lads! The Sergeant-Major was abune sax-feet afore; he'll be bigger than ever noo!"

"Eh, but Marget will be a prood woman" says I. "She was aye terriple beelt-up in her loon, Roddie!"

"We maun go up to Montquhir anes-errand an' see them, Bawbie" says Sandy. "I'll go an gi'e the harness a bit snod-up juist this very minute"; and aff he set an' his cronies wi' him. There's nae aff-pet wi' Sandy when he tak's a thing intil his heid.

"Weel, to mak a lang story short, to Montquhir we had to go—rizzen be't or nane—the very neist day; Sandy, the Smith, Nathan an' me an' Donal'. A bonnie day it was! The tender green o' the wids was like a drink o' fresh water on a stoury efternune, an' the whistle o' the caller wind amon' their branches was as heartsome as the gurgle o' a bairnie's lauch.

When we landed at Montquhir, here was the Sergeant-Major standin' at the yett, smokin' his pipe, lookin' as kingly an' commandin' as ever; carryin' his seventy odd winters as lichtly as Maggie—that's Roddie's little lassockie; she's a fell taed noo, of course—wou'd carry a bunch o' maysies.

"Sandy! Bawbie!" he said, stappin' ootower to meet's. "What airt's the wind in the day ava that it's blawn ye this gate?"

Sandy ga'e the reinds a twine into Donal's curpin, jamp doon, an' shook hands wi' Roderick something terriple, peyin' nae farrer heed to ether horse or cairt. If it hadna been Nathan, we'd a' been heels-ower-gowrie i' the ditch; Donal's that fond o' a green moofu'.

"An' hoo's Marget?" says I, efter Roderick had lifted me oot o' the cairt, juist as I've seen him do when I was a roid young coign, say——ow, weel, a fell twa-'r-three year syne noo!

"Aye haudin' the road an' juist witterin' awa; but naething to brag aboot," said Roderick. "But here she is, see!" he added, as Marget cam' hirplin' doon the yaird.

I can tell ye, it wasna lang till Marget had the kettle an' frying-pan singin' on the fire, an' the benhoose table laden wi' pozels o' her ain scones an' bannocks, an' bowls lippin' foo o' sweet milk. She didna hain the kitchen, I ashure ye! An' we did tak' oor tea! Haud your tongue! D'ye ken, the fresh air made me that hungry that I was nearhand black affrontit at my ain appiteet. An' Nathan stack in till I was akinda fley'd at him. But Marget was aye handin' him the ither sheed o' breed, laden wi' sweet butter an' grozer-jeel'; an' Nathan had a crap for a' corn.

Hoosomever, we a' enjoyed oor tea by-ordinar' weel; an' syne Marget drew inby the sofa an' we got a' set roond the fire, the Sergeant-Major in his ain big chair, wi' Sandy opposite him, an' the rest o's atween them.

"Ay; it's a great honour," said Roderick, reaching up to the chumla for his pipe, an' takin' a prood, half-waefu' glint o' the row o' medals that hang below his father's picture.

"It is!" said the Smith, gettin' ready his cutty to bear Roderick company in a reek. "Your father wou'd ha'e been a prood man this day, had he lived to see't."

"Ay; an' I think this is what grandfather prayed for for forty year, Smith," said the Sergeant-Major. "He is, I'm pretty sure, if no' a prood, a happy man this day, if he kens o' this. An' I believe he does," he added in a voice like's he was pronouncin' a benediction, "though it's aucht-an-fifty year noo sin' they happit him in his grave owerby at Redstane."

D'ye ken, when I was a young kimmer I had aye a feelin', when I was speakin' to Roderick Burns—that was afore he listed an' gaed awa to the Crimea—that he cou'd ha'e ta'en me an' putten me in his pooch. He was that magerfu'; I never met his marrow! The soond o' his voice had a bum in't like the wind in the wids o' the Guynd; an' his big, saft grey e'e glinted as gin a lamp was lichtit in his heid. It's as fac's ocht, d'ye ken, he aye made me feel akinda mauchtless—although a kinder-hearted man never stappit. That's a lang time syne noo; but, wou'd ye believe it, the very same feelin' cam' ower me when he spak' o' his grandfather.

"He focht at Camperdown, didna he?" speered Sandy.

"He focht at Camperdown," repeated Roderick. "An' a weel-faur'd chield he maun ha'e been," he added, blawin' a moofu' o' reek into the lum, an' starin' into the heart o' the fire. "There was fully sax-feet o' him, Sandy; Admiral Duncan himsel' said that Roderick Burns, Sergeant o' Marines on the 'Belliqueux,' was aboot the only man in his fleet that he wou'dna care to tackle single-handed. An' the Admiral—as ye've nae doot heard tell—was as brave, as big, an' as bonnie a Scotsman as ever focht for his native land."

"I mind weel o' hearin' your father speak of'en o' Admiral Duncan an' Lord Northesk," says I. "An' the wey he spak o' your grandfather was aye something byordinar'."

"Ay, Bawbie," said Roderick, wi' a twinkle in his e'e that reminded me o' lang-syne; "gin my grandmither had been as gleg a hand at the pen as you, she cou'd hae written a scrift aboot her man weel wirth readin'. He was nearhand as winderfu' a character as Sandy himsel'."

"You've been a fechtin' family," said the Smith. "Your grandfather focht at Camperdown; your father was at Waterloo; you gaed through the Crimea an' the Mutiny yoursel'; an' noo here's young Roderick gotten the Victoria Cross! I'm thinkin' there's no' many families in Scotland can brag o' sik a story. What sent ye a' into the fechtin' business ava?"

"That's a story that gangs back to the Mutiny at the Nore; an' there's nane livin' the day that can tell the whole o't," answered Roderick. "If you wanted to rouse grandfather's dander, you had juist to mention the Nore. He used to say that Parker an' the rest got nae mair than they deserved; but he thocht some o' the doited dunderheids at the Admiralty wou'd ha'e been nane the waur o' a bit hangin' at the same time. He got into some pickle ower the heid o't; an', even efter Camperdown, there was a stramush, and grandfather cam hame. His father died within a twa-r-three days o' his hame-comin', an' his mither was left her leefu' lane. The fowk at the heid o' affairs in the Navy made some enquiry efter grandfather, an' were tell'd that Roderick Burns was deid. They thocht it was grandfather, an' there was nae mair wird o't. But baith Duncan o' Camperdown an' Northesk kent a' the story, an' they were here, baith o' them, aneth this very roof, oftener than ance."

"Michty me! D'ye say so?" says Sandy, gowpin' up at the rafters wi' his moo wide open, an' his hands up like Dominie Sampson. "By faigs, lads; this is a hoose wirth bidin' in!"

"There was some mystery aboot it," continued Roderick. "My father didna ken the exact particulars; but he aye said it was naething dishonourable. An' it cou'dna ha'e been; for Admiral Northesk an' Captain Inglis o' Redhall—that was him that commanded the 'Belliqueux' at Camperdown, an' said, juist as they were signallin' to begin the battle,—'Damn thae signals! Up wi' the hellum an' into the middle o' them'—baith o' them stood at grandfather's graveside; an' Northesk said to Mester Powrie, the minister, when he was biddin' grannie good-bye, 'A British Admiral, goin' into the stiffest battle he micht ever face, could wish for no better man than Sergeant Burns to stand at his shoulder on the upper deck.' That I've been tell'd; but this I ken—that my father listed an' focht at Waterloo to please his father; an' when grandfather was on his death-bed he said to my father, 'You'll gi'e ane o' your loons to your country, Roderick'; an' that's hoo I cam to see bloody battles in the Crimea, an' wi' Sir Colin in the days o' the Mutiny."

"Ay," brook in Sandy, wi' a pech o' relief—he'd been listenin' wi' moo, een an' ears wide open—"Sir Colin was a general wirth while speakin' aboot. Man, if we'd only haen him ootbye i' the noo, Mester Kruger, an' the feck o' thae Boer billies, wou'd hae been brakin' stanes in Perth gyle gin this time. We've muckle need o' a little o' the Balaclava kind o' thing oot aboot Sooth Africa, Roderick. We maun ha'e some o' you auld 'Thin Red Line' billies reekit oot an' sent to the Transvaal yet, Sergeant. We have Mester Cobb doon in Arbroath, an' Sergeant Jago in Montrose, an' a curn mair, besides yoursel. I'm thinkin' you billies cou'd timmer up a puckle Boers the richt gate yet, auld age an' athegither."

Roderick blew a ring o' reek in the air, an' his lauch was like the soond o' a bugle. "We've a fell curn grand generals at hame, Sandy," says he, "writing to the noospapers, or sellin' tatties, for that pairt o't. Experts, I see they ca' some o' them. Weel, I'm mibby no' muckle o' a judge; but it's my opinion that the British sodger—ay, an' the British general an' a'—is what he has aye been, the bravest an' best in the world. That, as Marget here wou'd say, is the clash o' the countryside in every land o' the earth. Ay, an' Mester Cobb's aye toddlin' aboot, is he?" he added efter a whilie.

"He is that; an' winderfu' fleet an' hardy," said the Smith.

"Ay, ay," said Roderick, takin' anither look into the fire. "Nane o's is likely to forget that October mornin' in a hurry."

"You mean Balaclava?" said Sandy.

"Balaclava," repeated the Sergeant-Major. "But, man, when ye come to think o't, there's michty little atween victory and defeat sometimes. If the Rooshians had haen anither donal o' vodka—that was the whisky they drank— that mornin', there's nae sayin' but Sir Colin's 'Thin Red Line' michta been ca'ed a' to crockineeshin, an' him sent hame just like Gatacre."

"Bide ye noo, Roderick," I says, says I. "By golly, lad, if ye begin to rin doon the 'Thin Red Line' Sandy 'ill be on to Donal's back chairgin' you himsel. He has a grand picture o't in the backshop at hame, an' he lectures everlastin' aboot Balaclava to all an' sundry. I'll swag, Sergeant, but you'll better ca' canny."

"Nane o' your ornamental lees, noo, Bawbie," says Sandy. "Roderick's richt eneuch. Isn't Burns that says somewey—

> Genius frae madness is no' far awa,
> There's michty little atween the twa.

"That's in my schoolbook," said Nathan, "but that's no' the wey o't. It's something aboot a thin partition wa'."

"You're richt eneuch, birkie," said the Sergeant-Major to Nathan. "You'll be a man afore your mither yet, my gallant lad. But dinna mistak me," he added, turnin' to the Smith an' me wi' a wave o' his hand. "I ken weel what the auld 93rd was in the days o' the Crimea. Better sodgers —if it werena mibby an antern ane or twa here an' there—never pulled the trigger o' a musket; although they said hereaboot at the time that we had in the regiment the rakin's o' the Scoorinburn o' Dundee an' o' Croall's Wynd in Arbroath. An' when we left Plymouth in the 'Himalaya' there's nae doot there were some gey like radgers amon's. They were dreeled into grand fechtin' stuff afore Balaclava, hooever. But think o' a line twa deep bein' set up to stop a thoosand o' the best cavalry in the Rooshian airmy. Man, it lookit like settin' up a red-stane dyke to haud back the sea."

"I wou'dna doot but there mibby micht be something in what you say," says Sandy.

"They cam thunderin' doon like a winter flood in the nairro' o' the Gannochy," continued Roderick. "The growl o' their oncomin' fury was like the rum'le o' hell aneth oor feet; the very earth was tremblin'. I took a bit gley alang the line an' saw the feathers in the busbies o' the 93rd quiver like's they'd been shaken wi' the wind. It was the boys diggin' their heels in the turf an' settin' their heids like men wi' the sough o' death soondin' in their ears."

"That's it; that's exactly it!" said Sandy, jerkin' forrit his heid, an' steekin' his niv's like's he saw fifty Rooshians fleein' at him. "I've Mester Gibb's picture o't at hame. Man, Roderick, I'd gi'en a pound-note to been there!"

"Ay, Sandy," replied Roderick quietly, bringin' his hand across his broo; "if you'd been there you'd mibby gi'en twa pound-notes—gin you'd haen them—to be some ither wey."

"Ay, Sandy" said Cairncortie," "if you'd been there you'd gi'en the best teeth in your chafts to be back safe upon the front-end o' your tattie-cairt."

Cairncortie had come in while Roderick was speaking, alang wi' Tillyhiot an' Tympinny Tamson the joiner frae Wardnook.

"Inby, and sit ye doon" said Marget, as they cam' into the room. "Ye see," she says, turnin' to me, "a' kind o' characters get bilbie in this hoose."

"When the Rooshian cavalry swung aboot to get roond oor richt flank" continued Roderick—for he was back into the thick o' the battle again—"There were a fell puckle tume saddles an' troopers on fit gin that time — Sir Colin wheeled the Grenadier Company on its centre to the right, an' bent back his line till it was like a half-shut knife. The Rooshian General saw that he had met mair than his marrow, an' in a twinklin' his squadrons were awa back the wey they cam', leavin' a gey curn' deid an' wounded ahent them."

"That was something wirth ca'in' a battle" Sandy blurted oot, slappin' his hands on his knees. "Lyin' in trenches pappin' awa at ane anither on the sly; feech, that's no' war ava; it's mair like pee-koo!"

"But what I was to say, Sandy," Roderick gaed on, "was this — that, if the Rooshian cavalry had come on — an' I'm no' sure but an extra gless o' vodka the piece wou'd hae brocht them; the Rooshians cudna fecht wirth a doit excep' when they were half foo—oor 'Thin Red Line' wou'd hae run a gey sharpin'. If it had gane to pieces, a' the experts an' backshop generals in the kingdom wou'd hae been on to Sir Colin's tap, an' tell'd him an' a' the country what a gomeral he was. It's easy winnin' battles wi' ammunition oot o' an ink-bottle, Sandy, an' the enemy the maitter o' three thoosand miles awa'!"

Sandy saw brawly that Roderick had him; so, ha'in' naething to say, he took oot his hankie an' blew his nose.

"An' what aboot the wife that ga'e some o' the Turks a paikin' when they were fleein' through amon' the Highlanders to get oot o' the road?" says Tillyhiot.

"I've read aboot that in oor history at hame," said Nathan. "She was raised at them for rinnin' awa, the cooardie things 'at they were!"

"I saw her," said Roderick. "She was a glib-tongued tague, I can tell ye. It set a roar o' a lauch richt through the regiment to hear an' see her yalpin' an' layin' frae her amon' the sneakin' dogs. I saw her gi'e ae muckle dosent snotter a fung wi' her fit that garr'd him play skloit a' his len'th, an' he up an scuddit like a maukin withoot sayin' a wird. They said she cam' frae the Gallowgate o' Glesca; her langitch seemed to me to ha'e a flavour o' Lochee aboot it. It was aboot as strange a sicht as ever was seen on a battlefield — a woman lampin' sodgers to get them to stand an' face up the enemy. But the Turks — the very fowk for whose sake French an' British blood was poured oot like water — the damned villains gaed an' robbit oor tents while we were facin' their foes an' fechtin' their battles!"

"The nesty footers" said Sandy, haudin' up his steekit niv. "If I'd been there I'd garr'd some o' the skrunts chowl their chafts."

"It's a winder to me that oor sodgers gaed on fechtin' when they saw what wirthless whaups the Turks were," said the Smith.

"There never was a wird o' insubordination that I heard," said the Sergeant-Major; "but when we were hurklin' doon in the trenches up ower the kuits amon' slush, wi' naething but teuch pork an' rum to eat an' drink — an' often michty little o' that — there was mony a British musket that wou'd hae turned on the Turks wi' as keen determination at the butt-end o't as sent its bullets up to the ramparts o' Sebastopol. The man in the ranks doesna think very often aboot the cause for which he fechts — an' mibby it's juist as weel for's a' that he doesna. 'For Queen and country' is enough for him. Wi' that cry on his lips the British sodger has garr'd the world winder of'ener than ance. Tak' my word for't, billies, he's as fit for his task the day as ever he was in the days o' Wellington or Sir Colin."

"You're richt!" says Sandy, startin' up aff his seat. "You've heard me say that, Smith—

> 'Their's not to reason why,
> Their's not to make reply,
> Their's but to do an' die '—

Ah, Balaclava! Was there ever sik a battle?"

"It wasna a battle," Roderick broke in; "it was a day o' splendid madness. The fey bluid seemed to hae gotten into the heid o' every officer an' man in the field. If Sir Colin's 'Thin Red Line' was a risk, Scarlett's chairge wi' the Heavies was a reckless temptin' o' Providence. Man, the Brigade disappeared amon' the Rooshian squadrons like fox-hunters intil a wid. It was a winder they ever cam' oot. As for the chairge o' Cardigan an' the Light Brigade, that was the maddest but most magnificent exploit ever seen on a British battlefield. I've seen mony a sodger drunk wi' the wine o' war—it tak's a strong heid to cairry muckle o' that drink—but at Balaclava the whole British force was delirious wi' valour. You speir at Mester Cobb the first time you meet him, an' he'll tell you that half-a-dizzen times some o's had to grip youngsters in the 93rd by the cuff o' the neck to keep them frae rushin' oot an' chairgin' the Rooshian cavalry!"

"An' did you no' see the Chairge of the Light Brigade, Roderick?" I speered.

"No" said he; "that took place on the ither side o' the hill; but I saw the remains o't that nicht when we were oot buryin' oor deid. Ay; there was the makin' o' mony a wearyfu' hame in that day's wark, Bawbie—mony a weel faur'd fellow—baith British an' Rooshian—lyin' stark an' still wi' nane to speir 'Wha's ocht him?' If ever I got greit-hearted, it was that forenicht as I helped to bury Lieutenant Abercrombie, as brave an' braw a lad as ever wore a cockit bonnet. Ay; ay!" said the Sergeant-Major; an' he lichit a spunk atween the ribs an' sat lookin' into the flame o't, wi' his pipe in the ither hand, croonin' to himsel'—

> "Oh, wat ye no my hert was sair
> When I happit the mouls on his yellow hair;
> Oh, wat ye no my hert was wae
> When I turned aboot an' went my way!"

"Eh, sirce, ay," says Marget, in a waefu' voice; "it maun be a mournfu' sicht a battlefield. I wiss my laddie were hame again to his wife an' bairnies, an' his soord an' gun laid by. I'm sure, sodger's wife an' mither though I be, nae woman ever prayed mair anxiously than me for the day when, as the auld Paraphrase says—

> "No longer hosts encount'ring hosts
> Shall crowds of slain deplore;
> They hang the trumpet in the hall
> An' study war no more."

"Oh, but Roddie 'ill sune be back, Marget," said the Smith, layin' his hand on her shuder; "an' a gey prood woman you'll be. I'm thinkin' the boddom o' the greybeard 'ill be turned to the rafters that day. I'm no' growkin' for a biddin'; but I'll wad a groat, if I'm spared, ye may lippen to me bein' here to help awa' wi' a donal o' its contents. Ay, Marget, an' gin his country shou'd need him, when Roddie's litlan grows to be a man—an' may God spare an' bless him—his grannie, I ken, is no' the woman that wou'd refuse to gi'e, for Queen an' Fatherland, anither Roderick yet!"

There was a glimmer o' a tear in Roderick's e'e as Marget an' the Smith spak; but his mooth closed ower his pipeshank like a vice; an' I cou'dna help sayin' to mysel'—"Thank God, oor beloved Queen an' country ha'e little to fear as lang as we can breed an' bring up sodgers like Sergeant-Major Burns!"

AT HOME—COVE HA'EN, ARBROATH

ABROAD—SOUTH ESK. LONGFORD. TASMANIA

From Water-Colour Sketches by   *Miss L. Macdonald, M.A. Lond.*

THE ANGUS MUSTER-ROLL MARCH.

By the Hon. Mrs F. J. BRUCE of Seaton

THE ANGUS MUSTER-ROLL MARCH.

THE ANGUS MUSTER-ROLL MARCH.

THE ANGUS MUSTER-ROLL MARCH.

THE ANGUS MUSTER-ROLL MARCH.

THE ANGUS MUSTER-ROLL MARCH.

THE ANGUS MUSTER-ROLL MARCH.

From Chalk Drawing by   Helen B. Mill.

PORTRAITS OF ANGUS OFFICERS, TROOPERS, &c.

PORTRAITS OF ANGUS OFFICERS

IN

BRITISH REGIMENTS AND NAVAL BRIGADES

AND OF

ANGUS OFFICERS, TROOPERS, &c., IN COLONIAL AND VOLUNTEER FORCES

ENGAGED IN SOUTH AFRICAN WAR.

1899-1900.

Commander Ogilvy
Captain Lyulph Ogilvy
Trooper David Mitford
Lieut. Malcolm Lyon
Lieut. Clement Mitford

LIEUT. BALLINGALL. LIEUT. MUDIE.
LIEUT. COLLIER. LIEUT. MACGREGOR.

MAJOR LAING.
TROOPER STANLEY DUCAT.
CAPT. & ADJUT. WEIGHTON.
PTES. TOM, ALEC, & ANDREW McPHERSON.
TROOPER WILLIAM REID.

Trooper F. L. Scrymgeour Wedderburn

Trooper A. C. Anderson

Trooper C. Chalmers

Colonel Finlayson

Sergeant E. S. Vallentine

Lieut. A. Dickson

Trooper J. E. Chalmers

The Muster-Roll of Angus.

CAPT. J. M. ROBERTSON.
W. MURRAY GUTHRIE, M.P. TROOPER S. B. JOLLY.
PTE. D. J. SCOTT, M.S.C. PTE. MAXWELL BALFOUR.
TROOPER J. McL. DERRICK, IMPERIAL YEOMANRY.

TROOPER D. L. PATULLO. CORP. JOHN J. CABLE.
DR LOUIS IRVINE. DR D. M. GREIG. DR INVERARITY.
TROOPER NIBLOCK-STUART. COL.-SERGT. A. CHEYNE.

Pte. F. Bertie. Pte. J. M. Reid. Pte. A. Kidd. Pte. W. Walker. Pte. T. Ferguson. Pte. R. M. Baxter. Pte. J. Duncan.
Bugler J. Quinn. Pte. J. Norwell. Pte. A. Mathewson. Pte. J. M. Duncan. Pte. N. M. Welsh. Pte. D. Fraser. Pte. J. Scrimgeour.
Pte. J. Ogg. Sgt. D. S. Sime. Cpl. R. C. Skinner. Pte. W. Millar. Pte. R. R. Campbell.

ACTIVE SERVICE SECTION 2nd Jan. 1900
3rd V.B. THE BLACK WATCH

Pte. J. Kelly.　Pte. J. Gray.　Pte. A. Greig.　Bugler A. Chalmers.　Pte. J. Duncan.　Pte. H. Harris.
Lce.-Cpl. D. Florence.　Pte. J. Jack.　Pte. W. Cosgrove.　Pte. J. Cameron.　Pte. H. Low.　Lce.-Cpl. A. Malcolm.
Cpl. J. Burt.　Lce.-Sgt. G. Brander.　Sgt. J. Gegan　Lieut. H. K. Smith.　Lce.-Sgt. L. Bisset.　Cpl. W. Carnegie.　Cpl. W. Donaldson.

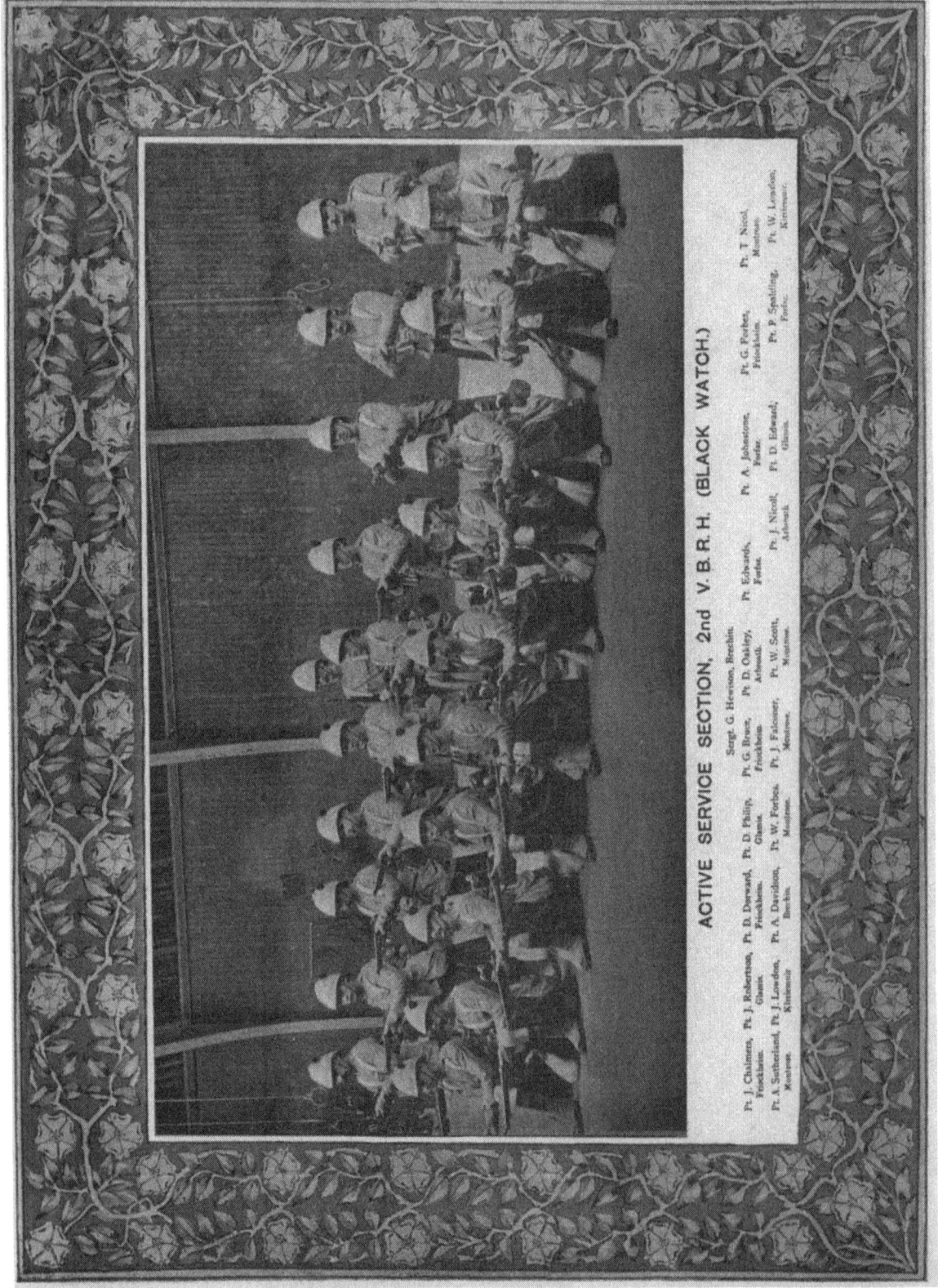

ACTIVE SERVICE SECTION, 2nd V.B.R.H. (BLACK WATCH.)

Sergt. G. Hewison, Brechin.

Pt. J. Chalmers, Friockheim. Pt. J. Robertson, Glamis. Pt. B. Dorward, Friockheim. Pt. D. Philip, Glamis. Pt. G. Bruce, Friockheim. Pt. D. Ogilvy, Arbroath. Pt. Edwards, Forfar. Pt. A. Johnstone, Forfar. Pt. G. Forbes, Friockheim. Pt. T. Nicol, Montrose.

Pt. A. Sutherland, Montrose. Pt. J. Lowdon, Kirriemuir. Pt. A. Davidson, Brechin. Pt. W. Forbes, Montrose. Pt. J. Falconer, Montrose. Pt. W. Scott, Montrose. Pt. J. Nicoll, Arbroath. Pt. D. Edwards, Glamis. Pt. P. Spalding, Forfar. Pt. W. Lowdon, Kirriemuir.

PORTRAITS OF ANGUS NON-COMMISSIONED OFFICERS
AND RANK AND FILE.

PORTRAITS

OF

ANGUS NON-COMMISSIONED OFFICERS AND
RANK AND FILE

IN

BRITISH REGIMENTS

ENGAGED IN SOUTH AFRICAN WAR.

1899-1900.

DRIVER WM. ROBERTSON, R.F.A.
Distinguished Service Medal for Heroic Effort to save the Guns at Colenso.

The Muster-Roll of Angus.

The Muster-Roll of Angus.

The Muster-Roll of Angus.

The Muster Roll of Angus.

184   The Muster-Roll of Angus.

NOTES ON ANGUS OFFICERS, COLONIALS VOLUNTEERS, &c.

NURSE E. MABEL BICKERDYKE,

Grand-daughter of the late Angus Calder, Arbroath; served on Staff of General Hospital (No. 8), Bloemfontein.

NOTES

ON
OFFICERS IN BRITISH REGIMENTS & NAVAL BRIGADES,
AND
OFFICERS, TROOPERS, &c, IN COLONIAL AND VOLUNTEER FORCES.

The Number at end of each Note indicates the Page upon which Portrait may be found.

AIRLIE, EARL OF—David William Stanley Ogilvy, Lieut.-Colonel, commanding 12th (Prince of Wales Royal) Lancers; son of the seventh Earl of Airlie and Hon. Henrietta Blanche (daughter of second Lord Stanley of Alderley.) Born, 1856; educated at Eton. Lieutenant's Commission, 1875; Major of 10th Royal Hussars, 1885; Lieut.-Colonel of 2nd Dragoon Guards (Queen's Bays); served in the Afghan War, 1878 (Medal); in Egypt, 1884 (Medal); and in Nile Expedition, 1884-85; wounded at Abu Klea and at Metammeh; twice mentioned in despatches (Brevet-Major and two clasps.) Lord Airlie's honours include the Afghan and East Soudan Medals with Clasps, the fourth-class Medjidie, and also two Clasps for the Nile Expedition. Lord Airlie went to South Africa in command of the 12th Lancers, of which regiment he was gazetted Lieutenant-Colonel in 1897. During the war he was several times mentioned in despatches, his services at a critical moment during the battle of Magersfontein, when he dismounted two squadrons and checked the enemy, coming in for special mention. In the thick of the fight wherever his troop was called upon, Lord Airlie was frequently under fire; he was severely wounded in the fight at Welkom on 4th May. He recovered speedily under the devoted care of the Countess, who attended him at Bloemfontein; he rejoined his regiment in the beginning of June, and died a soldier's death in action near Pretoria on 12th June. A braver soldier or more intrepid cavalry officer never served his Queen. The Earl of Airlie maintained, with great distinction, the highest military traditions of the name he bore, and his kindness of heart and generous treatment of his tenantry maintained other family traditions not less honourable and popular. Wherever he was known, Lord Airlie's death was heard of with deep regret; in Forfarshire it was felt amongst all classes with the keen sorrow of personal bereavement. The one consolation lay in the fact that he had died as, one can well believe, he would have wished to die had it been his to choose—in action, at the head of his men, and with his face to the foe. Lord Airlie was one of Scotland's representative Peers, and a Deputy-Lieutenant of his native county. He was Hon. Colonel of the 3rd (Dundee Highland) Volunteer Battalion Black Watch (Royal Highlanders), and took a keen and generous interest in the affairs of the Battalion. The portrait in this volume is from a photograph by Charles Knight, Aldershot. [137

ANDERSON—Alex. C. Anderson, 12 Windsor Street, Dundee. Trooper, "C" Squadron, Plumer's Rhodesian Regiment. [147

ANGUS—Private G. C. Angus. Active Service Section, 1st V.B.R.H. [155

BAIRD—Trooper J. W. Baird, Downfield, Dundee. Fife and Forfar Contingent Imperial Yeomanry. [149

BALFOUR—Maxwell Balfour, 118 Cheyne Walk, Chelsea, London, son of James R. Balfour, Leven, and grandson of the late John Ogilvie, solicitor, Dundee. Served in the South African War in Cyclist Section, C.I.V. [151

BALLINGALL—Lieut. Henry Miller Ballingall. Born April, 1878; third son of ex-Provost Ballingall, Ardarroch, Dundee, J.P., D.L.; educated at Clifton Bank, St. Andrews, High School, Dundee (where he held the Ballingall Gold Medal for gymnastics for two years), and Edinburgh University. Lieut. for two years in 16th Middlesex R.V. (London Irish Rifles); commission in the Royal Garrison Artillery, June, 1899; appointed to No. 15 Company Southern Division "Siege Train" for South Africa in November, 1899. [145

BAXTER—Private R. M. Baxter. Active Service Section, 1st V.B.R.H. [157

BELL—Trooper W. Bell. Fife and Forfar Contingent, Imperial Yeomanry. [149

BERTIE—Private F. Bertie. Active Service Section, 1st V.B.R.H. [157

BIRRELL—Ernest James Birrell, second son of the late Andrew Birrell, farmer, Cardean, Meigle, and Whitestonelaw, Dundee. Got military training in C.M.R., and joined B.S.A. Police at commencement of South African War; served under Colonel Plumer. [152

BISSET—Lance-Sergeant L. Bisset. Active Service Section, 3rd V.B.R.H. [158

BLAIR—Captain Arthur Blair, A.D.C., K.O.S.B. Joined army March, 1890; Lieutenant, 1893; *Aide-de-camp* to Major-General Hildyard, October, 1899; Captain, 1900. Served in Burmah and in Soudan campaign under Lord Kitchener; present at the battle of Atbara; holds British-Soudan Medal and Khedive's Medal. Served in South African War on the staff of Major-General Hildyard, commanding the 2nd Brigade, 1st Division, of South African Field Forces. [142

BLAIR—Lieutenant Hew Francis Blair, Lincolnshire Regiment of Militia. Served in South Africa with the Behar Troop of Lumsden's Horse. Lieutenant Blair is the eldest son of Colonel Henry Blair, R.E., who is brother of Colonel Blair-Imrie of Lunan, and his heir-presumptive. [141

BLAKENEY—Robert Blakeney, 1 James Place, Broughty Ferry, latterly of Johannesburg. Volunteer in Bethune's Mounted Infantry. [153

BRANDER—Lance-Sergt. G. Brander. Active Service Section, 3rd V.B.R.H. [157

BROWN—Quarter-Master-Sergeant J. G. Brown, Craighill, Dundee; Fife and Forfar Contingent Imperial Yeomanry. [149

BRUCE—Private G. Bruce, Friockheim. Active Service Section, 2nd V.B.R.H. [159

BRUCE—George M. Bruce, Dundee. Corporal, Imperial Light Infantry. [153

BURT—Corporal J. Burt. Active Service Section, 3rd V.B.R.H. [158

CABLE—Corporal John Joseph Cable, eldest son of William Cable, Teston, Maidstone, and grandson of the late John Cable, Arbroath. Served with the 2nd Dorset Imperial Yeomanry. [154

CAMERON—Private J. Cameron. Active Service Section, 3rd V.B.R.H. [158

CAMPBELL—Private R. R. Campbell. Active Service Section, 1st V.B.R.H. [157

CARGILL—David Cargill, son of David Cargill, Longhaugh, Dundee. Educated at Dundee and Crieff. Captain of 20th Company Boys' Brigade. Served as Trooper in Fife and Forfar Contingent of Imperial Yeomanry. [149

CARGILL—Corporal D. Cargill, Toryhaugh, Dundee. Fife and Forfar Contingent Imperial Yeomanry. [149

CARNEGIE—Captain the Hon. Robert Francis Carnegie, third son of Earl of Southesk, K.T. Born 6th May, 1869; educated at Eton; joined London Scottish while studying for army in London; passed into militia,

3rd Battalion Gordon Highlanders, in 1887; commissioned 2nd Battalion Gordon Highlanders in June, 1890; special certificate as best shot amongst officers of the corps, 1893. In command of "Gordon" section of Highland Company Mounted Infantry in South Africa in 1896 at the time of Matabele War; returned to regimental duty, 1897; sailed to India with his regiment in September, 1898; and was appointed extra A.D.C. on Viceroy's staff; rejoined his battalion, 1899; arrived in Natal in October, 1899, and was sent at once to Ladysmith. Captain Carnegie showed great presence of mind and courage, and was severely wounded in the great attack by the Boers on Ladysmith on 6th January, 1900. A powerful drawing by Mr Melton Prior of Captain Carnegie's exploit at Ladysmith on 6th January, 1900 is included in this volume. Captain Carnegie, with ten Gordons, rushed the position at Cæsar's Camp which the Boers had captured, and, by great daring, was successful in putting the enemy to flight and rescuing Lieutenant Hunt Grubbe, who had been trapped and captured by the Boers. Captain Carnegie led his men gallantly and shot down four of the enemy before he fell wounded by four bullets. [138

CARNEGIE—The Hon. Ian Ludovic Andrew Carnegie, Midshipman, H.M.S. "Powerful." Born 30th September, 1881; godmother, H.R.H. Princess Louise, Duchess of Argyll; god-fathers, General Andrew Wauchope, C.B., C.M.G., and Lord Carnegie; third son of the late ninth Earl of Northesk, Ethie Castle. Went to Ladysmith with Naval Brigade under Capt. the Hon. Hedworth Lambton, R.N.; slightly wounded. On the return of H.M.S. "Powerful" to this country, Midshipman Carnegie was the recipient of handsome presents in Hampshire. From the inhabitants of Longwood he received a fine pair of field glasses, together with an illuminated address, "as a memento of the siege of Ladysmith," while the inhabitants of Owlesbury gave him a silver flask inscribed—"Presented by the people of Owlesbury to Midshipman Ian Carnegie, Her Majesty's ship 'Powerful.' Her guns saved Ladysmith, October, 1899, to February, 1900." The Queen received the Naval Brigade from H.M.S. "Powerful," which served at Ladysmith and elsewhere in South Africa, at Windsor, on Wednesday, May 2nd. Midshipman Carnegie has been rated for early promotion on qualifying for Lieutenant. [138

CARNEGIE—Corporal W. Carnegie. Active Service Section, 3rd V.B.R.H. [158

CHALMERS—Trooper John Ernest Chalmers, son of Patrick Chalmers of Aldbar. Trooper in Colonel Baden-Powell's Rhodesian Field Force under Colonel Plumer; served in Matabele War in Sir F. Carrington's Division. Born, 1874; educated, Inverness; and had military training in Lancashire Fusiliers. [147

CHALMERS—Trooper Cecil Wolseley Chalmers, son of Patrick Chalmers of Aldbar. Trooper in Colonel Baden-Powell's Rhodesian Field Force, Colonel Plumer's Regiment. Holds medal for Matabele War, 1896. Born, 1876; educated, Inverness and Haileybury College. [147

CHALMERS—Private J. Chalmers, Friockheim. Active Service Section, 2nd V.B.R.H. [159

CHALMERS—Bugler A. Chalmers. Active Service Section, 3rd V.B.R.H. [158

CHEVALLEY—Trooper Frank F. Chevalley, son of the late Capt. and Adjt. Chevalley, 1st F.V.A. Educated, Hawick and Dundee. Was preparing for entering army when South African War started, when he enlisted in Fife and Forfar Contingent of Imperial Yeomanry. [149

CHEYNE—Alex. Cheyne, formerly of Kirriemuir. Quartermaster Sergeant, Ceylon Mounted Infantry. Served in Malta, India, and Ceylon, in Gordon Highlanders. [154

CLAYHILLS—Lieutenant George Clayhills, 1st Battalion, East Lancashire Regiment, 1900. Born 1878; educated at Cheltenham and Trinity College, Cambridge. Entered army

1899; sailed for South Africa, January, 1900. Fourth son of Thomas Clayhills, Esq., Darlington, and nephew of Captain Clayhills Henderson, of Invergowrie, R.N. [141

COLLIER—Lieutenant Bertram W. Collier, son of Thomas Collier, Esq., Broughty Ferry. Born 1874; educated, Crieff and Rugby; entered army, 1894; first Lieutenant, 24th Regiment, South Wales Borderers; gazetted, February, 1894; served two years in Gibraltar, and three years in India; sailed January 13, 1900, for South Africa with second battalion of his regiment. [145

COSGROVE—Private W. Cosgrove. Active Service Section, 3rd V.B.R.H. [158

CROCKART—James H. Crockart, 12 St Peter's Place, Montrose. Private, Cape Town Volunteer Highlanders. [153

DARLING—Lieutenant John Collier Stormonth-Darling; son of Patrick Stormonth-Darling of Lednathie, Kirriemuir; grandson of the late John Collier, Panlathie. Gazetted January, 1900, second Lieutenant K.O.S.B. Educated at Cordwallis, Maidenhead, and Loretto, and served in Mounted Infantry Detachment of the Queen's Edinburgh R.V. [142

DAVIDSON — Private A. Davidson, Brechin. Active Service Section, 2nd V.B.R.H. [159

DAVIDSON—Private J. L. Davidson, Montrose. Active Service Section, 2nd V.B.R.H. [155

DAWSON—Trooper M. Dawson, Ferry Road, Dundee. Fife and Forfar Contingent Imperial Yeomanry. [149

DERRICK—J. M'Leod Derrick. Served in 70th Company Imperial Yeomanry Sharpshooters' Corps. Appointed leader of his sub-section. [151

DEWAR—Thos. Finlayson Dewar, Hill Terrace, Arbroath, eldest son of Dr J. A. Dewar, Arbroath. Educated, High School, Arbroath, Aberdeen, and Edinburgh; B.Sc. 1888, M D. 1890; Surgeon-Captain Army Medical Reserve, 1889; Surgeon-Captain Forfar Light Horse. Enlisted as Trooper in the Fife and Forfar Unit of the Imperial Yeomanry. Was appointed during war to medical superintendency of the Sixth Battalion of Imperial Yeomanry. [148

DICKSON — James Dickson, son of David Dickson, gardener, Castle Roy, Broughty Ferry. Served as Trooper in Glasgow Contingent of Imperial Yeomanry. [152

DICKSON—Arthur Dickson, junr., National Bank House, Montrose. Born, 1874; son of Arthur Dickson, Montrose; educated, Montrose and Edinburgh; Commission, 2nd V.B.R.H., 1892; Lieutenant in Reserve of Officers for Land Forces, 1896; passed School of Instruction at Chelsea Barracks, 1895. Joined Ceylon Contingent of Mounted Infantry for service in South African War. [147

DONALDSON—Corporal W. Donaldson. Active Service Section, 3rd V.B.R.H. [158

DORWARD — Private D. Dorward, Letham. Active Service Section, 2nd V.B.R.H. Died in hospital at Cape Town. [159

DUCAT—Stanley Ducat, M.B., C.M., son of Mr William Ducat, Warslap, Arbroath. Trooper in Lumsden's Light Horse. [146

DUNCAN—Private J. Duncan. Active Service Section, 3rd V.B.R.H. [158

DUNCAN—Private J. Duncan. Active Service Section, 1st V.B.R.H. [157

DUNCAN—Private J. M. Duncan. Active Service Section, 1st V.B.R.H. [157

EDWARD—Private D. Edward, Glamis. Active Service Section, 2nd V.B.R.H. [159

EDWARDS—Private Edwards, Forfar. Active Service Section, 2nd V.B.R.H. [159

EDWARDS — Private A. Edwards. Active Service Section, 1st V.B.R.H. [155

FALCONER—Private J. Falconer, Montrose. Active Service Section, 2nd V.B.R.H. [159

FENWICK—Trooper J. Fenwick, Nethergate, Dundee. Fife and Forfar Contingent Imperial Yeomanry. [149

FERGUSON—Private T. Ferguson. Active Service Section, 1st V.B.R.H. [157

FERRIER — David L. Ferrier, of Arbroath. Served as Stretcher-Bearer in Field Ambulance Corps with Buller's forces in Natal. Long well-known as a prominent cricketer in Forfarshire. [152

FINDLAY—Trooper G. C. Findlay, Downfield, Dundee. Fife and Forfar Contingent Imperial Yeomanry. [149

FINLAYSON — Colonel Robert A. Finlayson, grandson of the late Robert Finlayson, postmaster, Arbroath. Educated in Edinburgh; went to South Africa in 1875; granted Commission in Scots Corps in Kimberley in 1890, and saw active service in Bechuanaland. The Scots Corps amalgamated with the Kimberley Rifles, in which regiment Colonel Finlayson served during the siege. [147

FLORENCE — Lance-Corporal D. Florence. Active Service Section, 3rd V.B.R.H. [158

FORBES—Private W. Forbes, Montrose. Active Service Section, 2nd V.B.R.H. [159

FORBES — Private G. Forbes, Friockheim. Active Service Section, 2nd V.B.R.H. [159

FORREST—Colin L. Forrest, Brechin, Sergeant in Brabant's Horse. [153

FRANCIS—Trooper G. A. Francis, West Seaton, Arbroath. Fife and Forfar Contingent Imperial Yeomanry. [149

FRASER—Private D. Fraser. Active Service Section, 1st V.B.R.H. [157

GARDYNE — Captain Alan David Greenhill-Gardyne, eldest son of Lieutenant-Colonel Greenhill-Gardyne of Finavon, Forfarshire (and of Glenforsa, Argyllshire), and grandson of the 9th Viscount Strathallan. Gazetted, February, 1888; Captain, 2nd Gordon Highlanders. Served with the Chitral Relief Force, 1895. Took part in action at Malakand Pass, &c. Has the Indian Frontier Medal (1895) and Clasp. [141

GARDYNE—Walter Greenhill Gardyne, son of Lieut.-Col. Greenhill-Gardyne of Finavon. Served as Trooper in Fife and Forfar Unit of Imperial Yeomanry. [149

GEGAN—Sergeant J. Gegan. Active Service Section, 3rd V.B.R.H. [158

GILROY — Captain Alistair Gilroy. Born, October, 1865; son of the late Alexander Gilroy, Dunalistair, Broughty Ferry; educated at Harrow; joined 11th Hussars February, 1884; gazetted Captain, December, 1890; retired March, 1893; married Charlotte Evelyn Shepstone, grand-daughter of the late Sir Theophilus Shepstone, K.C.M.G., who annexed the Transvaal in 1877. Sailed for South Africa, February, 1900, as officer of the reserve of officers on special service. [143

GORDON — Lewis Gordon, Milksham, Wiltshire. Served as Trooper in Wilts. Contingent, Imperial Yeomanry. Youngest son of the late George Gordon of Donavourd, Perthshire. [150

GORDON—Trooper H. P. Gordon, Brechin. Fife and Forfar Contingent Imperial Yeomanry. [149

GRAY — Private J. Gray. Active Service Section, 3rd V.B.R.H. [158

GREIG—Private A. Greig. Active Service Section, 3rd V.B.R.H. [158

GREIG — David Middleton Greig C.M., F.R.C.S.E. Born, 1863; eldest son of the late Dr Greig, Dundee, who went through the Crimean War as Surgeon; educated, Dundee, St Andrews, and Edinburgh; graduated 1885; joined Army Medical Staff, 1886, and spent four years in garrison duty in Scotland and in India. Left army for civil practice in 1890; succeeded to his father's practice; Surgeon to Dundee Royal Infirmary, 1896. Enlisted for service on Medical Staff of Lord Roberts' Field Force in South African War. [154

GUTHRIE—Walter Murray Guthrie, M.P. for Bow and Bromley. Born, 1867; younger son of D. C. Guthrie, Craigie, Forfarshire;

Stratford House, 11 Stratford Place, London, W.; partner in firm of Chalmers, Guthrie & Co., Ltd., Colonial Merchants, London. Volunteered for service as secretary and manager to American Field Hospital for South Africa. Mr Guthrie holds a commission in the Queen's Bodyguard for Scotland—the Scottish Archers—and this uniform he wears in photograph given in this volume. [151

HARRIS—Private H. Harris. Active Service Section, 3rd V.B.R.H. [158

HEWISON—Sergeant G. Hewison, Brechin. Active Service Section, 2nd V.B.R.H. [159

HIGH—Private E. S. High. Active Service Section, 3rd V.B.R.H. [155

HUNTER—Hope Hunter, Bonnington, Arbroath. Private, London Scottish Volunteers attached to 2nd Gordon Highlanders. [150

INVERARITY—Dr James Moffat Inverarity, Forfar. Educated, Forfar and Glasgow. Resident House Surgeon in Glasgow Royal Infirmary. Enlisted for service in South African War as Surgeon to the 4th Battalion Scottish Rifles. [154

IRVINE—Louis G. Irvine, Maritzburg, Natal; son of the late Rev. Walter Forbes Irvine, minister, Arbroath. Educated at High School, Arbroath, and Edinburgh. M.B., C.M., and B.Sc. Served during South African War on Sir Wm. M'Cormack's medical staff. [154

JACK—Private J. Jack. Active Service Section, 3rd V.B.R.H. [158

JACKSON—Corporal George Erskine Jackson of Kirkbuddo. Born in India, 1872; only son of the late Deputy-Surgeon-General James Rawlinson Jackson of Kirkbuddo, Indian Medical Service. Educated in India and at Oxford; qualified as W.S. in Edinburgh, 1898; enlisted January, 1900, in City of London Imperial Volunteers (Mounted Contingent); Corporal in Mounted Contingent Queen's Rifle Volunteers Brigade (Royal Scots). [150

JOHNSTONE—Private A. Johnstone, Forfar. Active Service Section, 2nd V.B.R.H. [159

JOLLY—Stuart Blackie Jolly, son of Mr W. Jolly, H.M. Inspector of Schools. Served in the South African War in Colonel Hill's Scottish Yeomanry Corps of Sharpshooters. [151

KEITH—Alex. R. Keith, grandson of ex-Provost Keith, Arbroath, and youngest son of James Keith, C.E., Arbroath and London. Piper, London Scottish Rifle Volunteers attached to 2nd Gordon Highlanders. Appointed to the Pipe Band of the Gordons. [150

KEITH—Ernest C. Keith, Ivybank, Dundee Road, Broughty Ferry. Volunteer, Prince Alfred Guards. [153

KEITH—Henry M'Grady Keith, Ivybank, Dundee Road, Broughty Ferry. On the Provision Train between Port Elizabeth and Naauwpoort. [153

KELLY—Private J. Kelly. Active Service Section, 3rd V.B.R.H. [158

KENNEDY—Robt. Kennedy, Dundee. Trooper, Kitchener's Horse. [153

KERR—David B. Kerr, Madeira Street, Dundee; son of Peter Kerr of Gallowden. Trooper in B Company, Thorneycroft's Mounted Infantry. [153

KIDD—Private A. Kidd. Active Service Section, 1st V.B.R.H. [157

KIRK—Lieutenant John William Carnegie Kirk, 2nd Battalion Duke of Cornwall's Light Infantry; gazetted 2nd Lieutenant October, 1899. Lieutenant Kirk is the only son of Sir John Kirk, G.C.M.G., K.C.B., and grandson of the late Rev. James Kirk, minister of Barry, and afterwards of Arbirlot. His grandmother was the only daughter of Rev. Alexander Carnegie of Redhall, formerly minister of Inverkeilor. Lieutenant Kirk was wounded at Paardeberg. [141

LAING—Major D. T. Laing, Woodmyre House, Edzell; Major in the Rhodesian Horse. Major Laing has seen service in most of the wars in South Africa in recent years. In the Matabele War he was in command of the Belingwe Field Force, and was promoted Major for distinguished service; served during the South African War in Intelligence Department of Commander-in-Chief's staff, and was in command of Lord Roberts' bodyguard of forty picked Colonials. Major Laing holds two medals for service in South Africa, and has written a history of the Matabele War. [146

LAMB—Claude Carnegie Lamb, Beechwood, Dunkeld, son of David J. Lamb; second Lieutenant, 2nd Battalion Black Watch. Born at St Andrews, 1881; educated at Glenalmond and Sandhurst; gazetted, January, 1900. [144

LENNOX—Trooper C. F. Lennox, Morton Terrace, Lochee. Fife and Forfar Contingent Imperial Yeomanry. [149

LINDSAY—Major Walter Fullarton Ludovic Lindsay, R.A., second son of the late Captain Lindsay, 8th Hussars, and nephew of H. A. F. Lindsay-Carnegie of Spynie and Boysack. Gazetted as Lieutenant 28th January, 1875; captain, 1st January, 1884; Major, 27th January, 1892; served in the Egyptian War in 1882; present at Tel-el-Kebir, for which he holds medal with clasp and Khedive's star. Major Lindsay was in command of 75th Battery, R.A., under General Lord Methuen, and was mentioned by his General on 27th January as having "ignored a painful wound, and continued in command of his battery" at the battle of Modder River. It was Major Lindsay's battery that effectively silenced the Boer guns in two rounds at Belmont. Major Lindsay was also present at the battles of Graspan and Magersfontein. As indication of the perfection to which Major Lindsay has brought his battery, it may be mentioned that it has several times won the first prize for driving in the competition at the Agricultural Hall. [138

Low—Private H. Low. Active Service Section, 3rd V.B.R.H. [158

Low—Trooper D. T. Low, Millhead House, Arbroath. Fife and Forfar Contingent Imperial Yeomanry. [149

LOWDEN—Private W. Lowden, Kirriemuir. Active Service Section, 2nd V.B.R.H. [159

LOWDON—Private J. Lowdon, Kirriemuir. Active Service Section, 2nd V.B.R.H. [159

LUMSDEN—Lieutenant Charles Ramsay Lumsden, 1st Battalion Gordon Highlanders; second son of the late W. H. Lumsden of Balmedie, Aberdeenshire, and grandson of the late Thomas Renny-Tailyour of Borrowfield. Entered army July, 1899; present at the battle of Magersfontein. [143

LYELL—David Lyell, son of the late Alexander Lyell of Gardyne. Served as engineer with the Royal Engineers. [153

LYON—Lieutenant the Hon. Malcolm Bowes Lyon, 2nd Life Guards; seventh and youngest son of the Earl of Strathmore, Lord-Lieutenant of Forfarshire; born, April, 1874; educated at Eton and Trinity College, Cambridge; joined 3rd Battalion Durham Light Infantry, 1893; gazetted to the 2nd Life Guards, 1895. On the outbreak of South African War he volunteered for active service, and was attached as Lieutenant to 10th Royal Hussars; served under General French in Cape Colony. Lieutenant Malcolm Lyon is exceptionally popular; an expert sportsman, a finished horseman and keen soldier. On leaving for the Front he was accorded a most enthusiastic send-off from Glamis station in October, in which pleasing expression was given to the respect in which Lord Strathmore and his family are held by their Forfarshire tenantry and neighbours. (Photograph by Thomson, 70 Grosvenor Street, London, and half-tone block by Swan Electric Engraving Co.) [139

MACDOUGALL—Trumpeter J. MacDougall, Dundee. Fife and Forfar Contingent Imperial Yeomanry. [149

MACGREGOR — Lieutenant Walter William MacGregor, 84 Cromwell Road, London; great-grandson of the late Dr Gibson, Montrose; Lieutenant, 2nd Battalion Gordon Highlanders; gazetted March, 1897; present at battle of Elandslaagte; wounded 6th January, 1900, during Boer attack on Ladysmith. [145

MACLEAN—Lieutenant Donald Charles Hugh MacLean, Royal Scots, 2nd Battalion; first commission, 28th September, 1895; second son of Major-General Charles MacLean, C.B., C.I.E., late Consul-General in Persia; and grandson of the late Peter Bairnsfather of Dumbarrow. Lieutenant MacLean is younger brother of the late Lieutenant Hector MacLean, who fell mortally wounded at Laudakai on the Indian frontier in August, 1897, while heroically rescuing two wounded brother-officers who were in great jeopardy, and who, had he survived, would have received the Victoria Cross. [140

M'GRADY—Walter Watson Hughes M'Grady. Born, 1873; son of ex-Lord Provost M'Grady, Dundee; educated, Dundee and Blairlodge. Formerly Lieutenant 1st V.B.R.H. Served as Trooper in Fife and Forfar Contingent of Imperial Yeomanry. [149

M'GRADY—Edgar Arthur M'Grady. Born, 1874; son of ex-Lord Provost M'Grady, Dundee; educated, Dundee and Blairlodge. Formerly Lieutenant 1st V.B.R.H. Served as Trooper in Fife and Forfar Contingent of Imperial Yeomanry. [149

M'INTOSH — Private J. M'Intosh. Active Service Section, 1st V.B.R.H. [155

M'KENZIE—John M'Kenzie, son of William M'Kenzie, Academy Flour Mills, Montrose. Engaged for some years with Kaffrarian Milling Coy., King William's Town. Served with Mounted Rifle Contingent. [152

M'PHERSON—Tom, Alexander, and Andrew M'Pherson, sons of the late Oliver M'Pherson, *Dispatch*, Forfar. Privates in Queenstown Rifles with Gatacre's Division, under Brigadier-General Brabant. [146

MALCOLM—Lance-Corpl. A. Malcolm. Active Service Section, 3rd V.B.R.H. [158

MATHEWSON—Private A. Mathewson. Active Service Section, 1st V.B.R.H. [157

MERRY—Lieutenant Frederick Hallard Merry, R.A.M.C., son of George Ross Merry, M.A. Oxon., LL.D., Rector, High School, Dundee. Born 1874; educated High School, Dundee, University College, Dundee, and University of Edinburgh; trained at Royal Victoria Hospital, Netley; entered army, 1899; attached to 2nd Hampshire Regiment, which forms part of the 7th Division in South African Field Force. [142

MILLAR—Captain Robert Hoyer Millar, V.D., The Links, Montrose, son of the late Christian Hoyer Millar, of Blair Castle, Fife. Captain and Hon. Major, 2nd V.B.R.H.; joined Queen's Edinburgh in 1874, and 2nd V.B.R.H., 1876. Appointed Captain of Volunteer Company of his Battalion for service in South Africa. [148

MILLAR—Private W. Millar. Active Service Section, 1st V.B.R.H. [157

MILLIKIN—Trooper J. C. Millikin, Drumore, Broughty Ferry. Fife and Forfar Contingent Imperial Yeomanry. [149

MITFORD—Lieutenant Clement Mitford, eldest son of A. B. Freeman-Mitford, C.B., of Batsford, Gloucestershire, and of the Lady Clementine Mitford, second daughter of David, 7th Earl of Airlie. Gazetted, November, 1899, second Lieutenant 10th Royal Hussars. [139

MITFORD—Trooper David Mitford, second son of A. B. Freeman-Mitford, C.B., and the Lady Clementine Mitford. Trooper in Oxfordshire Imperial Yeomanry; orderly to General Brabazon; slightly wounded. [139

MOFFET—Major Granville E. Moffet, M.B.C.M. (Aberdeen), D.P.H. (Cantab.) Address—Castle Street, Brechin; Major, R.A.M.C.; Commission January, 1885. Major Moffet served in Soudan campaign; attached to 2nd Seaforth Highlanders in the South African War; subsequently in charge of

No. 4 Field Hospital, Orange River. Senior medical officer with Colonel Pilcher's force in reconnaissance from Belmont, 3rd December, 1899. [141

MUDIE—Lieutenant T. C. Mudie, son of the late James Mudie, Craig-gowan, Broughty Ferry; born, 1880; educated in Broughty Ferry and at the Fettes College; passed into Sandhurst; Lieutenant in Royal Scots; gazetted 12th August, 1899; left for South Africa early in November, 1899; and joined General Gatacre's force in Cape Colony. [145

NICOLL—Private J. Nicoll, Arbroath. Active Service Section, 2nd V.B.R.H. [159

NICOL—Private T. Nicol, Montrose. Active Service Section, 2nd V.B.R.H. [159

NORWELL—Private J. Norwell. Active Service Section, 1st V.B.R.H. [157

OAKLEY—Private D. Oakley, Arbroath. Active Service Section, 2nd V.B.R.H. [159

OGG—Private J. Ogg. Active Service Section, 1st V.B.R.H. [157

OGILVIE—Trooper C. J. W. Ogilvie, Yr. of Coul, Alyth. Fife and Forfar Contingent Imperial Yeomanry. [149

OGILVY—Commander Frederick Charles Ashley Ogilvy, third son of Sir Reginald Ogilvy, Bart., A.D.C. to the Queen, Baldovan House, Strathmartine, Forfarshire. Born, 1866; cadet, 1880; Midshipman H.M.S. "Britannia," 1882; Lieutenant, 1888. In October, 1893, he was appointed 1st Lieutenant and Torpedo Lieutenant in H.M. Ship "Polyphemus," and in January, 1897, he was given a similar post on H.M. Ship "Defiance"; while in March of the following year he was transferred as 1st Lieutenant and Torpedo Lieutenant to H.M. Ship "Terrible." Lieutenant Ogilvy landed with H.M.S. "Terrible," at Durban, November, 1899; joined Natal Field Force (General Buller's) as Lieutenant in command of Battery of six 12-pounder naval guns; took part in action near Colenso, 15th September, 1899, and gained special mention in General Sir Redvers Buller's despatches as having rendered "excellent service." For his distinguished service at Colenso, Lieutenant Ogilvy was promoted to be Commander, and was called to Windsor, along with the other officers of H.M.S. "Powerful" on his return home. Subsequently appointed Commander of H.M.S. "Terrible." [139

OGILVY — Hon. Lyulph Gilchrist Ogilvy, Captain in Brabant's Horse. Born, 1861; second son of David, 7th Earl of Airlie. Volunteered and served with the American army in Cuba in the Spanish-American War. Captain Ogilvy is a rancher in Colorado. He volunteered for service in South African War. [139

OGILVY—Charles James Wedderburn-Ogilvy, eldest son of J. A. Wedderburn-Ogilvy of Ruthven. Enlisted as Trooper in Fife and Forfar Light Horse Contingent of Imperial Yeomanry; sailed with the Yeomanry for South Africa; died on voyage from an attack of pneumonia, and was buried at sea. [149

PARKER—Private A. Parker, Arbroath. Active Service Section, 2nd V.B.R.H. [155

PATTULLO—David Langlands Pattullo, son of the late Mr Pattullo, Hatton Mill, Friockheim. Served as Trooper in the West Kent Contingent of the Imperial Yeomanry. [154

PHILIP—Private D. Philip, Glamis. Active Service Section, 2nd V.B.R.H. [158

PIRIE—Alexander Stuart Pirie, St Andrew House, Brechin. Served as Private in Active Service Section of 1st V.B. Gordon Highlanders. [152

QUINN—Bugler J. Quinn. Active Service Section 1st V.B.R.H. [157

RAIT—Lieutenant Walter Garnet Rait, only son of Colonel Rait, C.B., of Anniston, Arbroath. Born, 1878; educated at Rugby; second Lieutenant 1st Battalion King's Own Scottish Borderers; gazetted, 3rd August, 1898; godson of Field-Marshal The Right Honourable Viscount Wolseley, K.P., G.C.B., G.C.M.G. Went through the South African War with his regiment; present at Battle of Karee; died of enteric fever at Wynberg Hospital, 22nd June, 1900. Memorial service—attended by Provost and Town Council of Arbroath —held in Arbroath Parish Church on 1st July, 1900. [138

RAMSAY — Lieutenant Nigel Neis Ramsay, eldest son of Sir James Ramsay, Bart. of Bamff, Alyth. Born, March, 1876; educated at Cargillfield, Edinburgh, and at Winchester, and passed into Sandhurst in 1895; left June, 1896, after winning Sword of Honour; second Lieutenant 2nd Battalion Black Watch; gazetted Lieutenant September, 1896; sailed for South Africa with his Battalion, and served under General Lord Methuen; killed at the battle of Magersfontein, December 11, 1899. [140

REID—William Reid, son of the late Provost Reid, Arbroath. Trooper in Lumsden's Light Horse. [146

REID—Private J. M. Reid. Active Service Section, 1st V.B.R.H. [157

RENNY—William Charles Renny, 8 Douglas Terrace, Broughty Ferry. Served as Trooper in the Fife and Forfar Unit of the Imperial Yeomanry; three years 2nd Lieutenant in Tay Division, Submarine Engineers, Broughty Ferry. [149

ROBB — Trooper J. C. Robb, Springfield, Arbroath. Fife and Forfar Contingent Imperial Yeomanry. [149

ROBERTS—John Roberts, electrical engineer, Durban; son of Andrew Roberts, Montrose, and nephew of ex-Bailie Strachan, Arbroath. Engaged during the war in managing flashlight and other electrical appliances used by the field force.

ROBERTSON—J. M. Robertson; born, Newtyle, 1865. Joined Angus Rifles in 1881; Captain in Command of Mounted Infantry of Port Elizabeth Town Guard. [151

ROBERTSON—Lieutenant Alexander Brown Robertson, 1st Battalion Cameron Highlanders. Born, 1878; son of Lord Dean of Guild Robertson, J.P., Dudhope House, Dundee; educated at Dundee and Edinburgh; Commission in 3rd Seaforth Highlanders, 1897; transferred to Cameron Highlanders, January, 1899; promoted First Lieutenant, October, 1899. [144

ROBERTSON—Private J. Robertson, Glamis. Active Service Section, 2nd V.B.R.H. [159

ROMILLY—Lieutenant Bertram Henry Samuel Romilly, Lieutenant 3rd Battalion Scots Guards; son of Samuel Henry Romilly and Lady Arabella Charlotte, daughter of the Right Hon. Earl of Southesk, K.T. Born in 1878; gazetted Second Lieutenant, March, 1898; Lieutenant, December, 1899; sailed for South Africa, January, 1900, with draft of Reservists to reinforce 1st Battalion Scots Guards at Modder River camp under General Lord Methuen, C.B., K.C.V.O. [140

ROSE—Alexander Simpson Rose, son of the late Rev. Donaldson Rose, East Free Church, Brechin. Educated at Brechin Public School; studied medicine at Edinburgh University; took his degrees; M.D. 1883; received his Commission, 1881; served in Egypt, 1882, as adjutant of Field Hospital No. 6; present at Kassassin and Tel-el-Kebir; afterwards at Suakim; served on Medical Staff Royal Victoria Hospital; Netley; afterwards in Mooltan, India; Major in R.A.M.C., 2nd Scottish Rifles; holds medal bronze and star, and clasp for services in Egypt, 1882-84. Major Rose was wounded at Potgieter's Drift on 7th February, 1900. [144

SCOTT—David Jobson Scott, medical student, son of Rev. Robert Scott, M.A., Craig, Montrose. Appointed to serve in South Africa in connection with "Edinburgh and East of Scotland Field Hospital" under Professor Chiene. [151

SCOTT—Private W. Scott, Montrose. Active Service Section, 2nd V.B.R.H. [159

SCOTT—Trooper A. Scott, Broughty Ferry. Fife and Forfar Contingent Imperial Yeomanry. [149

SCOTT—Trooper J. B. Scott, St Andrews. Fife and Forfar Contingent Imperial Yeomanry. [149

SCOTT—Trooper J. G. Scott, Perth Road, Dundee. Fife and Forfar Contingent Imperial Yeomanry. [149

SCRIMGEOUR—Private J. Scrimgeour. Active Service Section, 1st V.B.R.H. [157

SEMPLE—Trooper J. Semple, Mains of Farnell, Brechin. Fife and Forfar Contingent Imperial Yeomanry. [149

SHIELL—John Anthony Shiell, son of the late John Shiell of Cairney, solicitor, Dundee. Received military training in Rugby School Cadet Corps and Cyclist Corps of Oxford University Rifle Volunteers; enlisted in the Active Service Section of Oxfordshire Light Infantry 1st V.B. [150

SHIELL—Trooper Arnold Shiell, fifth son of John Shiell, Brechin, factor to the Earl of Dalhousie. Born, 1878; educated Trinity College, Glenalmond; while there he was a member of the Cadet Corps attached to the Black Watch. In 1897 he won the Wedderburn Vase and Stirling Cup. Joined the Fife and Forfar Contingent of the Imperial Yeomanry. [149

SIME—Sergeant D. S. Sime. Active Service Section, 1st V.B.R.H. [157

SKINNER—Corporal R. C. Skinner. Active Service Section, 1st V.B.R.H. [157

SMITH—Captain Harry Kebel Smith, 3rd (Dundee Highland) Volunteer Battalion Black Watch (Royal Highlanders); fifth son of Colonel William Smith, V.D., J.P., Binn Cottage, Dundee. Born at Newport-on-Tay, November 21st, 1877; educated at the High School and University College, Dundee, and at Edinburgh; appointed chief in an extensive brewery in Canada, September, 1897. On 17th December, 1899, when it was known that the services of Volunteers would be accepted for South Africa, Lieutenant Smith wired from St John, New Brunswick, offering his services in any capacity, and was shortly afterwards selected as subaltern in the Volunteer Active Service Company of the Black Watch, with which he now serves in South Africa; gazetted Captain, 3rd V.B.R.H., April, 1900. [148

SOOTE—Captain Cecil Speed Soote, Reres House, Broughty Ferry; son of the late James Soote; East Yorkshire Regiment; joined Royal Scots Guards, December, 1886; transferred to East Yorkshire Regiment, November, 1899; in active service in South Africa in November, 1889, and October, 1891. [143

SOUTAR—Andrew Watson Soutar, second son of Mrs Soutar, Addison Place, Arbroath. Served in South African War with Kimberley Light Horse. [152

SPALDING—Private P. Spalding, Forfar. Active Service Section, 2nd V.B.R.H. [159

SPREULL—Farrier-Sergeant A. Spreull, Ferntower, Dundee. Fife and Forfar Contingent Imperial Yeomanry. [149

SPRUNT—Private T. Sprunt. Active Service Section, 3rd V.B.R.H. [155

STANSFELD—Lieutenant John Raymond Evelyn Stansfeld, nephew of Captain Stansfeld of Dunınald, Montrose. Educated in Army class, Uppingham School; passed into Sandhurst, and on leaving received Sword of Honour; Second Lieutenant 2nd Gordon Highlanders; first commission in October, 1899; sailed for South Africa in December, 1899, with 1st Battalion of his Regiment, and went on to Estcourt and joined force under General the Right Hon. Sir Redvers Buller, V.C., G.C.B. [140

STUART—James Niblock-Stuart, son of Rev. J. Niblock-Stuart, minister of First Charge, Montrose. Served in South African War under General Gatacre with Cape Mounted Rifles, in which he enlisted in 1897. Enteric fever, brought on by poisoned water, for which four Boers were shot, prostrated numbers of the Mounted Rifles, Mr Stuart among them. Several died, but young Stuart has recovered, [154

STUART—John Stuart, St Andrew's House, Brechin. Served in South African War with Royal Pioneer Railway Regiment. The Royal Pioneer Regiment was composed of Johannesburg men who volunteered their services during the war to make and mend railways and guard communications. [152

STURROCK—Trooper J. P. Sturrock, Dundee. Fife and Forfar Contingent Imperial Yeomanry. [149

SUTHERLAND—Private A. Sutherland, Montrose. Active Service Section, 2nd V.B.R.H. [159

SUTHERLAND—Daniel Sutherland, 4 Gellatly Street, Dundee. Private in the Natal Volunteer Ambulance Corps. [153

SUTTIE—George Suttie, Durban; Gunner in the Natal Field Artillery; third son of the late James Suttie, Arbroath. Served with force under General Buller. [152

SWEENEY—Private J. G. Sweeney. Active Service Section, 3rd V.B.R.H. [155

THOMSON—Lieutenant Angus Eric Methven Thomson, grandson of George Addison Cox, of Beechwood, Dundee. Born May 24th, 1880; educated at Epsom College and the English College, Bruges; entered the army, from the West of Scotland Artillery, as Second Lieutenant of the 1st Essex Regiment, November, 1899; served with his regiment in the South African War. He was wounded at the Battle of Paardeberg, February 18th, 1900. [144

THOMSON—Lieutenant George Addison Lister Thomson, grandson of George Addison Cox, of Beechwood, Dundee. Born October 10th, 1876; educated at Charterhouse and the Royal Academy, Gosport; entered the army from the Militia as Second Lieutenant of the 1st Suffolk Regiment in May, 1897; Lieutenant April 28th, 1899. [142

THOMSON—Corporal D. T. Thomson. Active Service Section, 3rd V.B.R.H. [155

TOSH—Lieutenant Elmslie Tosh, only son of Mr Alex. Tosh, C.A., Dundee. Born 1872; educated, Dundee; served as Trooper in Natal Mounted Police. Qualified as C.A. on return home from South Africa, and became partner with his father in business. Selected to command second detachment of Active Service Volunteers from Dundee. [155

TROUP—Midshipman James Gardiner Troup, H.M.S. "Terrible," son of Rev. G. E. Troup, M.A., West Free Church, Broughty Ferry. Born 1883; educated at Broughty Ferry, High School, Dundee, and at Bournemouth; joined H.M.S. "Britannia," May, 1897; passed out of "Britannia" in August, 1898, as midshipman to H.M.S. "Mars"; appointed to H.M.S. "Terrible," September, 1899. Attached to South Natal Field force (General Buller's), and served with Naval Brigade at Colenso, &c. [144

VALENTINE—Captain Alastir A. Valentine, son of W. D. Valentine, Auchterhouse. His mother is first cousin to the Right Hon. Joseph Chamberlain. He was educated at St Andrews, and afterwards privately, and is a director of Valentine & Sons, Ltd., Dundee, Edinburgh, and London; joined 1st V.B.R.H., 1892; commissioned, 1894; selected as Lieutenant in Volunteer Active Service Company, Black Watch, in which he served. Gazetted Captain, 1st V.B.R.H., April, 1900. [148

VALLENTINE—Sergeant Edwin J. Vallentine, son of ex-Provost Vallentine, British Linen Co. Bank, Brechin. Sergeant Vallentine went through the last Matabele War with the Rhodesian Horse, Belingwe Field Force, under Major Laing. He was a mining engineer on the Rand, and at the outbreak of present war enlisted as Corporal in Thorneycroft's Mounted Infantry; was present at the Battle of Spion Kop, and was promoted Sergeant for distinguished service. [147

WALKER—Private W. Walker. Active Service Section, 1st V.B.R.H. [157

WATT—William Martin Watt, son of Rev. Hugh G. Watt, D.D., St Enoch's, Dundee. Educated, Dundee; in training as C.E. with Messrs Johnstone & Rankine, C.E.

Glasgow; enlisted in Queen's Own Glasgow Royal Yeomanry, and was made leader of his sub-section. [150

WEBSTER—Gustavus William Webster, 32 Milner Street, London; son of George Kennedy Webster, Bengal Civil Service, and grandson of the late George Webster, Sheriff Clerk of Forfarshire. Served as Trooper with the 61st Company Imperial Yeomanry (Paget's Horse.) [150

WEDDERBURN—Major Alexander Scrymgeour-Wedderburn. 9th Battery Royal Field Artillery; brother of Henry Scrymgeour-Wedderburn of Wedderburn. Entered army, December, 1878; served in the Egyptian Expedition, 1882; present at the battles of Kassassin and Tel-el-kebir; holds medal with clasp and bronze star; served in Indian frontier campaign, 1897-98; holds medal with three clasps; served with his regiment in South African War. [143

WEDDERBURN—Lieutenant Henry Scrymgeour-Wedderburn, eldest son of Henry Scrymgeour-Wedderburn of Wedderburn, Forfarshire, and Birkhill, Fife (Hereditary Royal Standard-Bearer of Scotland, Constable of Dundee), and grandson of the eighth Viscount Arbuthnott. Born 1872. Joined army 23rd December, 1893; accompanied his regiment, 1st Battalion Gordon Highlanders, to India in 1897, and was invalided home. He went through South African War with his regiment. [143

WEDDERBURN—Frederick Lewis Scrymgeour-Wedderburn, son of Henry Scrymgeour-Wedderburn of Wedderburn. Has spent his life since seventeen years of age in North-West Canada and Argentine. Enlisted as Trooper in corps raised by Mr Henry Somervell in Buenos Ayres, and arrived in South Africa, February, 1900. [147

WEDDERBURN — John Ogilvie Maclagan-Wedderburn, W.S. (yr. of Pearsie), eldest son of Dr A. S. Maclagan-Wedderburn of Pearsie; served as Trooper in the Lothians and Berwickshire Imperial Yeomanry. [152

WEIGHTON—Captain John Weighton, Pietermaritzburg, Natal, son of the late D. Weighton, Brax, Forfarshire. Captain and Adjutant, Natal Carbineers; served in Kaffir War in 1877; present at the battle of Umsintsana; served in Zulu War, and was appointed Commissariat Officer at Stager; holds Zulu War Medal. Joined General White's forces, and served in Ladysmith during the siege. [146

WELSH—Private N. M. Welsh. Active Service Section, 1st V.B.R.H. [157

YOUNG — Vet.-Lieutenant John Maclauchlan Young, F.R.C.V.S.; son of Dr Peter Young, Dundee. Educated, Dundee and Edinburgh; lecturer on Veterinary Hygiene, Aberdeen University. Vet.-Lieut. Fife and Forfar Contingent Imperial Yeomanry. [148

YOUNG — Edward Maule Young, Lincluden House, Dumfries, only son of the late Major Thomas Young of Lincluden (nephew of Fox Maule, 11th Earl of Dalhousie) and of Harriet Charlotte (niece of George, 12th Earl of Dalhousie). Educated at Cheltenham College, Sandhurst; gazetted, 1890; killed at the battle of Karee, Brantford, 29th March, 1900. [142

LIST OF NON-COMMISSIONED OFFICERS AND RANK AND FILE.

LIST

OF

ANGUS NON-COMMISSIONED OFFICERS & RANK & FILE IN BRITISH REGIMENTS

ENGAGED IN SOUTH AFRICAN WAR.

The Year given indicates date of first Enlistment; the Figures at end of each Note represent the Number of Soldier's Portrait. Where no Number is given, no Portrait has been obtainable.
w *indicates Soldier has been Wounded during the War.*

Adam, David, Guthrie Port, Arbroath; Drummer, 1st Black Watch—1888 [361

Adams, Cornelius, Links Cottages, Monifieth; Private, Black Watch—1898

Adams, Joseph, Links Cottages, Monifieth; Private, Black Watch—1899

Adams, Thomas, Bellfield Lane, Dundee; Private, Black Watch—1884 [230

Adamson, A., Kincardine Street, Montrose; Private, Black Watch—1887

Addison, James, Adela Villa, Brechin; Staff-Sergeant Farrier, 63rd Battery Royal Artillery—1885 [115

Aitken, John, Park Wynd, Dundee; Private, 1st Gordon Highlanders—1884 [240

Allan, A. Gair, King Street, Montrose; Corpl., Royal Horse Artillery—1892 [26

Allan, Hubert A., King Street, Montrose; Bombardier, Royal Artillery—1895 [82

Allan, Nicholas P., King Street, Montrose; Trumpeter - Sergeant, Royal Artillery—1887 [26

Allison, G. N., Fraser's Lane, Montrose; Private, Black Watch—1897 [162

Anderson, Alex., Overgate, Dundee; Private, 2nd Black Watch—1890

Anderson, James, Hilltown, Dundee; Private 3rd Battalion Perth Militia, Royal Highlanders—1899 [467

Anderson, John, High Street, Lochee; Private, 2nd Royal Highlanders—1897 [201

Anderson, John P., West Newgate, Arbroath; Lance-Corporal, Military Foot Police—1893 [41

Anderson, Tom, King Street, Ferryden; Private, Black Watch—1883

Armstrong, James, Derby Street, Dundee; Private, Royal Scots Fusiliers—1896 [428

Ballantine, Peter, Inverquharity, Kirriemuir; Private, Scots Guards—1890 [297

Bannerman, Thomas C., Commerce Street, Arbroath; Lance Corporal, Black Watch, 2nd Battalion—1897 [62

Barrett, Edward, Dallfield Walk, Dundee; Private, Scots Guards—1895 [291

Bastion, James, Douglas Street, Dundee; Private, Highland Light Infantry

Batchelor, Alec. C. Pole Street, Dundee; Private, Scottish Rifles—1897 [498

Bates, William, Hunter Street, Dundee; Private, 2nd Black Watch—1884 [243

Bathie, William, Lilybank Road, Dundee; Private, 1st Gordon Highlanders—1888 [200

Beagin, Francis, Kinloch Street, Dundee; Private, King's Own Scottish Borderers—1887. Medals — Egyptian and Star; Chitral [395

Beattie, A., Queen Street, Montrose; Private, Highland Light Infantry [324

Beattie, Andrew, Links Cottages, Monifieth; Lance-Corporal, 1st Battalion Cameron Highlanders—1896. Two Medals and 2 Clasps [37

Beattie, David, Peddie Street, Dundee; Private, 1st Highland Light Infantry—1893 [311

Beattie, John, Blackscroft, Dundee; Gunner, Royal Field Artillery—1887 [479

Beattie, John, Ryehill Lane, Dundee; Private, 2nd Black Watch—1888

Beattie, Mungo, Small's Lane, Dundee; Private, 2nd Royal Highlanders [194

Beattie, Robert, Wilkie's Lane, Dundee; Driver, Royal Field Artillery—1889 [302

Beedie, David, Kinnaird Place, Brechin; Private, Gordon Highlanders—1890 [66

Belford, John S., Kinnaird Place, Brechin; Private, Royal Highlanders—1888 [166

Bell, David, Reform Street, Kirriemuir; Private, 2nd Royal Highlanders—1888 [154

Bell, John, Pole Street, Dundee; Private, Black Watch—1889; *w* Magersfontein and Paardeberg [392

Bell, J., West High Street, Forfar; H.M.S. "Powerful"

Bennett, George A., Derby Street, Dundee; Private, 2nd Royal Highlanders—1890 [360

Bett, A., Zoar, Forfar; Private, Black Watch; killed.

Bews, George, West High Street, Forfar; Private, Black Watch—1886 [164

Bissett, David F., Barrack Street, Dundee; Sergeant, 2nd Black Watch. Two clasps and one star [426

Black, David, Gallowlaw, Panbride; Private, Gordon Highlanders—1892. Medal and Three Bars (Chitral Campaign, &c.) [112

Black, James, Westmuir, Kirriemuir; Lance-Sergeant, 1st Royal Scots—1893 [138

Black, Robert, Carnoustie; Private, Black Watch

Blacklaw, John, Watson Street, Dundee; Private, Gordon Highlanders — 1892. Medals—Chitral and Dargai

Blacklaw, Philip, Watson Street, Dundee; Private, Scots Guards—1899

Boath, James, Ponderlaw Lane, Arbroath; Lance-Corporal, 1st Cameron Highlanders—1897. Medals—Khedive and Egyptian (Atbara and Omdurman) [67

Boath, James, Hospital Wynd, Dundee; Private, 3rd Gordon Highlanders—1892

Bokey, Louis, Park Lane, Dundee; Private, 2nd Scottish Rifles—1876

Bowes, John, Blackness Road, Dundee; Private, 2nd Black Watch

Bowman, J., Eastern Sunnyside, Forfar; Private, Black Watch

Boyd, William Ferry, Albert Street, Lochee; Private, 2nd Black Watch—1898 [452

Boyle, John, High Street, Lochee; Private, 2nd Royal Highlanders—1885

Brady, Henry, West High Street, Lochee; Private, Highland Light Infantry—1889

Brady, Robert, Campbell Street, Dundee; Private, Seaforth Highlanders [436

Braid, David, Nursery Feus, Forfar; Private, 2nd Royal Highlanders—1886 [195

Brannan, George, Hilltown, Dundee; Private 1st Highland Light Infantry—1898 [289

Brannan, J., Monifieth; Private, Royal Highlanders

Bremner, James, Dundee; Private, Seaforth Highlanders; killed at Koodoosberg

Bremner, Robert, Wallace Street, Arbroath; Lance-Corporal, Cameron Highlanders—1896. Medal, with Clasps for Atbara and Omdurman [63

Bremner, William, West Queen Street, Broughty Ferry; Royal Horse Artillery—1895 [84

Broadley, Francis, North Church Street, Lochee; Private, 2nd Seaforth Highlanders—1888. Medal and Clasp—Chitral [181

Brierty, Robert Clifford, Union Street, Maxwelltown, Dundee; Private, 2nd Scottish Rifles—1891 [253

Brodie, Frank, Garland Place, Dundee; Private, 2nd Black Watch [248

Brodie, Mungo, Hospital Wynd, Dundee; Private, 79th Queen's Own Cameron Highlanders—1894. Medals—Khedive and Egyptian (Atbara and Omdurman) [506

Brougham, John, Applegate, Arbroath; Corpl., 1st Highland Light Infantry—1888 [31

Brown, A., Lilybank Road, Dundee; Private, 2nd Argyll and Sutherland Highlanders—1890

Brown, David S., St James' Road, Forfar: Royal Field Artillery—1881

Brown, James, Lochee Road, Dundee; Private, 2nd Black Watch—1890 [451

Brown, James, Charles Street, Dundee; Private, 2nd Black Watch—1891; w. Medals—Atbara and Omdurman [495

Brown, Robert, High Street, Lochee; Private, 2nd Royal Highlanders. Fatally wounded at Magersfontein [189

Brownlee, James, Horsewater Wynd, Dundee; Private, 2nd Scottish Rifles—1884 [400

Bruce, Henry M'G., Wilkie's Lane, Dundee; Private, 3rd Royal Highlanders—1894

Bryan, Robert, Foundry Lane, Dundee; Private, 2nd Black Watch—1880

Bunce, John, Coupar Street, Lochee; Private, Royal Highlanders [484

Burke, Charles, Ladyloan, Arbroath; Private, 2nd Gordon Highlanders—1894. Medals—India (Chitral Campaign) Medal and 2 Bars [39

Burke, John, Ladyloan, Arbroath; Private, Scots Guards

Burnett, James, Keptie Street, Arbroath; Private, 1st Gordon Highlanders—1886 [28

Burnett, John O., River Street, Brechin; Private, Scots Guards—1888 [278

Burnett, John, Paterson Street, Duncan's Bridge, Dundee; Private, 3rd Gordon Highlanders—1878 [235

Burnett, Robert, Bakers' Wynd, Arbroath; Private, Gordon Highlanders—1898

Burnett, William B., Legaston, Friockheim; Private, 2nd Black Watch—1898; w [198

Butchart, Robert, North Grimsby, Arbroath; Private, Seaforth Highlanders

Calder, Thomas, Arbroath; Volunteer, Thorneycroft's Mounted Infantry [471

Cameron, Arthur, Hannah Street, Arbroath; Private, Black Watch—1889 [95

Cameron, David C., Howard Street, Arbroath; Corporal, Black Watch—1888; w [1

Cameron, Fred. G., Dundee; Corporal, 2nd Seaforth Highlanders. Killed at Koodoosberg.

Campbell, James, Tod's Land, Broughty Ferry; Private, Black Watch—1897

Campbell, John, Jun., Green Street, Forfar; Corporal, 1st Royal Dragoons—1897 [369

Campbell, John L., Argyll Cottage, Brechin Road, Forfar; Gunner, 18th Battery, Royal Field Artillery—1898 [329

Candie, James, Arnhall, Edzell; Private, Black Watch. Killed at Paardeberg.

Cargill, Alexander, Lunan; Private, Border Regiment—1891. Medal—India [36

Cargill, David, Union Street, Arbroath; Private, 79th Cameron Highlanders

Cargill, Joseph H., Links Cottages, Monifieth; Private, Royal Highlanders—1891 [128

Carnegie, L., Mill Street, Montrose; Private, Black Watch—1889; w [145

Carroll, Cornelius, Constable Street, Dundee; Private, 2nd Black Watch—1896 [387

Carroll, Francis, Blackness Road, Dundee; Private, Royal Highlanders—1896 [386

Carroll, James, Constable Street, Dundee; Private, 2nd Scottish Rifles—1888 [220

Cassick Owen, Dundee; Private, 2nd Black Watch—1889

Cassidy, James, Brewery Lane, Dundee; Private, 2nd Royal Highlanders—1900 [420

Cassidy, Patrick, Monifieth; Gunner, Forfar and Kincardine Militia

Cavanah, Thomas, John Street, Dundee; Driver, Royal Horse Artillery—1890

Chalmers, George, Whitehill, Forfar; Private, Royal Scots Fusiliers

Cheyne, George, Kirriemuir; Private, 1st Gordon Highlanders—1897 [167

Chisholm, George, Lyon Street, Dundee; Private, 2nd Royal Munster Fusiliers—1891 [402

Christie, Alexander, Maryton, Kirriemuir; Private, Argyll and Sutherland Highlanders—1898 [100

Christie, George, Hannah Street, Arbroath; Private, 21st Royal Scots Fusiliers

Christie, James, Lindsay Street, Arbroath; Private, Royal Scots Guards

Christie, James, Sidney Street, Arbroath; Private, Cameron Highlanders — 1891. Medals—Soudan and Egyptian with 2 clasps [146

Christison, D., Lochee; Colour-Sergeant, Argyll and Sutherland Highlanders. Killed at Magersfontein

Clark, Alex. William Street, Dundee; Private, Royal Scots Greys—1895 [368

Clark, George, Lindsay Street, Arbroath; Private, 79th Cameron Highlanders

Cockburn, Robert, Foundry Lane, Dundee; Private, 2nd Royal Highlanders—1890 [419

Coen, Michael, Cowgate, Dundee; Private, 3rd Black Watch

Cogan, Peter, Tindal Wynd, Dundee; Private, 2nd Lincoln Regiment—1889

Coleman, Patrick, Hospital Wynd, Dundee; Private, 2nd Seaforth Highlanders—1892. Killed at Paardeberg [255

Collins, Michael, Scouringburn, Dundee; Private, Army Service Corps—1894

Collins, David, Fergus Square, Arbroath; Lance-Corporal, Cameron Highlanders—1897. Medal—Omdurman [91

Connell, Henry, Tulloch Crescent, Dundee; Private, 2nd Royal Irish Fusiliers—1890 [328

Connelly, Francis H., Hunter Street, Dundee; Private, Black Watch—1891 [483

Connelly, John, Todburn Lane, Dundee; Private, 3rd Black Watch—1890

Conning, William, Gray's Square, Dundee; Drummer, 3rd Black Watch—1895

Conway, James R., Wilkie's Lane, Dundee; Private, 3rd Battalion Royal Highlanders—1894 [438

Conway, William, City Road, Dundee; Private, 1st Coldstream Guards—1894

Connon, John, Blackness Square, Dundee; Private, Royal Scots—1884 [327

Connor, Owen, Whorter Bank, Lochee; Gunner, Edinburgh Artillery—1895 [410

Cook, William, Union Place, Dundee; Private, 3rd Royal Highlanders—1887 [211

Coonan, John, Coupar Street, Lochee; Private, Royal Scots Fusiliers—1885. Medal and clasp—Burmah [422

Cooper, Walter, Arbroath; Private, 1st Scots Guards—1895 [25

Cossans, Alexander G., Lochland Street, Arbroath; Private, Black Watch—1887 [357

Couttie, John, Bridge Street, Brechin; Private, Army Service Corps—1896 [168

Couttie, John I., Benvie Road, Dundee; Private, Royal Scots Fusiliers — 1885. Medal and clasp—Burmah [304

Coutts, D., Castle Street, Montrose; Troop-Sergeant, Scots Greys—1893 [22

Cowan, Arthur, Abbotsford Place, Dundee; Private, Highland Light Infantry—1889 [286

Cowie, D., Gibson Place, Montrose; Private, Black Watch—1886 [155

Cowie, W., Northesk Road, Montrose; Private, Black Watch—1888 [159

Coyle, John, Ann Street, Dundee; Private, 2nd Scottish Rifles

Crawford, Andrew, Rowden's Alley, Dundee; Private, Black Watch—1891 [433

Crawford, Joe, Dundee; Private, Durban Light Infantry—1899 [275

Crawford, Robert, Lowden's Alley, Dundee; Corporal, 2nd Black Watch—1889

Crawford, Thomas, Links Cottage, Monifieth; Private, Highland Light Infantry [274

Cree, Andrew, James Street, Dundee; Private, Gordon Highlanders—1884 [441

Crichton, John, Scouringburn, Dundee; Private, Black Watch—1886 [442

Crowe, Albert, Abbot Street, Arbroath; Private, Black Watch

Culross, William, Fleuchar Street, Dundee; Private, Royal Highlanders—1892; *w*

Cumming, John, King Street, Montrose; Lord Lovat's Scouts

Currans, Joseph, Urquhart Street, Dundee; Private, 2nd Royal Highlanders—1898

Cuthbert, J., Murray Street, Montrose; Lance-Corporal, Gordon Highlanders — 1895. Medal—Chitral [21

Dailly, James, Littlejohn Street, Dundee; Private, 2nd Royal Scots Fusiliers—1885

Dakers, A. M., North Street, Montrose; Private, Royal Scots—1888

Daly, Hugh, Blackness Road, Dundee; Private, Black Watch—1888

Dargie, David, Alexander Street, Dundee; Driver, 14th Field Battery, Royal Field Artillery—1898

Davidson, A., Lochee Road, Dundee; Private, Scots Guards. [455

Davidson, David, Russell Street, Dundee; Private, 1st Scots Guards—1890 [372

Davidson, John S., River Street, Brechin; Private, 3rd Gordon Highlanders

Davidson, Robert, Catherine Street, Dundee; Corporal, King's Own Scottish Borderers—1886. Medal—Egyptian Star and Medal for Gemaiza [456

Dear, Alex., Canmore Lane, Forfar; Private 79th Cameron Highlanders—1885. Medals—Khedive Star and Medal—1885

Devine, Samuel, Princes Street, Dundee; Sergeant, 3rd Black Watch—1893

Diack, George, Belgrave Terrace, Lochee; Private, 2nd Black Watch—1888. Medal—Matabele War, 1893-4 [271

Dickson, Alfred, Northesk Road, Montrose; Trooper, Royal Horse Guards—1891 [281

Dillon, James, E. Henderson's Wynd, Dundee; Lance-Corporal, Highland Light Infantry—1893 [285

Dilly, Stuart, Lordburn, Arbroath; Private, 42nd Black Watch—1889; w [3

Dolan, Michael, Glebe Street, Dundee; Bandsman, 2nd Black Watch—1892 [407

Dolan, Wm., Dundee; Private, 2nd Black Watch—1892 [250

Donachie, Wm., Arthur Street, Dundee; Private, 1st Gordon Highlanders—1893. Medal — Dargai; Bars — Punjab, Tirah [173

Donachie, W., Arthur Street, Dundee; Private, 1st Gordon Highlanders—1892. Medal for Dargai; Two Clasps—Tirah and Punjab [182

Donald, David, Rosebank, Arbroath; Private, King's Own Scottish Borderers — 1888. Medals—Chitral and Chin Lushai [512

Dorans, Neil, Union Street, Maxwelltown, Dundee; Private, 2nd Black Watch [508

Douglas, Robert, Ferry Street, Montrose; Private, 2nd Cameron Highlanders—1899

Dowling, David, Overgate, Dundee; Private, 2nd Black Watch—1894

Downie, David, Watson Street, Dundee; Private, 1st Gordon Highlanders—1893. Medals—Chitral and Dargai Clasps [228

Downie, John, Arthur Street, Dundee; Lance-Corporal, 3rd Royal Highlanders—1895

Downie, John, Kirriemuir; Private, 1st Seaforth Highlanders—1894 [153

Downie, William, Lowson's Park, Carnoustie; Private, Argyll and Sutherland Highlanders—1889 [52

Drysdale, W., Ann Street, Dundee; Private, Royal Highlanders. Killed at Magersfontein [193

Dudley, Joseph, Watson's Lane, Dundee; Private, Royal Highlanders—1891 [261

Duff, Andrew, Edward Street, Dundee; Private, 2nd Royal Highlanders—1898

Duffy, John, Hawkhill, Dundee; Private, 25th King's Own Scottish Borderers. Medal and Star—Egyptian (Suakin)

Duncan, James, Rose Street, Lochee; Private, Argyll and Sutherland Highlanders—1891 [356

Duncan, R. S., Northesk Road, Montrose; Private, Black Watch—1898

Duncan, William F., Duke Street, Arbroath; Private, 1st Battalion 79th Cameron Highlanders—1892. Medals—Medal and Two Bars (Atbara and Omdurman) [64

Duncan, —, Pugeston Brick Works, Montrose; Sapper, Royal Engineers

Dye, James, Annfield Road, Dundee; Private, 2nd Black Watch—1891

Easson, D., Alexander Street, Dundee; Private, Gordon Highlanders — 1898. Died of dysentery.

Edwards, J., Victoria Street, Montrose; Private, Black Watch—1882 [76

Edwards, William, R., Burnside, Forfar; Lance-Corporal, 2nd Black Watch—1900 [110

Egan, M., Small's Wynd, Dundee; Private, Scots Guards—1893

Elder, David, Barrack Street, Dundee; Gunner, Royal Artillery—1888 [404

Elder, John, Auchlishie, Kirriemuir; Private, Royal Scots Greys—1893 [15

Evans, David, Blackness Road, Dundee; Private, 2nd Black Watch—1896 [196

Evans, Thomas, James Street, Dundee; Private, 3rd Dragoon Guards—1889 [365

Ewan, Frederick, Victoria Terrace, Dundee; Corporal, Argyll and Sutherland Highlanders—1880 [308

Ewan, Francis, Cotton Road, Dundee; Private, Gordon Highlanders—1897 [185

Fairbairn, Thomas, Dundee; Private, Black Watch—1892; *w*

Fairley, James, Kincardine Street, Dundee; Private, Black Watch—1892 [312

Fairweather, James, Park Wynd, Dundee; Private, Seaforth Highlanders—1894 [315

Farrell, James, East Whorterbank, Lochee; Private, 3rd Royal Highlanders—1891

Farrell, J., Bell Street Lane, Dundee; Lance-Corporal, Royal Highlanders—1884

Farrell, John, Albert Street, Lochee; Private, 71st Highland Light Infantry — 1890. Medal and 2 Clasps (Indian).

Farquhar, John, Charles, and Willie, son-in-law and grandsons of Mrs. Robertson, British Buildings, Ladyloan, Arbroath; Members of Kimberley Town Guard during the seige

Fawcett, John, Wolseley Street, Dundee; Corporal, 2nd Scottish Rifles—1888 [379

Fearn, Stewart, New Road, Forfar; Private, 2nd Argyll and Sutherland Highlanders—1894. Medal—Punjab Frontier, 1897-98 [2

Feeney, James, Albert Street, Lochee; Private, 3rd Black Watch—1890 [338

Fergusson, D., Monifieth; Private, Black Watch

Ferguson, Joseph, Wilkie's Lane, Dundee; Private, 2nd Black Watch

Ferrier, A., Dundee Road, Forfar; Private, King's Own Scottish Borderers

Ferrier, James, Green Street, Arbroath; Private, Black Watch—1887. Medal for Matabele War [9

Ferry, Francis, Logie Street, Lochee; Private, 2nd Black Watch—1891 [197

Fidler, Edward, Todburn Lane, Dundee; Corporal, 3rd Gordon Highlanders—1897

Flynn, Edward, Rose Lane, Dundee; Private, 2nd Scottish Rifles—1884 [423

Flynn, James, Blackness Road, Dundee; Private, 1st Gordon Highlanders—1887 [481

Folan, James, Small's Lane, Dundee; Private, 42nd Black Watch—1897 [184

Folan, Michael, Small's Lane, Dundee; Drummer, 42nd Black Watch—1892 [183

Forat, William, East Mill Wynd, Arbroath; Lance-Corporal, Border Regiment—1888

Forbes, Alex., Hawkhill, Dundee; Private, Scottish Rifles—1890 [466

Forbes, David, Union Street, Brechin; Sapper, Royal Engineers [30

Forbes, James, Dens Brae, Dundee; Private, 1st Black Watch—1890 [259

Forbes, James, Lochland Street, Arbroath; Driver, Royal Field Artillery—1894 [18

Forbes, John, Union Street, Brechin; Sapper, Royal Engineers [30

Forbes, Wm., Park Avenue, Dundee; Corporal, Royal Scots Greys—1891

Forbes, William. Kinnaird Street, Brechin; Private, 2nd Royal Highlanders—1899; *w* [59

Ford, William, Panmure Street, Arbroath; Private, 1st Cameron Highlanders—1897 Medals—Soudan (2) [55

Ford, William A., Palmer Street, Arbroath; Private, 2nd Gordon Highlanders—1894 Medal—Dargai [511

Forrester, Alex., Ogilvie Street, Dundee; Private, 2nd Scottish Rifles—1888 [279

Forsyth, James, Rosebery Street. Dundee; Private, Highland Light Infantry—1894 [391

Fox, James, St Roque's Lane, Dundee; Private, Royal Scots Fusiliers—1884. Medal—Burmah [352

Fox, Owen, Powrie Place, Dundee; Sergeant, Royal Field Artillery [336

Fraser, Clark R., Wallace Street, Arbroath; Private, 2nd Black Watch—1897 [96

Fraser, David, Rosebrae, Arbroath; Driver, 39th Battery Royal Field Artillery [597

Fraser, J., Carnegie Street, Montrose; Private, Black Watch—1891 [330

Fraser, William, Brechin; Sergeant, Black Watch [209

Fraser, William, Carcary, Farnell; Sergeant, Royal Highlanders—1889 [79

Fyfe, Wm., Rosebank Road, Dundee; Private, 42nd Highlanders—1887 [212

Garvie, Patrick, Whorter Bank, Lochee; Private, 42nd Black Watch—1886

Gavin, William, Ogilvie Road, Dundee; Private, 3rd Gordon Highlanders—1871 [191

Gellatly, James, Lochee Road, Dundee; Private, 2nd Scottish Rifles—1887 [501

Gibb, William, Holm Head, Edzell; Private, Gordon Highlanders

Gibson, John, Cairnie Place, Arbroath; Bombardier, 4th Battery Royal Field Artillery—1877. Medals—Khedive and Victoria [43

Gilhooley, B., Monifieth; Private, Gordon Highlanders

Gilhooley, Thomas Dolan, Monifieth; Private, Black Watch Militia

Gilkison, Samuel, Clepington Street, Dundee; Private, Royal Highlanders [399

Glass, James, Blackness Road, Dundee; Private, 1st Cameron Highlanders—1885. Medal—Egyptian and Star [225

Glass, Victor, Westgate, Friockheim; Lance-Corporal, 1st Cameron Highlanders—1892. Medals—Atbara, Omdurman [176

Goodall, A., Zoar, Forfar; Trooper, Scots Greys

Gordon, John, Panmure Street, Arbroath; Lance Corporal, Queen's Own Cameron Highlanders—1897. Medals—British and Soudan [161

Gordon, John, Kirk Wynd, Kirriemuir; Private, 2nd Royal Highlanders—1899.

Gordon, John, Peddie Street, Dundee; Driver, Royal Artillery

Gordon, Wm. B., Dundee; Private, Kings Own Scottish Borderers—1884; Medals—Egyptian and Star [448

Gordon, William N., Elm Bank, Kirriemuir; Private, 1st Gordon Highlanders—1893. [24

Gorman, Wm., Hospital Wynd, Dundee; Private, 2nd Royal Highlanders—1880

Gracie, William, Brechin Road, Forfar; Private, 1st Scots Guards—1895 [126

Graham, Francis, Foundry Lane, Dundee; Private, Gordon Highlanders [177

Graham, D., Wellington Place, Montrose, Private, Highland Light Infantry—1890. Medal—Indian Frontier [53

Graham, James, Ponderlaw Lane, Arbroath; Piper, 1st Cameron Highlanders—1890. [68

Graham, W., Little Nursery, Montrose; Private, Black Watch

Graham, Wm., Meiklemill, Brechin; Gunner, 42nd Battery Royal Artillery—1893 [34

Grant, David, Jordstone, Meigle; Corporal, 2nd Royal Highlanders—1896 [103

Gray, Edwin, River Street, Brechin; Private, Argyll and Sutherland Highlanders—1888 [120

Gray, Jas., Blackness Road, Dundee; Private, Argyle and Sutherland Highlanders—1884. Killed at Roodepoort [450

Gray, Owen, Overgate, Dundee; Private, King's Own Scottish Borderers—1898

Grear, Walter, Wilkie's Lane, Dundee; Private, 1st Gordon Highlanders—1885 [445

Green, George, St Andrew Street, Dundee; Private, West Kent Regiment — 1871. Fought at Majuba in 1881 [210

Green, Thomas, Kinnaird Street, Dundee; Private, Royal Scots Fusiliers — 1885. Medal—Burmah [497

Grewer, A., Lunanhead, Forfar; Private, Black Watch

Griffiths, Joseph, Union Street, Lochee; Private, King's Own Scottish Borderers—1885 [460

Guild, David C., East Union Street, Arbroath; Private, King's Own Scottish Borderers; formerly Sergeant in Cameron Highlanders; re-enlisted in 1894. Medal—Egyptian and Star [411

Gurney, Albert, South Road, Lochee; Sergeant Black Watch—1892 [175

Guthrie, John L., Guthrie Hill, Arbroath; Private, 1st Gordon Highlanders, 1888. Medal—Chitral and Bar [123

Guthrie, William, Airlie Street, Kirriemuir; Private, 42nd Black Watch [104

Haddon, W., Montrose; Private, Black Watch —1890; w [86

Haddon, William, Wardmill Road, Arbroath; Private, 1st Battalion Highland Light Infantry—1892 [119

Hagan, James, Hilltown, Dundee; Driver, Royal Field Artillery—1890 [219

Hagan, William, Milne's East Wynd, Dundee; Private, 2nd Black Watch—1892 [405

Hannah, Chas., Barngreen, Arbroath; Private, Royal Scots Fusiliers

Hannah, John, Green Street, Arbroath; Private, Black Watch

Halkett, Richard, Hospital Wynd, Dundee; Lance Corporal, 2nd Black Watch. Killed at Bloemberg, May 26

Harris, A., Reform Street, Montrose; Private, Black Watch—1898; w [169

Harris, H., North Street, Montrose; Private, Black Watch—1898 [78

Harris, John, Forebank Road, Dundee; Private, 2nd King's Own Scottish Borderers—1883. Medal—Egyptian and Star [493

Harrison, James, Small's Wynd, Dundee; Lance-Corporal, Black Watch—1899 [417

Harrison, Samuel, Bernard Street, Dundee; Private, King's Own Scottish Borderers—1885. Medal—Egyptian and Star

Harrison, Samuel, Watson's Lane, Hawkhill, Dundee; Private, King's Own Scottish Borderers—1885 [491

Hart, John, Seagate, Dundee; Private, Black Watch—1888 [321

Hart, John, Mid Street, Lochee; Private, Gordon Highlanders—1886. Medal—Chitral [252

Hay, David, Hunter Street, Dundee; Private, Black Watch—1885 457

Hay, John, Marshall Street, Lochee; Private, King's Own Scottish Borderers—1892. Medal and Three Bars—Indian Frontier

Heather, Benjamin, Poet's Lane, Brechin; Private, 2nd Royal Highlanders—1897 [80

Heenan, John, Marshall Street, Lochee; Private, 42nd Royal Highlanders [272

Henderson, David, Campbell Street, Lochee; Private, 1st Gordon Highlanders—1893. Medal and Two Bars—Indian Frontier [231

Henderson, Joseph, Walton Street, Dundee; Private, 2nd Seaforth Highlanders—1892. Medal and Two Clasps—Atbara and Omdurman

Henderson, Robert R., Milnbank Road, Dundee; Private, 2nd Black Watch—1890 [375

Hendry, James, Poet's Lane, Brechin; Private, 1st Gordon Highlanders—1890 [20

Henry, John, Dundee; Private, Seaforth Highlanders—1891. Medal—Chitral; w [260

Herron, Wm., Ann Street, Dundee; Bombardier Quarter-master, 11th Field Battery, Royal Artillery—1889 [458

Herschell, David, Leonard Street, Arbroath; Private, 2nd Black Watch—1899

Herschell, William, Leonard Street, Arbroath; Private, 2nd Black Watch—1889 [333

Herschell, — Northesk Road, Montrose; Private, Gordon Highlanders—1895. Medal—Chitral [490

High, D., Montrose; Private, Black Watch. Killed at Magersfontein.

Hill, David, North Street, Forfar; Private, 42nd Black Watch—1877 [408

Hogg, Andrew, Catherine Street, Dundee; Private, Scots Greys—1890. Medal—Indian Frontier

Holden, Henry, Rosebank Street, Dundee; Private, 2nd Royal Highlanders—1897. Killed at Magersfontein [287

Hopkins, James, Caldrum Street, Dundee; Private, 1st Highland Light Infantry—1890. Medal—Dargai.

Hotson, A., Queen Street, Montrose; Private, Royal Scots—1895 [16

Hughes, John, Flyght's Lane, Lochee; Private, 2nd Black Watch—1898

Hughes, P., Flyght's Lane, Lochee; Private, 2nd King's Own Scottish Borderers—1891. Medal—Chitral

Hughes, Thos., Flyght's Lane, Lochee; Private, 2nd Black Watch—1897

Hutcheson, William, Westhall Terrace, Dundee; Private, 2nd Scots Guards—1893

Inglis, James, Catherine Street, Dundee; Private, Gordon Highlanders—1892. Medal and Clasps for Dargai [229

Inglis, Henry, Catherine Street, Dundee; Private, Scots Fusiliers—1898

Irons, Peter, Alyth; Private, Black Watch—1889; w

Irvine, John W., Maryton, Kirriemuir; Private, 2nd Royal Highlanders—1891 [102

Irvine, Wm., Poet's Lane, Brechin; Private, 1st Gordon Highlanders—1890. Chitral Medal and Clasp

Jack, Alex., Maxwelltown, Dundee; Private, 2nd Seaforth Highlanders — 1891. Two Medals [227

Jackson, Wm., Kinnaird Street, Dundee; Private, 3rd Royal Highlanders—1891

James, Charles, Hunter Street, Dundee; Lance-Corporal, Royal Highlanders—1890. Killed at Modder River [323

Jamie, Alex., Gravesend, Arbroath; Private, 2nd Battalion Scottish Rifles—1892 [144

Jamieson, John Simpson, Fergus Street, Arbroath; Private, 1st Battalion Cameron Highlanders — 1894. Medals—Egyptian and two Clasps; and Queen's "Sudan" Medal [19

Janes, Alex. B., Brechin Road, Arbroath; Private, Royal Scots Greys—1892 [33

Johnston, C. Stuart, Shore Wynd, Montrose; Private, Gordon Highlanders—1895 [92

Johnstone, A., Bell Place, Forfar; Driver, 31st Company Army Service Corps

Johnstone, Adamson, Robert Street, Forfar; Corporal, 2nd Volunteer Battalion Royal Highlanders—1890 [307

Johnstone, David D., Rattray's Land, Monifieth; Private, Black Watch Militia—1897

Johnstone, John, West Wynd, Dundee; Private, 2nd Black Watch—1890 [459

Johnstone, John J. D., Rattray's Land, Monifieth; Private, 1st Gordon Highlanders—1889. Medal and three Clasps—Indian Frontier [108

Jolly, D., Castle Street, Montrose; Private, Black Watch—1888

Jordon, Thomas, Taylor's Lane, Dundee; Gunner, 87th Field Battery Royal Artillery —1885 [461

Keating, William, Blackness Road, Dundee; Private, 2nd Scottish Rifles—1888 [489

Keegan, William, Henderson's Wynd, Dundee; Sergeant, Highland Light Infantry—1889 [347

Keenan, John, Marshall Street, Lochee; Sergeant, 3rd Royal Highlanders—1875 [284

Keill, John, West Wynd, Dundee; Private, King's Own Scottish Borderers—1891 [290

Keillor, J., North Church Street, Lochee; Private, Scots Guards [454

Keith, James L., Dundee Road, Broughty Ferry; Private, Black Watch—1898 [303

Keith, Wm., Hays Lane, Arbroath; Private, 26th Cameronians, Scottish Rifles—1889 [44

Kelman, George, Dundee; Private, Black Watch—1898; w

Kelly, Alexander, Pitfour Street, Dundee; Private, 2nd Black Watch—1887 [295

Kennedy, James, Polepark Road, Dundee; Driver, 50th Field Battery Royal Artillery —1890. Medal—Punjab, 1897-98 [224

Kennedy, James, Lunanbank, Inverkeilor; Private, Black Watch—1896 [74

Kennedy, John, Albert Street, Dundee; Private, 2nd Highland Light Infantry— 1889 [301

Kennedy, Thomas, North Tay Street, Dundee; Private, King's Own Scottish Borderers. Two Medals and one Star (Egyptian) [314

Kidd, James, Watson's Lane, Dundee; Private, 3rd Black Watch—1891

Kidd, William, Inverkeilor; Corporal, 14th Hussars—1888 [101

Kidney, John, Kemback Street, Dundee; Private, Black Watch—1890 [238

King, Alexander, Hunterspath Farm, Arbirlot; Lance-Corporal, Seaforth Highlanders— 1898; w [127

King, Joseph, Polepark Road, Dundee; Private, 25th King's Own Scottish Borderers —1885 Medal and Star [502

King, Robert, Arbroath; Private, Black Watch

Kirkland, James, Campbell Street, Lochee, Private, 1st Kings Own Scottish Borderers [425

Kirkwood, James, Kincardine Street, Montrose; Private, Royal Irish Lancers—1889. Killed at Magersfontein [69

Kirkwood, John, Wolsley Street, Dundee; Drummer, 2nd Black Watch—1890 Died of wounds after Magersfontein [353

Kirkwood, J., Kincardine Street, Montrose; Private, Black Watch—1899. Killed at Magersfontein [131

Knight, David, Links Cottages, Monifieth; Private, Black Watch—1886 [40

Kynoch, D., Union Street, Brechin; Private, Gordon Highlanders — 1892. Medal—Indian Frontier and two Clasps [335

Laburn, David, Dallfield Walk, Dundee; Sergeant, Black Watch—1885 [254

Laing, David C., St Peter Street, Dundee; Private, Queen's Own Cameron Highlander—1887 [398

Laird, Alexander, Albert Street, Dundee; Private, Black Watch—1885 [389

Laird, Allan, Albert Street, Dundee; Private, 7th Dragoon Guards—1891 [374

Laird, James, Robert Street, Forfar; Private, 2nd Royal Highlanders—1889 [505

Lamb, Alexander, Constitution Road, Dundee; Private, 3rd Battalion Gordon Highlanders, 1881

Lamb, James, Mid Wynd, Dundee; Private, 2nd Royal Highlanders—1890 [306

Lamont, Ecclesgreig, Montrose; Trooper, Scots Greys

Langton, Joseph, Foundry Lane, Dundee; Private, King's Own Scottish Borderers—1899 [350

Lawrence, Charles, Lochland Street, Arbroath; Private, 1st Battalion Cameron Highlanders—1896 Medal and Two Bars—Atbara and Omdurman [51

Lawrie, Arthur, Maulesbank Cottage, Carnoustie; Private, Royal Highlanders—1891 [65

Leonard, Wm., Well Road, Dundee; Sergeant, 1st Royal Scots Fusiliers—1890. Medal and two Clasps—Indian Frontier [362

Leroy, Louis, Taylor's Lane, Dundee; Private, 2nd Black Watch—1889 [236

Lindsay, Charles, Dundee; Quarter-Master-Sergeant, 1st Gordon Highlanders—1886 Medals—Chitral and Tirah [313

Lindsay, David P., Wellgate, Kirriemuir; Corporal, 2nd Royal Highlanders—1889; w [156

Lindsay, D. Montrose; Private, Black Watch

Lindsay, J., Hill Street, Montrose; Private, Royal Army Medical Corps—1899 [381

Lochead, Shepherd's Loan, Dundee; Private, 2nd Seaforth Highlanders. Medal—Chitral [463

Logan, Robert, Links Cottages, Monifieth; Private, 2nd Gordon Highlanders—1896 Medal and Two Clasps for India [11

Lord, William M., Duthie Street, Kirriemuir; Private, 2nd Royal Highlanders—1899 [121

Lorimer, Angus, Overgate, Dundee; Private, 3rd Black Watch—1897 [414

Low, David, Barnhead, Old Montrose; Private, 2nd Royal Highlanders—1888

Lowdon, James, Glamis Road, Kirriemuir; Corporal, 2nd Seaforth Highlanders—1891 Medal for Chitral. Killed at Magersfontein [105

Lowrey, Edward, B., Watson Street, Dundee; Private, 1st Royal Welsh Fusiliers—1887 Medal—Hazarah [280

Lundie, Alex., Barngreen, Arbroath; Private, 1st Royal Scots—1892 [56

Lusby, George, Blackscroft, Dundee; Private, 1st Royal Scots [217

Lynch, Patrick, Foundry Lane, Dundee; Private, Scottish Rifles—1888 [377

Lynch, Thomas, Mid Wynd, Dundee; Private, Black Watch—1890

M'Ardle, John, High Street, Arbroath; Private, Medical Staff—1899 [380

M'Artney, Patrick, Blackness Road, Dundee; Private, 3rd Argyll and Sutherland Highlanders

M'Cabe, Bernard, Larch Street, Dundee; Private, 3rd Royal Highlanders—1890

M'Cabe, Henry G., Lawrence Street, Dundee; Private, 2nd Royal Scottish Fusiliers—1890 [499

M'Connell, Thomas, John, Isla Street, Dundee; Private, 2nd Black Watch—1897 [322

M'Connell, Wm. J., John Street, Dudhope Crescent, Dundee; Gunner, Royal Artillery

M'Cormack, James, Albert Street, Lochee; Private, Scots Rifles

M'Cracken, David S., Ashton Place, Dundee; Private, 1st Gordon Highlanders — 1888 Medal—Chitral [319

M'Cracken, David, Ure Street, Dundee; Private, 1st Gordon Highlanders—1888. Medal—Chitral [447

M'Cusker, F., Monifieth; Private, Argyll and Sutherland Highlanders

M'Donach, James, City Road, Dundee; Private, 1st King's Own Scottish Borderers—1884. Medal — Egyptian and Clasp; Khedive Star

M'Donald, Alex., St Rogue's Lane, Dundee; Lance-Corporal, 1st Gordon Highlanders—1890. One Medal and Three Clasps—Chitral, Punjab, Tirah [283

M'Donald, James, Castle Lane, Dundee; Sergeant, 3rd Gordon Highlanders—1891 [221

M'Dowell, Alexander, Smithy Croft, Arbroath; Private, Black Watch

M'Ewan, John, Brown Street, Dundee; Private, 21st Royal Scottish Fusiliers—1888 [513

M'Ewan, Peter, West Port, Dundee; Driver, Royal Artillery [340

M'Farlane, Alexander, Hilltown, Dundee; Private, Royal Scots—1875

M'Farlane, James, Small's Lane, Dundee; Private, Royal Field Artillery—1891 [300

M'Farlane, James, Polepark Road, Dundee; Gunner, Royal Field Artillery

M'Farlane, Thomas, West High Street, Forfar; 78th Battery Royal Field Artillery—1892 [367

M'Farlane, Wm, Small's Lane, Dundee; Royal Field Artillery—1895 [299

M'Gann, J., Monifieth; Private, Black Watch

M'Gann, Thomas, Union Street, Dundee: Private, 3rd Royal Highlanders—1890

M'Garry, John, D., Market Street, Brechin; Lance-Corporal, Royal Highlanders—1899. Promoted after Magersfontein [72

M'Gee, James, Hill Street, Dundee; Private, 4th King's Royal Rifles — 1885. One Medal—Burmah [397

M'Gillivray, Wm., T., Mitchell Street, Dundee; Private, 2nd Black Watch—1890; w

M'Govern, Thomas, Peddie Street, Dundee; Private, 1st Highland Light Infantry—1886. Two Medals—India [305

M'Grath, Francis, Dundee; Gunner, 78th Field Battery, R.A.—1890 [264

M'Gregor, George, Dundee; Private, Black Watch—1892; w

M'Gregor, James, Annfield Road, Dundee; Lance-Corporal, 1st Scots Guards—1891 [430

M'Gregor, J., Yeaman Street, Forfar; Trooper, 7th Dragoon Guards

M'Guillan, Owen, Kinnaird Street, Dundee: Private, 3rd Black Watch [449

M'Gurty, Francis, Mills W. Wynd, Dundee; Private, Royal Highlanders—1886 [245

M'Hardy, James, Lilybank Road, Dundee; Private, Black Watch—1888 [332

M'Hardy, William, Hill Street, Dundee; Private, Royal Scots Fusiliers—1885. Medal —Burmah [412

M'Inally, Bernard, Arthur Street, Dundee; Private, Black Watch—1898; w [393

M'Inally, William, Burnside Street, Dundee; Private, 71st Highland Light Infantry—1888

M'Intosh, Albert, Liff Road, Lochee; Private, Gordon Highlanders — 1892. Medal—Dargai and Clasp

M'Intosh, John, Liff Road, Lochee; Private, Gordon Highlanders — 1892. Medals—Chitral and Dargai (and Clasp)

M'Intyre, James, Russell Street, Dundee; Private, 42nd Royal Highlanders—1884 [205

M'Kay, John, Princes Street, Dundee; Trooper, 6th Dragoon Guards—1888 [345

M'Kelvie, George, Polepark Road, Dundee; Private, Royal Highlanders—1894

M'Kelvie, Wm., James Street, Dundee; Private, 2nd Black Watch—1889; w [206

M'Kenna, Charles, Monifieth; Private, Argyll and Sutherland Highlanders—1890. Medal with Clasp (Tirah); w [46

M'Kenna, Francis, Links Cottages, Monifieth; Private, Gordon Highlanders — 1893. Medal with two Clasps [46

M'Kenzie, James T., Overgate, Dundee; Private, 3rd Black Watch—1899

M'Kenzie, Alexander, Overgate, Dundee; Corporal, Royal Highlanders—1898

M'Kernan, John, Lyon's Close, Dundee; Private, 2nd Black Watch

M'Kinnes, Alexander, Queen Street, Forfar; Private, Cameron Highlanders

M'Kinnes, Allan, Queen Street, Forfar; Private, Cameron Highlanders

M'Kinnon, Roderick, Park Street, Arbroath; Lance-Corporal, Royal Scots Fusiliers—1899

M'Laren, —, Whitehills, Forfar; Private, Seaforth Highlanders

M'Laren, Edward, High Street, Dundee; Driver, Army Service Corps—1894

M'Laren, George, Balgay Street, Lochee: Private, Gordon Highlanders—1879. Medal in Luchi War

M'Laren, James, Brewery Lane, Dundee; Private, Argyll and Sutherland Highlanders—1884

M'Lauchlan, Dugald, Anchor Place, Westhaven; Private, Gordon Highlanders—1889 [12

M'Lauchlan, John, Watson Street, Dundee; Private, Black Watch—1891 [265

M'Lean, Alfred, Ann Street, Arbroath; Private, Scottish Rifles

M'Lean, Henry, Lochee Road, Dundee; Private, Royal Scots Fusiliers—1890 [326

M'Lean, George, Rosebank Street, Dundee; Private, 2nd Black Watch — 1890; w One Medal—Matabele War [192

M'Lean, Worthy J., Alpha Place, Forfar; Private, Seaforth Highlanders—1898 [151

M'Leish, David, St Mary Street, Arbroath; Driver, 67th Field Battery, Royal Artillery —1897 [4

M'Leish, Stephen, St Mary Street, Arbroath; Private, 17th Lancers

M'Luskie, George, Campbell Street, Lochee; Private, 1st Gordon Highlanders—1892. Medal and Two Bars — Chitral, Tirah, Dargai [288

M'Manus, James, Hilltown, Dundee; Private, Royal Highlanders—1889 [406

M'Millan, John, Arbroath; Quarter-Master Sergeant, Staff (Roberts')—1883, in Argyll and Sutherland Highlanders. Medal for Ashantee [124

M'Neilly, Joseph, Scouringburn, Dundee; Private, 2nd Seaforth Highlanders—1889 [440

M'Phee, J., Queen Street, Broughty Ferry; Private, 1st Gordon Highlanders—1886; w Medal and Bars for Chitral—Punjab and Tirah [439

M'Phee, Terrance, Queen Street, Broughty Ferry; Private, 1st Gordon Highlanders—1886. Medals — Dargai, and Egyptian Campaigns; w [130

M'Robbie, Alex., Chapel Lane, Broughty Ferry; Private, Argyll and Sutherland Highlanders—1895; w [129

M'Robbie, George, Chapel Lane, Broughty Ferry; Private, Black Watch—1899

M'Robbie, James, Chapel Lane, Broughty Ferry; Private, Argyll and Sutherland Highlanders—1897

M'Rudden, John, Applegate, Arbroath; Private, Black Watch

Macleod, Alex., Stirling Street, Dundee; Lance-Corporal, 2nd Black Watch—1897 [485

Macpherson, Wm., Burnside Cottage, Kirriemuir; Colour-Sergeant, Argyll and Sutherland Highlanders—1884 [98

Macfarlane, James, Craigie Street, Dundee; Driver, 38th Battery Royal Field Artillery —1890 [293

Mackie, J., St Mary Street, Dundee; Private, 13th Hussars—1897 [358

Madden, Peter, Cotton Road, Dundee; Private, 2nd Royal Highlanders—1883

Malcolm, James, Coupar Street, Lochee; Private, Royal Highlanders—1886 [435

Malcolm, W., Hillside, Montrose; Sergeant, 2nd Black Watch—1892; w [71

Mann, Allan P, Letham Mill, by Arbroath; Private, Black Watch—1887 [125

Mann, J., Letham Mill, by Arbroath; Private, Black Watch

Marnie, John, Seagate, Montrose; Private, Black Watch—1893 [160

Marr, David S., David Street, Broughty Ferry; Private, 1st Seaforth Highlanders—1895

Marshall, David, Fleuchar Street, Dundee; Private, 2nd Black Watch—1888 [503

Marshall, H., Mill Street, Montrose; Private, King's Own Scottish Borderers

Marshall, James, Peep o' Day Lane, Dundee; Private, Black Watch—1890 [222

Marshall, Matthew, Hilltown, Dundee; Lance-Corporal, 1st Cameron Highlanders—1885 [418

Martin, Alex., St Mary Street, Dundee; Private, Royal Artillery—1888 [429

Martin, John, Russell Street, Dundee; Private, Cameron Highlanders—1885. Medal and Star—Nile Expedition [510

Martin, John, Larch Street, Dundee; Private, 3rd Royal Highlanders—1897

Martin, Robert, Caldrum Street, Dundee; Private, 1st Gordon Highlanders—1889. Medal and Bar [262

Martin, Wm., Garland Place, Dundee; Private, 1st Scots Guards [249

Matthew, Alexander, Dundonald Street, Dundee; Private, 2nd Royal Scottish Fusiliers —1891 [401

Matthew, John, Links Cottages, Broughty Ferry; 1894 [170

Matthews, James, Overgate, Dundee; Private, 18th Hussars—1895

Matthews, Patrick, West Port, Dundee; Private, 2nd Scottish Rifles—1888 [427

Maxwell, Andrew, Poet's Lane, Brechin; Gunner, Royal Artillery—1886

Maxwell, Henry, Private, 2nd Black Watch. Killed at Magersfontein

Maxwell, Henry, Arbroath; Private, Black Watch. Killed at Magersfontein

Maxwell, Hugh, Poet's Lane, Brechin; Private, 2nd Royal Highlanders — 1890. Killed, Magersfontein [58

Maxwell, J., Arbroath; Private, 2nd Black Watch; *w*

Maxwell, Ralph, Poet's Lane, Brechin; Private, Royal Highlanders—1890

Meek, David D., Green Street, Arbroath; Private, 42nd Black Watch—1889 [143

Meikle, David B. H., Ure Street, Dundee; Private, 1st Highland Light Infantry—1888 [188

Melville, David, Middle Brighty, Murroes; Private, Gordon Highlanders—1884 One Medal, 2 Bars, and 1 Star [35

Melville, David, Middlebrighty, Duntroon; Private, Gordon Highlanders. One Medal and Two Clasps [403

Melville, James, Rose Street, Dundee; Private, 1st Gordon Highlanders—1884 [270

Melville, James, Hunter Street, Dundee; Private, Royal Scots Fusiliers—1884 [432

Melville, Peter, Dallfield Walk, Dundee; Private, King's Own Scottish Borderers — 1885. One Medal, One Star, One Bar [486

Millar, Alexander, Foundry Lane, Dundee; Private, 2nd Royal Highlanders — 1892 [266

Millar, Alexander, Alyth; Sergeant, Black Watch—1890; *w*

Millar, Wm., Scouringburn, Dundee; Private, 3rd Royal Highlanders—1890 [437

Miller, William Patterson, Lilybank Road, Dundee; Private, 2nd Seaforth Highlanders —1891 [226

Mills, Thomas, Bain's Square, Dundee; Private, Royal Highlanders—1884

Milne, David, East High Street, Forfar; Sapper, Royal Engineers—1894 [70

Milne, David E., Mains of Logie, Forfarshire; Private, Argyll and Sutherland Highlanders — 1888. Medals, 2 Indian. Killed, Magersfontein [158

Milne, James, Rood Street, Kirriemuir; Private, 2nd Gordon Highlanders—1897 [13

Milne, James, Ogilvie's Road, Dundee; Private, 2nd Royal Highlanders—1885 [415

Milne, John W., North Grimsby, Arbroath; Sapper, 23rd Company Royal Engineers— 1897; *w* [163

Milne, William, East High Street, Forfar; Royal Horse Artillery—1896 [49

Milton, James, Wilkie Lane, Dundee; Private, 2nd Black Watch—1884 [216

Minnock, Thos. C., Blackness Road, Dundee; Private, 2nd Seaforth Highlanders—1895 Medal—Cretan War [480

Mitchell, A., Dallfield Walk, Dundee; Private, 42nd Black Watch [179

Mitchell, David, Montrose Street, Brechin; Private, 2nd Royal Highlanders—1895 [147

Mitchell, George, Kinnaird Place, Brechin; Private, Gordon Highlanders — 1881. Medals—Egyptian, Khedive Star, and three Clasps [75

Mitchell, George, Dudhope Crescent Road, Dundee; Private, Black Watch — 1885 [496

Mitchell, George, Albert Street, Dundee; Private, Black Watch—1885 [384

Mitchell, James, Wilson Street, Lochee; Corporal, Gordon Highlanders—1899

Moir, D., North Street, Forfar; Private, Black Watch; w

Moir, John, Robert Street, Arbroath; Private, Black Watch—1888; w [152

Moir, William, North Street, Forfar; Sergeant, 2nd Gordon Highlanders—1890; w [109

Moir, Market Street, Montrose; Private, King's Own Scottish Borderers

Moncur, David, Gardiner Street, Dundee; 17th Royal Engineers—1896 [475

Moon, George, North Tay Street, Dundee; Sergeant, 3rd Royal Highlanders [223

Mooney, D., Rosebery Street, Dundee; Private, 2nd Gordon Highlanders [277

Moonlight, Thomas, Woodville Feus, Arbroath; Private, 42nd Black Watch; w [334

Moore, Thomas, Camperdown Street, Lochee: Private, Royal Highlanders—1889 [446

Morris, James, Kirriemuir; Private, 2nd Black Watch—1898. Killed, Magersfontein [23

Morris, Wm., Gladstone Place, Forfar; Private, 1st King's Own Scottish Borderers

Morrison, A., King Street, Montrose; Private, Black Watch—1887 [81

Morrison, Robert, Gray Square, Dundee; Private, Royal Highlanders—1894 [421

Morrison, W., New Wynd, Montrose; Private, Black Watch—1889 [339

Morton, James, Robert Street, Forfar; Lance-Corporal, 1st Scots Guards—1898 [6

Mowatt, A., Montrose; Private, 2nd Seaforth Highlanders—1890; w

Mudie, David, Watt Street, Dundee; Private, Royal Highlanders—1885 [263

Mudie, James, Dens Road, Dundee; Private, Black Watch—1899. Died from wounds received at Lynburg

Muir, Geo., Reform Street, Arbroath; Private, Black Watch—1887 [359

Munro, David W., Union Street East, Arbroath; Private, Royal Scots Greys—1884 [32

Munro, Robert, Pennycook Lane, Dundee; Lance-Corporal, 2nd Black Watch. Mentioned in despatches for recovering the body of Lord Winchester out of firing line at Magersfontein [276

Murdoch, R., Brechin; Private, 2nd Royal Highlanders; w

Murray, R., Southesk Street, Montrose; Royal Engineers—1896 [93

Murphy, Daniel, Hill Street, Dundee; Gunner, Royal Artillery—1889 [241

Neave, Charles, St James Road, Forfar; Private, 2nd Black Watch—1898. [89

Neish, David, St Mary Street, Dundee; Private, 2nd Battalion Black Watch—1894

Neish, George M'L., Mid Road, Hilltown, Dundee; Lance-Sergeant, 3rd Royal Highlanders—1897 [349

Nicoll, Alexander, Caldrum Street, Dundee; Private, Royal Field Artillery—1898 [258

Nicoll, Alex., Crocket's Buildings, Brechin; Private, Argyll and Sutherland Highlanders—1893 [57

Nicoll, Andrew, Caldrum Street, Dundee; Private, 2nd Royal Highlanders — 1899 [258

Nicoll, James, Kinloch Street, Dundee; Private, Black Watch—1892 [218

Nicoll, Wm. S., St Vigeans; Private, King's Royal Rifles.—1898. Died of fever in Ladysmith [132

Nisbet, William, South Road, Lochee; Private, 2nd Black Watch—1888 [175

Nixon, James, Blackness Road, Dundee; Private, Royal Highlanders [416

O'Brien, Patrick, Dundee; Private, 1st Durham Light Infantry—1899. Medal—One, and Three Clasps [500

O'Neill, Richard, Union Street, Maxweltown; Private, 2nd Royal Irish Fusiliers—1889

Ogg, Alexander, Arbroath; Private, 2nd Battalion Black Watch—1892 [474

Ogg, John G., Brechin Road, Arbroath; Private, 42nd Black Watch—1892. Killed at Magersfontein [42

Ormond, D., St James Road, Forfar; Private, Cameron Highlanders.

Orr, Thomas, John Street, Dundee; Private, Royal Highlanders. [494

Page, Peter, Crescent Lane, Dundee; Private, 2nd Scottish Rifles—1888. Killed at Spion Kop

Palles, Joseph, Watson's Lane, Dundee; Private, Royal Army Medical Corps—1895 [186

Parker, David, Leonard Street, Arbroath; Private, Royal Scots Fusiliers—1888 [99

Paterson, John, Montrose Street, Brechin; Private, 1st Highland Light Infantry—1889 Medal for India [376

Patterson, David, Strathview, Edzell; Private, Scots Guards

Patterson, David T., Union Street, Brechin; Private, 2nd Royal Highlanders

Patterson, David T., Carsebarracks, Forfar; Private, Black Watch—1889 [118

Patterson, James, Strathview, Edzell; Private, Black Watch. Killed at Magersfontein

Paton, Peter, King Street, Ferryden; Private, Black Watch—1896 [73

Pattullo, James R., Eglinton Place, Broughty Ferry; Private, Scots Greys—1893 [38

Pert, J., Shore Wynd, Montrose; Private, Black Watch—1899. Killed at Magersfontein

Petrie, Charles, Lochland Street, Arbroath; Private, Black Watch—1889 [61

Petrie, Edward R., West High Street, Forfar; Private, 1st Battalion Scots Guards—1895 [139

Petrie, John, S. Grimsby, Arbroath; Private, Argyll and Sutherland Highlanders—1888 [157

Petrie, William, Forfar; 1st Royal Scots [142

Phillip, George P., Derby Place, Broughty Ferry; Private, 2nd Battalion Scottish Rifles—1888; w [409

Phin, J., or Lindsay, Kinloch Place, Dundee; Private, 1st Cameron Highlanders—1885 Medals—Soudan (3 and 1 Star) [316

Plummer, Robert, Wolseley Street, Dundee; Gunner, Royal Artillery—1879 [203

Pont, Charles L., Mid Road, Dundee; Trooper, Royal Scots Greys—1891 [180

Potter, G., Dundee; Private, Black Watch; w

Powrie, John, Benvie Road, Dundee; Private, 11th Hussars [468

Printy, Edward, Watt Street, Dundee; Private, 2nd Gordon Highlanders—1894. Killed at Elandslaagte [233

Prophet, Robert, West Whorter Bank, Lochee; Private, 3rd Battalion Gordon Highlanders

Quigley, Charles, Ashton Place, Dundee; Royal Army Medical Corps. Medals—3 for Soudan. Assisted to bring in Kitchener when wounded in Soudan

Quin, Patrick, Dundee; Private, Black Watch —1898; w

Quinn, Edward, Ann Street, Dundee; Private, 3rd Royal Highlanders

Rae, J., North Street, Forfar; Private, Black Watch

Ramsay, Ernest, North Street, Forfar; Private, Black Watch—1897; w [116

Rattray, L. C., Montrose; Private, Black Watch; w

Reid, Alex., Malcolm Street, Dundee; Private, Argyll and Sutherland Highlanders—1888

Reid, George, Dundee; Sergeant, Bechuanaland Rifles (formerly Private in Dundee Highlanders)

Reid, James, Montrose; Corporal, Royal Artillery—1878 [94

Reynolds, Joseph, St Mary Street, Arbroath; Private, 21st Royal Scots Fusiliers

Reilly, James, Hunter Street, Dundee; Private 3rd Royal Highlanders—1888

Richmond, William, Albert Street, Lochee; Private 21st Royal Scots Fusiliers—1884. Medal—Burmah [443

Riley, Peter, Polepark Road, Dundee; Private, Royal Scots Fusiliers—1885 Killed near Ladysmith [337

Ritchie, Alex. M'A., Blackscroft, Dundee; Drummer, 1st Argyll and Sutherland Highlanders—1896 [213

Ritchie, James, Dundee; Private, Gordon Highlanders

Ritchie, Thos., 64 Hilltown, Dundee; Private, 2nd Black Watch—1887 [244

Robb, Wm. F., Caldrum Street, Dundee; Private, 1st Royal Scots—1892

Robbie, Alexander, Kirriemuir, latterly Utinhage, South Africa; Corporal, Utinhage Volunteers

Roberts, William F., Wellbraehead, Forfar; Lance-Corporal 42nd Royal Highlanders —1888; w [117

Robertson, Daniel C., Wellgate, Dundee; Private, 1st Black Watch—1885 [477

Robertson, David, John Street, Dundee; Private, 2nd Seaforth Highlanders—1886 [214

Robertson, George H., Leysmill; Private, 2nd Royal Highlanders — 1898. Killed at Magersfontein [204

Robertson, John, Carnoustie; Private, Royal Scots Fusiliers

Robertson, Joseph, King Street, Broughty Ferry; Private, Royal Artillery [14

Robertson, Laurence, H. C., St Mary Street, Dundee; Ordinary Seaman, H. M. S. "Terrible," R.N.—1896 [268

Robertson, William, Monifieth; Driver, 7th Royal Field Artillery—1897. Received Distinguished Service Medal for heroic conduct in trying to save the guns at Colenso. He was wounded, but recovered speedily. His conduct was described by General Sir C. F. Clery as one of the most intrepid deeds of the whole war.—[Page 162

Robertson, Wm. R., Dens Road, Dundee; Drummer, 2nd Black Watch—1890; w [296

Robertson, W. D., Castle Street, Montrose; Private, Black Watch—1896 [113

Rosemond, John, Burnside Street, Dundee; Corporal, 4th Argyll and Sutherland Highlanders [331

Ross, Allan, St James' Road, Forfar; Private, Seaforth Highlanders—1885. Medal and 2 Clasps. Killed at Paardeberg [137

Ross, David, Fergus Street, Arbroath: Private, 1st Black Watch—1886 [344

Ross, James, Hunter Street, Dundee; Private, 2nd Royal Scots Fusiliers—1885 [509

Ross, Robert, Montrose Street, Brechin; Private, Army Service Corps—1897 [366

Ross, Walter, Logie Street, Lochee; Private, 12th Royal Lancers [390

Rourke, Wm., Cowgate, Dundee; Private, 1st Gordon Highlanders—1889 [294

Row, James Hay, Mid Street, Lochee; Private, Black Watch—1889 [239

Rowell, John, Albert Street, Lochee; Private, Scots Guards—1899 [202

Rutherford, Alex., Barbers' Croft, Arbroath; Private, Black Watch

Samson, Andrew L., Glenisla; Private, 2nd Royal Highlanders. Died of fever

Sandeman, Charles, Kidd Street, Dundee; Lance-Corporal, 3rd Black Watch—1895 [514

Sands, William, Constable Street, Dundee; Private, 1st King's Own Scottish Borderers —1885 Medal—Egyptian and Star [215

Scott, Abraham, Larch Street, Dundee; Private, Royal Highlanders—1890

Scott, Andrew, Lyon's Close, Dundee; Private, Royal Highlanders—1886

Scott, James, Union Place, Lochee; Private, Black Watch—1888 [396

Scott, James M. J., Hill Street, Arbroath; Private, Black Watch—1897; w [97

Scott, William N., Ireland Street, Carnoustie; Bombardier, Siege Artillery—1888 [5

Scullin, Ambrose, Scouringburn, Dundee; Private, Royal Highlanders—1888 Killed at Magersfontein [234

Shand, W., Dundee; Private, Seaforth Highlanders

Sharples, James, Princes Street, Dundee; Private, 1st Royal Scots—1892

Shaw, Henry, Dundee; Private, Black Watch —1889; w

Sheriff, Charles, Rosebery Street, Dundee, Private, 71st Highland Light Infantry— 1889. Medals—Five from the A.T.A. India, for fidelity [462

Sheret, David, Fraser's Lane, Montrose; Private, Black Watch [77

Shepherd, John R., Albert Street, Forfar; Private, Highland Light Infantry—1894

Short, John, Larch Street, Dundee; Private, 3rd Battalion Royal Highlanders—1888 [207

Simpson, Alexander, Arbroath; Corporal, 26th Cameronians—1890 [7

Simpson, Alexander A., Glamis Road, Forfar; Private, 2nd Black Watch—1898; w [88

Simpson, Thomas, Wolseley Street, Dundee; Private, Royal Highlanders—1899. Killed at Paardeberg [232

Sinclair, James, Caldrum Street, Dundee; Private, 2nd Royal Highlanders—1891 [413

Sinclair, James, River Street, Brechin; Lance-Corporal, 2nd Royal Highlanders—1897 [90

Skelly, John, Watson's Lane, Dundee; Private, 42nd Royal Highlanders—1887 [237

Skelley, Peter, Dens Brae, Dundee; Private, 3rd Argyll and Sutherland Highlanders—1894

Sloggie, J., Panmure Road, Montrose; Private, Black Watch—1898 [325

Sloan, Wm., Dens Road, Dundee; Private, Royal Highlanders—1890 [171

Smart, James, Clerk Street, Brechin; Private, 2nd Royal Highlanders—1899

Smart, Wm., Blackness Road, Dundee; Private, Highland Light Infantry—1891 [247

Smart, Wm. D., Glengate Street, Kirriemuir; Lance-Corporal, King's Own Scottish Borderers—1887. Medal—Egyptian. [140

Smith, Alexander, Cotton Road, Dundee; Bandsman, 15th Hussars—1892

Smith, David, Montrose Street, Brechin; Trooper, 10th Hussars—1893 [45

Smith, Edward, Leonard Street, Arbroath; Private, 2nd Seaforth Highlanders—1890 [165

Smith, Edward, Sim's Land, Lochee; Private, 3rd Royal Highlanders

Smith, Isaac, Marketgate, Arbroath; Private, 2nd Cameron Highlanders—1898 [343

Smith, James, Arbroath Road, Dundee; Private, 2nd Royal Highlanders; w [388

Smith, James, Fergus Square, Arbroath; Private, Black Watch

Smith, James (or Shields), Rosebank Street, Dundee; Private, 3rd Gordon Highlanders

Smith, Joseph, Fraser's Lane, Montrose; Private, Gordon Highlanders — 1880. Medal—Chitral [83

Smith, William, Blackscroft, Dundee; Private, 1st Gordon Highlanders—1890. Medal—Chitral; Bar—Punjab; Bar—Tirah [298

Smith, Wm. D., Hillbank Road, Dundee; Private, 2nd Seaforth Highlanders—1888 Medal and Clasp—Hazarah; Medal with Clasp, 1895 [256

Smith, William, Albert Street, Lochee; Private, 1st Gordon Highlanders—1888. Medal—Dargai [487

Souter, George, Caldrum Street, Dundee; Private, 3rd Gordon Highlanders [444

Spalding, George, Peep o' Day Lane, Dundee; Private, 1st Gordon Highlanders — 1883 Egyptian Medal, 1 Star, and Clasps, Kerbekan and Nile Expedition [424

Spalding, James, Dallfield Walk, Dundee; Piper, Royal Scots Fusiliers—1890 [348

Spence, Andrew W., Claypots Cottages, Broughty Ferry; Private, 1st Gordon Highlanders—1889 [85

Stark, Alex., Links Cottages, Broughty Ferry; Private, Seaforth Highlanders—1888; w [135

Stark, Alexander, Ravensby Feus, Carnoustie; Private, Seaforth Highlanders—1888; w Medal—Chitral

Strachan, James, Hospital Wynd, Dundee; Private, Royal Highlanders—1883

Strachan, J., Monifieth; Private, Black Watch

Strachan, R., Academy Square, Montrose; Private, Black Watch—1898

Steel, Wm., Whorter Bank, Lochee; Private, 2nd Black Watch—1898 [373

Stephen, Alex., Southesk Street, Brechin; Gunner, Royal Artillery—1896 [54

Steven, James, Alexander Street, Dundee; Corporal, 3rd Battalion Royal Highlanders—1894 [482

Stevenson, Frank, Garland Place, Dundee; Private, King's Own Scottish Borderers—1896 [346

Stevenson, George, Garland Place, Dundee; Pipe-Major, King's Own Scottish Borderers [309

Stevenson, James, Duthie Street, South Kirriemuir; Private, 2nd Royal Highlanders—1899; w

Stewart, David, North Ellen Street, Dundee; Private, 2nd Black Watch—1889 Killed at Magersfontein [371

Stewart, David C., Dundee; Gunner, 82nd Battery Royal Field Artillery—1888 [355

Stewart, George, Park Street, Arbroath; Private, 1st Gordon Highlanders—1890 [47

Stewart, Harry, Edzell; Private, Black Watch

Stewart, J., Logie Street, Lochee; Gunner, 36th Battery Royal Field Artillery—1885 [507

Stewart, John, Jamaica Street, Dundee; Private, 1st Queen's Own Cameron Highlanders—1892 [488

Stewart, John, Pole Street, Dundee; Private, 1st Cameron Highlanders—1885 [199

Stewart, Robert, Bog Lane, Arbroath; Private, 42nd Royal Highlanders—1885 [149

Stewart, T., Dudhope Street, Dundee; Private, 2nd Royal Scots Fusiliers—1897 [190

Stewart, T., Kinnaird Street, Dundee; Sergeant 3rd Gordon Highlanders—1893 [269

Stockman, George, Elliot Street, Arbroath; Private, 3rd King's Own Hussars—1891 [29

Stone, H., High Street, Montrose; Lance-Corporal, Gordon Highlanders—1898 [273

Stuart, George A., King Street, Broughty Ferry; Private, Black Watch—1897 [114

Sturrock, James, Queen Street, Forfar; Private, Royal Highlanders—1898

Sturrock, Wm., Hill Street, Dundee; Private, 1st Cameron Highlanders—1885 Medal—Egyptian and Star [473

Sutherland, Robert, Brook Street, Monifieth; Private, 1st Cameron Highlanders—1896. Medals—Soudan, with Clasp. [107

Suttie, David, Cleghorn Street, Dundee; Lance-Sergeant, 2nd Black Watch—1886 [208

Swan, George, Albert Street, Lochee; Private, Black Watch [464

Swan, John, Larch Street, Dundee; Gunner 5th Battery Royal Field Artillery—1887 [267

Sword, Thomas, Loons Road, Dundee; Gunner, Royal Artillery—1890 [492

Sword, Wm. Patterson, Hill Street, Dundee Private, Seaforth Highlanders—1898 [251

Tait, R. M., Dundee; Sergeant, 4th Rifle Brigade Mounted Infantry

Tarbat, A., Dundee Road, Forfar; Driver, Royal Field Artillery

Taylor, James, Robertson Street, Dundee; Private, 42nd Black Watch—1898 [383

Taylor, James, Whorterbank, Lochee; Private, Gordon Highlanders—1885 [187

Taylor, J., Monifieth; Lance-Corporal, Black Watch

Teviotdale, John, Dundee; Lance-Corporal, Black Watch—1898; *w*

Third, Daniel, Overgate, Dundee; Private, 1st Black Watch [469

Thom, David, Grove Street, Dundee; Private, Royal Highlanders—1884 [341

Thom, Henry, Kirriemuir; Private, 2nd Royal Highlanders—1893 [136

Thom, H., Canmore Lane, Forfar; Private, Black Watch

Thom, Robert, Wilson Street, Lochee; Private, 3rd Royal Highlanders—1879

Thomson, George, Tait's Lane, Dundee; Private, 1st Scottish Rifles—1884 [394

Thomson, James D., Union Place, Lochee; Private, 2nd Black Watch [318

Thomson, John, Lour, by Forfar; Gunner, 79th Battery Royal Artillery—1890 [50

Thomson, Joseph, Liff Road, Lochee; Driver, 41st Battery Royal Artillery—1885 [434

Thomson, Joseph, Strathmartine Road, Dundee; Private, Black Watch—1890 [122

Thomson, Stewart, Benvie Road, Dundee; Private, Scottish Rifles [282

Thomson, Thomas P., Greenordie, Lour, by Forfar; Sergeant-Farrier, 89th Battery Royal Artillery [50

Thornton, A. D., King Street, Broughty Ferry; No. 12 Hospital Ambulance Corps [10

Thornton, William T., King Street, Broughty Ferry; Bombardier, attached to 61st Howitzer Battery, Royal Field Artillery [48

Todd, Henry, Green Street, Forfar; Private, 1st Gordon Highlanders—1886 [111

Torrance, James, Horsewater Wynd, Dundee; Private, 2nd Scottish Rifles—1889 [342

Tosh, James, Shandford, Fern, Brechin; Trooper, 1st Life Guards—1894 [87

Tosh, W. S., Leys of Cossans, Glamis; Lance-Corporal, Royal Scots Greys—1895 [370

Trayner, James, Horsewater Wynd, Dundee; Private, Royal Highlanders—1888 [378

Vance, James, Church Street, Dundee; Private, Royal Scots Greys—1898 [364

Vance, William, Blackness Road, Dundee; Private, Royal Scots Greys—1888 [320

Veitch, William, Rosebery Street, Dundee; Sergeant, 2nd Black Watch—1894 [382

Walker, Alexander, River Street, Brechin; Sergeant, Royal Scots Fusiliers—1896 [8

Walker, David, 18 Dens Road, Dundee; Private, Black Watch

Walker, William, Church Street, Edzell; Private, Black Watch

Walker, William, Brechin; Private, Black Watch—1898; w

Wallace, Peter, West Mill Wynd, Arbroath; Driver, Artillery Divisional Staff

Ward, Patrick, St Peter Street, Dundee; Private, Royal Scots Fusiliers—1886 [453

Watt, David, Dunnichen, by Forfar; Private, Black Watch—1895; w

Watt, John, Palmer Street, Arbroath; Private, 79th Cameron Highlanders

Watt, T., Mill Street, Montrose; Corporal, Scots Guards—1891 [134

Watt, William S., East Queen Street, Broughty Ferry; Royal Scots Greys—1895; w [148

Watson, Alexander, River Street, Brechin; Trooper, 9th Lancers—1896. Died of fever at Wynberg [27

Watson, John R., Maule Street, Arbroath; Private, Gordon Highlanders—1897 [106

Watson, William, North Tay Street, Dundee; Highland Light Infantry [246

Webster, Alexander McC., Forfar, nephew of Mrs Flora Annie Steel; 1st Loyal North Lancashire — 1898. In command of armoured train, siege of Kimberley [133

Webster, George, East High Street, Forfar; Army Service Corps—1886 [141

Wedderspoon, Stewart, Kerr's Lane, Lochee; Private, Black Watch—1889 [310

Weir, George, Braik's Close, Brechin; Trooper, 18th Hussars—1896; w [60

Welch, James, Union Street, Maxwelltown, Dundee; Private, Royal Highlanders [465

Welsh, Michael, Lyon Street, Dundee; Private, 79th Cameron Highlanders

Wells, W., Claypots Road, Broughty Ferry; Private, 1st Cameron Highlanders—1896

Wheelan, James, Blackness Road, Dundee; Private, 3rd Royal Scots—1880

Whitton, R., St Mary Street, Dundee; Private, Highland Light Infantry—1894 [363

Whitehead, Thos., Elmbank, Broughty Ferry; Hartley's Cape Mounted Service Corps (attached to Highland Brigade) [317

Whyte, James, Monifieth; Private, Black Watch

Whyte, George, Market Street, Brechin; Private, 2nd Royal Highlanders—1889 [150

Wilkie, J., East High Street, Forfar; Private, Cameron Highlanders—1885. Medal and Star—Egyptian Campaign

Williamson, J., Montrose; Private, Black Watch; w

Wilson, George, Montrose; Private, Royal Scots Fusiliers—1886 [504

Wilson, John, Bernard Street, Dundee, Driver, Royal Field Artillery—1890

Wilson, Robert, Temple Lane, Dundee; Private, Royal Highlanders—1893. Killed at Magersfontein [174

Wilson, Robert, Dallfield Walk, Dundee; Sergeant, 2nd Royal Highlanders

Wishart, George, Howard Street, Arbroath [163

Wishart, John, Barrack Street, Dundee; Private, 2nd Black Watch—1887 [431

Wood, John, Links Cottages, Broughty Ferry; Private, Black Watch—1890

Woods John (or Harrison), Rosebank Road, Dundee; Gunner, 4th Mountain Battery, Royal Artillery—1896 [385

Wright, William, Campbell Street, Lochee; Private, Black Watch—1890 [257

Wynne, Owen, Lyon Street, Dundee; Private, Black Watch [351

Yeaman, John, Gravesend, Arbroath; Private, Gordon Highlanders

Young, John, Wilson Street, Lochee; Private, Highland Light Infantry—1892

Young, J., Brechin; Private, 2nd Royal Highlanders—1897. Killed at Magersfontein

Young, P., Yeaman's Land, Lochee; Private, Highland Light Infantry—1889 [476

Young, Thomas, Craigie Street, Dundee; Corporal, 2nd Scottish Rifles—1895 [354

LIST OF SUBSCRIBERS.

LIST OF SUBSCRIBERS.

Her Majesty the Queen.
H.R.H. The Princess Christian.
H.R.H. The Princess Louise, Duchess of Argyll.
H.R.H. The Duke of Connaught.
H.R.H. The Duke of York.

Aberdein, Francis, Garvocklea
Absolon, Misses, Wemyss, Forfar
Adam, John, 11 Guthrie Port, Arbroath
Adam, T. B., 37 Church Street, Brechin
Adam, Thomas, 16 Robertson Street, Glasgow (3)
Adamson, Robert, ex-Chief Constable of Forfarshire, Forfar
Adamson, William Shaw, of Careston
Addison, Miss, Kelso
Airlie, The Countess of (4)
Airlie, The Dowager Countess of (2)
Aitken, Alex., 2 Salisbury Place, Broughty Ferry
Aitken, Samuel, Imperial Hotel, Arbroath (2)
Alexander, Geo. M. B., 207 Caledonian Road London
Alexander, Hugh M., Denvon, Glamis
Alexander, James, 16 Wallace Street, Arbroath
Alexander, John, Ballindarg, Kirriemuir
Alexander, W., Hyde Park, Arbroath
Allan, Robert, Springbank Villa, Brechin (2)
Allan, Walter B., Scotland House, Sunderland
Allan, Wm., M.P., Scotland House, Sunderland (3)
Anderson, Miss, 39 West Newgate, Arbroath
Anderson, Miss, 33 Bryanston Square, London, W.
Anderson, Rev. James, Free Manse, Dyce
Anderson, John N,, solicitor, Stornoway
Anderson, Mrs Patrick, 12 Windsor Street, Dundee
Anderson, Miss Jean Y.,   do.,   do.
Anderson, Lockhart, G.,   do.,   do.
Anderson, Miss R C., 55 Rossie Street, Arbroath
Anderson, Mrs, 13 Dean Park Crescent, Edinburgh
Anderson, Dr, Heathbank, Brechin
Anderson, A D., Fernlea, Arbroath (2)
Anderson, Charles, 5 Castle Street, Brechin (2)
Anderson, David Woodhill, Carnoustie
Anderson, Henry G., 4 Putney Hill Park, London, S.W. (42)
Anderson, Miss Isabella, Bandoch, Inverkeilor (4)
Anderson, Dr J. Keith, Comely Bank, 2nd V.B.R.H., Arbroath
Anderson, James, 4 Elliot Place, Arbroath
Anderson, John, 69 Market Street, Brechin
Anderson, John P , Captain and Hon. Major, 2nd V.B.R.H.. Forfar
Anderson, J. S., builder, 28 Kyd Street, Arbroath
Anderson, Captain P. W., Derbyshire Regiment, Adjutant, 1st V.B.R.H., 12 Windsor Street, Dundee
Anderson, P. W., 43 Hill Street, Arbroath
Anderson, Captain T. Abbot, 6 Stanley Villas, Dundee
Anderson, Rev Thomas S., East Free Manse, Arbroath
Anderson, William, Bractullo, Idvies, Forfar
Anderson, William, solicitor, Brechin (2)
Anderson, William T., 42½ Cairnie Street, Arbroath
Annandale, Alexander, Den Nursery, Brechin (2)
Arbuthnott, The Dowager Viscountess, (4)
Arbuthnott, Mrs Capel Carnegie, Balnamoon, Brechin
Arbuthnott, Mrs Hugh L., 26 Cadogan Square, London, S.W.
Archer, William, Stonehaven
Armytage, Mrs Percy, 28 Hans Place, London
Artillery, 1st F.V., per Captain R. A. Mudie, Dundee
Austin, Robert D. J. Mein, Black Clachie, Barrhill, Ayrshire (6)
Bairnsfather, H. W., Beachwood, Coupar Angus
Ballantyne, Miss, Kinnordy House, Kirriemuir
Ballingall, Hugh, J.P., D.L., Ardarroch, Dundee
Ballingall, James B., LL.B., Advocate, Ardarroch, Dundee
Ballingall, Wm., M.A.F.C.S.,   do.,   do.
Balfour, Alexander, of Inchock, Arbroath (2)
Balfour, The Right Hon. A. J., M.P., First Lord of the Treasury
Balfour, David, 125 Hawkhill, Dundee (2)
Balfour, D. Hall, Bank of Scotland House, Forfar
Balfour, Mrs R., 178 High Street, Montrose
Balfour, R. R., 133 High Street, Montrose (2)
Balfour, William, 36 Victoria Street, Arbroath
Banks, William, 3 Hyndford Terrace, Dundee
Bannerman, The Right Honourable Sir Henry Campbell, G.C.B., Belmont Castle, Meigle
Barclay, James W., 5 Clarendon Place, Hyde Park Gardens, London, W. (2)
Barnett, David, Cargill Terrace, Forfar
Barrie, Charles, 49 Meadowside, Dundee
Barrie, J. M , 133 Gloucester Road, London (20)
Batchelor, Charles, Tofthill, Lochee
Batchelor, James T., Swan Street, Brechin (2)
Baxter, E. A., Kincaldrum, Forfar
Baxter, Mrs G. W., Ashcliff, Dundee (10)
Baxter, K. K., Portland, Oregon, U.S.A.

Beatt, Miss Helen M., 8 Glover Street. Arbroath
Beattie, Mrs, 61 Wilkie's Lane, Dundee
Beaumont, Christopher, Schoolhouse, Barry
Belford, James, *Guide* Office. Broughty Ferry (2)
Belford, W G., Solicitor, Dunbae House, Stranraer
Bell J Harriott, Belmont, Dundee (4)
Bell, John W.,   do.,   do.   (4)
Bell, Thomas, Hazelwood, Broughty Ferry (2)
Bell, Thos. Norman Jarvis, Hazelwood, Broughty Ferry
Bell, Mrs Thomas. Hazelwood, Broughty Ferry
Bell, John Ronald Jarvis, Hazelwood, Broughty Ferry
Bennet, Andrew, solicitor, Arbroath (2)
Benson, Mrs., 14 Cottesmore Gardens, Kensington, London, W.
Berry, J., P.G.M. Forfarshire, Dundee (2)
Bertie. William, 11 Springfield, Dundee (3)
Beveridge, Charles R., 32 Charlotte Square, Edinburgh
Birnie, Robert T., Chief Constable for Forfarshire
Black. G., gardener, Kinblethmont
Black. Miss Agnes, Arbroath
Black, John, Cortachy House, Kirriemuir
Black, Rollo S., 42 Lochland Street, Arbroath
Black. William, City Sawmills, Brechin
Black & Johnston, Brechin (2)
Blackburn, The Lady Constance, 11 Gloucester Place, Edinburgh
Blackley, Colonel, Army and Navy Club, Pall Mall, London, S.W.
Blair, Mrs Patrick. 11 Ainslie Place, Edinburgh (2)
Boase, W., Binrock. Dundee (4)
Boath, W. S, 10 Brothock Bridge, Arbroath
Booth, William, 91 High Street. Arbroath
Borthwick, William, Dunnichen
Bouick, J. B. Gowanbank, Craigie. Perth
Bowman, Mrs, 2 Meikle Mill, Brechin
Boyd, Rev. John, jr , 6 Charlotte Street, Perth
Boyd, Rev. John, D.D., The Manse, Kirriemuir
Brand, James, 172 Buchanan Street, Glasgow
Brand, John, Upland, Kinnoull
Brebner, James, 2 Scotswood Terrace, Dundee
Brodie, John, publisher, Arbroath
Brodie, Mr and Mrs Callender. of Idvies (2)
Brow, John C., 72 George Street. Glasgow (2)
Brown, Mrs, 11 Victoria Street, Arbroath
Brown, Sergeant Instructor, Brechin
Brown, A , Allan Park, Stirling
Brown, D. M., 80 High Street, Dundee (2)
Brown, John, Peasiehill, Arbroath (2)
Brown, Q.-M. Sergeant J., Imperial Yeomanry, Craighill, near Dundee
Brown, W. H., brewer, Dundee
Brougham, Mrs, Arbroath
Bruce, Miss, Bruce's Hotel, Carnoustie
Bruce, The Hon F. J. and Mrs, of Seaton (2)
Brumfitt, Mrs Richard, Newbiggen, Richmond, Yorkshire
Bryan, Henry, 19 Millgate, Arbroath
Buchan, W. B., 38 Union Street, Brechin

Buick, Captain John, 42 Glover Street Arbroath
Buist, Alex. J., Reres Mount, Broughty Ferry (2)
Buncle, T , & Co , *Guide* Office, Arbroath
Burden, Annie, 2 Windsor Terrace, Dundee
Burness, Mrs Robert. Leys of Boysack, Leysmill
Burnett, Alex.. *Chronicle* Printing Works, Montrose
Burnett, George, 11 Duncan Avenue, Scotstoun, Glasgow (2)
Burr, Rev. P. L., D.D., Manse of Lundie and Foulis, near Dundee (2)
Burrows, Miss. 4 Sussex Place, Hyde Park, London
Buyers, Mrs, Rowan Bank Brechin
Cable, John, 49 Billing Road, Northampton
Cables, Mrs. 32 Kyd Street, Arbroath
Cæsar, Rev. John. The Manse, Panbride
Cæsar, William, Lochty, Carnoustie (2)
Calder, Andrew R . Perth
Calder, David R., Ingleside, Arbroath
Calder, D. D., Keptie Street, Arbroath
Calder, John Gray, Ramsay Cottage, Arbroath (2)
Calder, William R., Glasgow
Cameron, W. J. W., 12 Clerk Street, Brechin
Campbell, Miss, 10 Dean Park Crescent, Edinburgh
Campbell, Rev. Colin, D.D., V.D., The Manse of Dundee
Campbell James, 36 Hill Street, Arbroath
Campbell, The Right Hon. James A , M.P., Stracathro, Brechin
Carey, George, c/o. Messrs Whishaw & Co., St. Petersburg, Russia
Cargill, Alexander T. Clifton, Bridge of Weir, Renfrewshire
Cargill, David S.. 45 Renfield Street, Glasgow (2)
Cargill, Francis, Bloomfield Cottage, Forfar
Carlow, Robert S., Gas Works House. Arbroath
Carmichael, G., Tay Mount, Broughty Ferry
Carnegie, Lord and Lady, Crimonmogate, Aberdeenshire (4)
Carnegie, Miss (late of Pitarrow), Edinburgh
Carnegie, Captain Alexander, Forebank, Brechin
Carnegie, C C. Strachan. of Tarrie (4)
Carnegie. Major Lindsay, 6 Playfair Terrace, St Andrews (2)
Carnegy, D. J., County Assessor, Forfar
Carnegie, Mrs Lindsay, Kinblethmont, Arbroath (12)
Carnegie, Miss Lindsay, 55 St George's Road, London, S.W.
Carnegie, The Hon. Launcelot, British Embassy, Berlin
Carnegy, P. A. W., of Lour, Forfar (2)
Carnegie, William, 6 North Grimsby, Arbroath (2)
Carrie, Miss, Rowan Bank, Carnoustie
Caw, Miss, Bank Street, Kirriemuir
Chalmers, Mr and Mrs, of Aldbar (6)
Chalmers, Miss, 6 Collingham Road, London (4)
Chalmers, Major, Gowanlea Cottage, Blairgowrie
Chalmers, John Binny, The Elms, Highgate Road, London, N.W. (2)
Chalmers, Colonel Norman G., late Queen's Own Cameron Highlanders (4)

Chapel, David. Caenlochan, Arbroath
Chaplin, Mrs Child, Kentucky House, Ipswich
Chaplin, Mr and Mrs J. H. A. Peebles, of Colliston (2)
Cheape, Mr and Lady Griselda, of Strathtyrum (2)
Cheape, Hon. Mrs J. C., Carron Lodge, St Andrews
Cheape, Miss, Luthockar, St Andrews
Christie, Mrs, The Manse, Auchmithie
Christie, Mrs, High Street, Arbroath
Christie, James P., 248 High Street, Arbroath
Christie, Wm. R., Queen's-gate Buildings, Inverness
Christie, W. E., M A., Collegiate School, Queens' Park, Glasgow
Clark, Rev. John A , The Manse, Brechin
Clark, J R. W., solicitor, Arbroath
Clark, John, 4 Hill Terrace, Arbroath
Clayhills, T , Southend, Darlington
Cleaver, Rev. Wilfred M., The Parsonage, Glamis Castle
Cleghorn, William, Bayfield, Broughty Ferry (2)
Cloake, W. H., Strathmore, Grove Park, Denmark Hill, London, S E.
Cloudsley, James, 13 Cullum Street, London (2)
Cobb, James, Dundee Road, Arbroath
Constable, C. W. N. B., of Wallace Craigie
Cook, James, plumber, High Street, Arbroath
Cooper, Mrs Walter, 44 Ernest Street, Arbroath
Cox, A. E., of Dungarthill, Dunkeld
Cox, Edward, of Cardean, Meigle (2)
Cox, Edmund C., Logie, Kirriemuir
Cox, George M., Beechwood, Dundee
Cox, Miss, Clement Park, Lochee (2)
Cox, W. H., of Snaigow, Dunkeld
Cochrane, Major A. H , of Dalnabreck, Perthshire
Collier, John and Miss, Hatton, Carnoustie (2)
Collier, Mrs, Auchessan, Crianlarich
Collier, Miss, Willow Grove, Broughty Ferry (4)
Colvill, Mrs, Seaton Road, Arbroath
Cooper, John, Inchcape, Epping, Essex, London, N.
Corsar, Miss Annie, 2 Alexandra Place
Corsar, C. W., Seaforth, Arbroath (3)
Corsar, Charles, Seaforth, Captain 1st F.V.A.
Corsar, David, The Elms, Arbroath (6)
Corsar, Major, 2nd V.B.R.H., Cairniehill, Arbroath (4)
Corstorphine, H., Victoria Street, Arbroath
Couper, Andrew, Brae of Pert, Laurencekirk
Couper, Frederick, of Douglasmuir
Couper, George G. D., 48 Blacket Place, Edinburgh
Couper, John, 16 Windsor Street, Dundee (2)
Couper, T. Duncraig, Dundee
Couttie, Mrs, 13 Benvie Road, Dundee
Couttie, Mrs A., 23 Bridge Street, Brechin
Coutts, James, 4 Hillend Road, Arbroath
Coutts, William, Castle Street, Forfar (2)
Cowper, Max., 34 Lincoln Road, E. Finchley London (12)
Craig, James B., 37 Millgate, Arbroath
Crawford, George, 6 Great Ormond Street, London
Crichton, Mrs J. S., Mansefield, Arbroath
Crichton, Mrs, of West Grange (4)
Crockart, D., 3 Shore, Arbroath
Crockart. David, Academy, Montrose
Crockart. James Hay, 12 St Peter's Place, Montrose
Croall, Miss, Arbroath
Crowder, Rev. A. E., B.A., St Mary's, Arbroath
Crow, David, Elmbank House. Letham, Forfar (2)
Crowe, David, 12 Dudhope Place, Dundee (2)
Crowe, George W. C.,   do.   do.
Cruickshank, Augustus W., of Langley Park
Cruickshank, John, jr., 13 Rosewood Terrace, Dundee
Cumming, Mrs, First Free Manse, Forfar
Cumming, Gregor, Brechin
Cunningham, Mrs W. O., Hillside, Bro'ty Ferry (2)
Cuthbert, James, Grange, Alloa
Dalhousie, The Earl of, (2)
Darling, Lord Stormonth. of Balvurran, Perthshire
Darling, P. Stormonth, of Lednathie, (2)
Darroch, Robert A., 25 High Street, Brechin
Davidson, J., 19 St David Street, Brechin
Davidson, Lieut.-Col. James, 2nd V.B., Kirriemuir
Davidson, J., manufacturer, Dens Works, Arbroath
Davidson, Robert, 57 Rossie Street, Arbroath
Davidson. Robert, S.S.C , 64 Frederick Street, Edinburgh
Davidson, J. M. 133 Ferry Road, Dundee
Davie, A., dentist, Arbroath
Dawson, David, 16 Strawberry Bank, Dundee
Dewar, D., Chief Constable, Dundee
Dewar, Dr James A., 13 Hill Terrace Arbroath
Dewar, Dr Thomas F., Imperial Yeomanry
Dewar, Dr W. J., 13 Hill Terrace, Arbroath
Deuchar, Robert, Shortridge Hall, Warkworth
Dickson, Adam, jr., 7 St Vigeans Road, Arbroath
Dickson, Arthur, solicitor, Montrose (2)
Dickson, Col. J. A., V.D., 2nd V.B., Woodville, Arbroath (2)
Dickson, Mrs J. F., Panbride
Dickson, J. G., Woodville, Arbroath
Dickson, Patrick, of Barnhill, Laurencekirk
Dods, Rev. G. Nisbet, 28 York Place, Perth (2)
Doig, Alex., 29 Jamieson Street, Arbroath
Doig, D , Tay Villa, 12 Cantwell Road, Plumstead, Woolwich
Don, Gilbert W., Clocksbriggs House
Don, Mr and Mrs John B., of Maulesden, Brechin (2)
Don, Robert B., The Lodge, Broughty Ferry
Donald, G. R., solicitor, Arbroath
Donaldson, Mrs, Scores Park, St Andrews
Dorward, Captain J. G., Nolt Loan Road, Arbroath
Douglas, David, Broadford Works, Aberdeen
Douglas, W. A.,   do.   do.
Douglas, W. C., of Brighton (3)
Driffield, Mrs C. G. T., Woodcroft, Prescot, Lancashire
Dron, Robert, Fothringham, Forfar
Ducat, William, Warslap, Arbroath
Ducat, Stanley, M.B., C.M., Arbroath.
Ducat, Alfred B., Arbroath
Ducat, W. F., Calcutta
Duff, Miss, Royal Infirmary, Dundee
Duke, David, Summer Bank, Brechin.

Duke, John, Lieut.-Col. 2nd V.B.R.H., Brechin
Duke, Robert, Bearehill, Brechin
Duke, Robert W., St Ninian's, Brechin
Duke, Rev. William. D.D., The Manse, St Vigeans
Duncan, A., postmaster, Arbroath
Duncan, John of Parkhill (8)
Duncan, A. R., of Sunnyside, Montrose
Duncan, George, Wellhill, Montrose
Duncan, James, of Jordanstone, by Meigle
Duncan, James, 2 St James Place, Brechin
Duncan, William quarrymaster, Carmyllie
Dundas, David, Chalmers Street Works, Arbroath
Duires, James, jr., joiner, Brechin
Durie, Wm., Abbey Road, Barrow-in-Furness
Duthie, James, 129 St Vincent Street, Glasgow
Easson, J. A., Whitehall Street, Dundee
Edward, Alf. S., R.B.A., 46 Fountayne Road, Stamford Hill, London, N.
Ehrlich, J. G., Douglas Hotel, Edinburgh
Elder, Mrs, 22 Barrack Street, Dundee
Elgin, The Countess of, C. I., Broomhall, Dunfermline
Ellis, Captain, Rosemount, Arbroath
Erskine, Mrs, of Linlathen, 14 Belgrave Crescent, Edinburgh
Esplin, W. K., Leysmill (2)
Ewen, John A., Conveth, Potters Bar, Middlesex
Ewen, John T., Millbank House, Forfar (2)
Fairlie, William, Bonhard, Arbirlot
Fairweather, Lieut. D. W., 2nd V.B.R.H., 2 Addison Place, Arbroath (3)
Fairweather, Frank, 33 Cairnie Street, Arbroath
Fairweather, Samuel, Hawthornbank (2)
Falconer, James, W.S., Edinburgh
Farmer, Sir William, Ascot Place, Ascot
Farquhar, Miss, Addison Place, Arbroath
Farquhar, Mrs, of Pitscandly, Forfar
Farquhar, Mrs D. O., Sunnyside, Reigate, Surrey
Fenwick, Mrs P., St Michael's Hotel, by Leuchars, Fife
Fenwick, Peter, 103 Nethergate, Dundee
Ferguson, P., 38 St Augustine's Villas, Highgate, London N. (2)
Fergusson, D. Scott, Union Bank of Scotland, Glasgow (2)
Fergusson, R. Arklay, of Ethiebeaton, Monifieth
Fergusson, W. H., The Buchties, Broughty Ferry
Ferrier, David, Thistle Hotel, Auchinblae
Ferrier, John Scott, 20 Blantyre Terrace, Edinburgh
Findlay, Charles, 9 Throgmorton Avenue, London
Findlay, David, 50 Keptie Street, Arbroath
Findlay, J. G., 6 Market Street, Brechin (2)
Findlay, William, Gunmaker, Kingston, by Forfar
Finlay, Mrs, St Helens, Trinity, Edinburgh
Finlayson, David, 64 Lexham Gardens, London, W.
Finlayson, James, Balcathie, Arbroath (2)
Fleming, Alexander D., 7 Panmure Street, Dundee
Fleming, Robert A., M.D., 10 Chester Street, Edinburgh
Fletcher, Fitzroy C., of Letham Grange (26)
Foote, Alexander, Mall Park, Montrose
Forbes, Edwin J. D., Fernbank, Clepington Road, Dundee
Forbes, Robert, 148 High Street, Arbroath (2)
Forman, Alexander G., W.S., 8 Heriot Row, Edinburgh
Forman, Miss, 6 Drummond Place, Edinburgh (2)
Forrest, Miss, 79 Keptie Street, Arbroath
Forrest, James B. L. Co Bank, Kirriemuir (2)
Foster, Mrs Johnston, Moor Park, Farnham, Surrey
Fothringham, Miss, Fothringham
Fothringham, W. Stewart, of Fothringham (4)
Francis, James, West Seaton (2)
Fraser, David, Architect, Carnoustie
Fraser, Gilbert, 39 Hill Street, Arbroath (2)
Fraser, Colonel G L., Kirkside, St Cyrus, Kincardineshire
Fraser, Miss M. E., 37 Cheyne Court, London, S.W.
Fraser, Mrs Patrick, 11 Dalhousie Terrace, Arbroath
Fraser, Norman, 28 Ogilvy Place, Arbroath
Fraser, Trustees of Patrick Allan, Hospitalfield, Arbroath (2)
Freeman, Alexander, Procurator-Fiscal, Forfar
Frere, Miss G. Bartle, 22 Bryanston Square, London, W.
Fullerton, Mrs Betsy, Benvue, Forfar
Galloway, D. Wishart, Brechin
Galloway, Robert, S.S.C., 41 Bruntsfield Gardens, Edinburgh
Galloway, W. F., Lily Cottage, Wellbank, by Dundee
Gammell, Col. J. H. H., of Lethendy, Meikleour (2)
Gammell, S. J., of Drumtochty Castle, Fordoun (2)
Gardyne, Lieut.-Colonel C Greenhill, of Finavon (2)
Gardyne, The Hon. Mrs Greenhill, Finavon (3)
Gardyne, J. W. Bruce, of Middleton, by Arbroath (4)
Gardyne, D. G. Bruce, 128 Sloane Street, London
Gauldie, James H., 9 Shandon Crescent, Edinburgh
Gavin, Hugh, 42 Hill Street, Arbroath
Geddes, John, 14 Applegate, Arbroath
Geekie, R., of Rosemount, Blairgowrie
Geyer, Hiermann J., 25 Perth Road, Dundee
Gibson, Mrs, Bankhead House, Forfar
Gibson, James, 36 Clerk Street, Brechin (2)
Gilbert, A. D 1 Princes Street, Arbroath
Gilmour, Sir John, Bart., of Montrave, Leven
Gilroy, Mrs, Castleroy, Broughty Ferry (2)
Gilroy, A. B., Castleroy, Broughty Ferry
Gilroy, Mrs, Alistair, Dallicot, Bridgenorth (3)
Gilroy, David R., Rowanbank, Broughty Ferry
Gilroy, George A., Rankeillour, Springfield, Fife
Gilruth, Mrs, Seaton, Auchmithie
Gilruth, J. D, M.B., Millgate, Arbroath
Glamis, Lord and Lady, Glamis Castle (2)
Glass, Mrs James, 11 Blackness Street, Dundee
Glen, James, Demondale, Arbroath
Gordon, Mrs, Threave Castle, Castle Douglas, N.B.
Gordon, Mrs, Ashludie, Monifieth
Gordon, Alexander D. L., Ashludie, Monifieth
Gordon, Major A. J., V.D., 1st F.V.A., Arbroath

Gordon, Miss, 8 Forres Street, Edinburgh (2)
Gordon, Captain and Lady F. Wolrige, Lawton House, Arbroath
Gordon, Miss I., 37 Queen's Crescent, Edinburgh (2)
Gordon, Mrs I. L., Trusta, Brechin
Gordon, John S., St Clement's, Forfar (2)
Gordon, Miss More, Charleton, Montrose
Gordon, Wm. St Clements, Forfar
Gordon, Col. W. A., V D., Angus Rifles, Arbroath
Gordon, Wm. J., W. S., Ferry House, Broughty Ferry
Gorrie, Dr, 148 Nethergate, Dundee
Gould, R. K., 2 West Newgate, Arbroath
Gowans, Wm., 111 Union Street, Glasgow
Grant, Provost and Mrs, Woodside, Arbroath (14)
Grant, Miss, Ogilvy Arms Hotel, Kirriemuir
Grant, Captain Forsyth, of Ecclesgreig, Montrose
Grant, George Smith, Auchorachan, Glenlivet
Grant, J. C., painter, 267 High Street, Arbroath
Grant, Wm., Balmoral Cottage, Arbroath (2)
Grant, Wm., 29 Howard Street, Arbroath
Grant, W. L., painter, 267 High Street, Arbroath
Gray, Mrs, of Carse Gray, Forfar
Gray, John Y., 4 Duff Street, Dundee
Greaves, Walter J., British Linen Bank, Arbroath
Greig, Miss, 1 Walker Place, Arbroath
Greig, James, 24 Bromar Road, Denmark Hill, London, S.E. (2)
Greig, James, Lindean, Perth Road, Dundee
Greig, Mrs Richard M'Gavin, Willowbrae, Dundee
Grewar, David W., 30 Gravesend, Arbroath
Grewar, James P., 62 Gravesend, Arbroath
Grimond, Alexander D., Dunmore, Dundee
Grimond, A. M., 1 Grosvenor Terrace, Dundee
Grimond, Mrs Joseph, Carbet Castle, Broughty Ferry
Grimond, Miss, Carbet Castle, Broughty Ferry
Grove, Miss, The College Hall, Byng Place, London
Grub, Rev. Charles, The Rectory, Montrose
Guthrie, Mrs. of Guthrie
Guthrie, Miss, St Mary's Tower, Birnam
Guthrie, Chas. J., Q.C., 13 Royal Circus, Edinburgh
Guthrie, D. C., of Craigie
Guthrie, James, Hope Park, Broughty Ferry
Haddon, Mrs, 24 Wardmill Road, Arbroath
Halden, Rev. Andrew, Manse, Inverkeilor (4)
Hall James, High Street, Brechin
Hall, William, Ethie Castle, Arbroath
Halley, E. B., 15 Belgrave Place, Edinburgh
Halley, J. H., Wallace Craigie Works, Dundee
Hamilton, C. G. Henderson, of Dalserf, Netherburn (2)
Hamilton, Geo G., Gowan Bank, Broughty Ferry
Harris, George, Millgate, Arbroath (2)
Harris, W. S., solicitor, 18 Westhall Gardens Edinburgh
Hay, Alex., solicitor, Ardloch, Forfar
Hay, David, Lunanbank, by Arbroath
Hay, John, S.S.C., 17 Hill Street, Edinburgh
Hay, John B, Windsor Terrace, Dundee
Henderson, Mrs, Upper Keith, East Lothian

Henderson, Mrs, 193 Blackness Road, Dundee (2)
Henderson, G. D. Clayhills, Captain R N, of Invergowrie, Dundee
Henderson, James, 22 Victoria Street, Arbroath
Hendry, Alexander, 1 Cairnie Place, Arbroath
Hendry, J. M, St Margaret's, Broughty Ferry
Herkless, Professor, St Andrews University
High, Miss, Tayview Place, Carnoustie
High, John C., High Street, Carnoustie
High, William, High Street, Arbroath
Hill, Charles, Sunnyside House, Forfar
Hill, Charles S, 22 Gowan Street, Arbroath
Hill, John C., Southwood Hall, Highgate, London, N. (2)
Hird, Alexander, Inchcape, Arbroath
Hobbs, James, The Knowe, Bothwell
Hogg, Miss, Mount Zion Brae, Arbroath
Hogg, Chas. P., C.E., 53 Bothwell Street, Glasgow
Hood, J F & Son, Arbroath (6)
Home, The Earl of K.T. (4)
Hood, Miss Lizzie, Westmuir, Kirriemuir
Horner, Miss 15 Embankment Gardens, Chelsea, London, S.W.
Howat, Rev James, Lochshade, Arbroath
Howden, Mrs. Mall House, Montrose
Howe, Alex., W.S., Moray Place, Edinburgh (2)
Hume, David, Barrelwell, Brechin (3)
Hume Robert, Addison Place, Arbroath
Hunt Rev J. M, Hill Road, Arbroath
Hutton, John, chemist 8 High Street, Brechin
Hunter, Douglas G., 32 Charlotte Square, Edinburgh
Hunter General, 87 Cadogan Gardens, London S.W.
Hunter, Miss, do., do.
Hunter, Miss, Arbroath
Hunter, G., Bonnington, Arbroath
Hunter, James, jr., of Horn, Willowbank, Carnoustie
Hunter, Lord Provost, Dundee
Hunter, W. O, 3 Drapers Gardens, Throgmorton Street, London, E.C.
Hutchison, David, 1 West Port, Arbroath
Hynd, James, North Mains of Ethie, Inverkeilor (2)
Hynd, Thomas M., Nether Kelly, Arbroath
Hynd, William, 12 Dudhope Place, Dundee
Imrie, Colonel Blair, of Lunan
Inglis Alexander, Post Office, Inverkeilor
Inverarity, James M., 10 Regent Place, Shawlands Glasgow
Inverarity, William S., jr., do do.
Inverclyde, The Lady, Castle Wemyss, Wemyss Bay
Ireland, James, East Balmirmer
Ionides, Mrs C., 7 Lansdowne Place, West Brighton
Irvine, Mrs William, 7 Poets' Lane, Brechin
Irvine, William B, Morgan Academy, Dundee
Jack, James F., 102 High Street, Arbroath
Jackson, Mrs J. R., Kirkbuddo House, Forfar (2)
Jackson, Major-General W., Folkestone
Jalland, Boswell G., Ochterlony House, Guthrie
Jamieson, Mrs, 35 Fergus Street, Arbroath
Jamieson, David, Lochton, Arbroath

Jamieson, James, Gowan Park, Arbroath (10)
Jamieson, Miss, 14 Buckingham Terrace, Edinburgh
Jamieson, John, of Denfield
Jamieson, Mr and Mrs James Auldjo, 14 Buckingham Terrace, Edinburgh (2)
Japp, William, of Broomhall, Glenisla
Jarman, J., Jarman's Hotel, Forfar
Jarron, J. A , Arbikie, Lunan
Jarvis Brothers, Forfar (2)
Jebb, Sir R. C., M.P., Springfield, Cambridge
Jeffrey, John D., 25½ West Abbey Street, Arbroath
Jenkins, Misses, 30 Jamieson Street, Arbroath (2)
Johnston, Alexander, junr., Woodbank, Forfar
Johnston, David, 35 Commerce Street, Arbroath
Johnston, Henry, Q.C , Sheriff of Forfarshire
Johnston, James, 15 Panmure Place, Montrose (2)
Johnston, William, 28 Victoria Street, Arbroath
Johnston, W., jr., Rosemount, Brechin
Keith, Jas., C.E., Dunottar, Brondesbury, London
Keith, Jas. B.,   do.   do.
Keith, Robert, Ivybank, West Ferry (4)
Kelly, Dr Richard, The Kepties, Arbroath (2)
Kelman, Mrs J , Rosebank Villa, W. Newport, Fife
Kermath, Wm R , Chestney House, St Andrews
Kerr, Mrs Oakbank, Madeira Street, Dundee
Kidd, Robert J.P , Broughty Ferry
Kidd, Wm , stationer, Whitehall Street, Dundee (2)
Kinloch, Sir John, Bart., M.P., of Kinloch, Meigle
Kinloch, Dowager Lady, Meigle House, Alyth
Kinloch, Major General Alexander A. A., of Logie, Kirriemuir
Kinloch, Miss, of Logie (4)
Kinnaird, The Lord, Rossie Priory, Inchture
Kinnear, Jas, M.A., Keptie Public School, Arbroath
Kinnear, Wm., M.B., C.M., 39 Tay Street Dundee
Kintore, The Earl of, G.C.M.G., 5 Portman Street, London, W. (2)
Kirk, Sir John, G.C.M.G., K.C.B., Wavertree, Sevenoaks, Kent (2)
Knowles, D. C., Brechin (2)
Kydd, Alex. B., Ferryden Farm, Montrose
Kydd, James, Scryne, Carnoustie
Kyllacky, Lord, 6 Randolph Crescent, Edinburgh
Lacey, The Lady Helen, 29 Cavendish Road, St John's Wood, London
Lackie, David, John Street, Montrose
Laing, Alex., Sydenham Terrace, Newcastle (2)
Laing, Dr David, Captain, 1st F.V.A., Maule Street, Arbroath
Laing, J. H. W , M.B., 9 Tay Square, Dundee
Laing, Thos. J. M'L., Binnericht, Dundee
Laird, Mrs, 47 Albert Street, Dundee (2)
Laird, W. G., Forfar
Lamb, Mr and Mrs, Lochmalony, Cupar Fife (2)
Lamb, David I., Beechwood, Dunkeld (2)
Lamb, John, Glencadam, Brechin (2)
Lamb, J. H., The Latch, Brechin
Lamb, Martin B , Argyle Street, Brechin
Lamb, W., Blindwells, by Arbroath
Laurence, J., 3-4 Charing Cross Mansions, Glasgow
Law, James, engineer, East Grimsby, Arbroath
Lawson, Wm , 28 Magdalen Yard Road, Dundee
Leadingham, David, Bishoploch, by Arbroath (2)
Lee, Sheriff, Magungie, Arbroath (2)
Leng, Sir John, Bart., M.P., Dundee (4)
Leslie, Mrs E. J., Lochlea, Arbroath (2)
Leslie, J. G., Millgate, Arbroath
Leslie, W. M., Marine Place, Hawkhill, Dundee
Lesslie, C. H., dentist, Arbroath
Leycester, Mrs, Tofthall, Knutsford (2)
Library, Public, Arbroath
Lindsay, Mrs, Cluny Place, off Perth Road, Dundee
Lindsay, Miss, 2 Gillespie Terrace, St Andrews
Lindsay, James, West Mains, Kinblethmont
Lindsay, Mr and Mrs D. C. Rutherford, of Ashintully Castle, Blairgowrie (4)
Lindsay, Robert, West Mains, Kinblethmont (4)
Lindsay, Thomas, 224 High Street, Arbroath
Lindsay, Lieut.-Col. W T., Glenthorpe, Cowley, Oxon
Littlejohn, David, 33 Commerce Street, Arbroath
Llangattock, Lord, The Hendre, Monmouth (2)
Locke, Robert, 14 Paton's Lane, Dundee
Long, Miss, Grand Parade, Portsmouth
Longair, William, 21 Albany Terrace, Dundee
Lord, George H , 26 Magdalene Yard Road, Dundee
Lorimer, Henry, 81 High Street, Arbroath
Low, Alexander, West Port, Arbroath
Low, James A , Glenesk, Bushhill Park, New Enfield, London, N
Low, James F., Monifieth
Low, James G , Cranesmeadow, Montrose
Low, Malcolm, St Margarets, Grovehill, South Woodford, W.
Low, Samuel M., Monifieth
Low, Walter, Strathmore, Tottenham, London (2)
Low, Mrs William, Taymount, Dundee
Low, William, Tighnamuirn Monifieth
Lowson, Mrs, 12½ West Port, Arbroath
Lowson, Miss, Annesley, Arbroath
Lowson, Alexander, Governor of Poorhouse, Forfar
Lowson, A. D., Elmbank, Arbroath (2)
Lowson, A. P , 72 Keptie Street, Arbroath
Lowson, George, Balgavies, Forfar (2)
Lowson, John, Thornlea, Forfar
Luis, Theo. G., Major 1st F.V. Artillery, Bloomfield, Lochee
Lumsden, Mrs, Balmedie, Aberdeenshire (4)
Lumsden, Colonel, Langley Park, Montrose
Lyall, Mrs C., Old Montrose, Montrose
Lyall, Herbert, of Old Montrose, Montrose
Lyall, David, of Gallery, &c , by Montrose
Lyell, Mrs, Gardyne Castle
Lyell, Alexander, of Gardyne
Lyell, David, Gardyne Castle
Lyell, Sir L , Bart., M.P , of Kinnordy (4)
Lyon, The Hon. Francis Bowes, Glamis Castle
Lyon, The Hon Patrick Bowes,   do.   do.
Malcolm, Andrew, Dunfermline
Malcolm, John D , 13 Portman Street, London, W.
Marr, Wm. T., Ladysmith Place, Step Row, Dundee

M'Bain, J. M., F.S.A, Scot., banker, Arbroath
M'Bain, Norman, Captain 1st F.V A , Arbroath
M'Bain, Henry, Captain, Surma Valley Light Horse, Sylket, India
M'Bain, Frank, tea planter, Sylket, India
M'Bain, Jas. A. D., Bombay
M'Bain, Maurice, Inspector, Scottish Provident Institution
M'Corquodale, D. A., Carnoustie
M'Crae, James M'Donald, *Guide* Office, Arbroath
M'Culloch, Alex., A.M. Inst. C.E., 25 Gayfield Square, Edinburgh
M'Donald, Sinclair G., 10 Clarendon Terrace, Dundee
Macdonald, W. K., Town Clerk, Arbroath (20)
Macdonald, J. M. L., of Wallabadah, New South Wales
Macdonald, H. L., do., do.
Macdonald, Miss Isabel, Wallabadah, New South Wales
Macdonald, Miss E. G., do., do.
Macdonald, R. L., do., do
Macdonald, C. L., do., do.
Macdonald, F. F., Windmill House, Arbroath (8)
Macdonald, Miss I. M., M.B., 47 Seymour Street, London W. (2)
Macdonald, Miss Louisa, M.A., The University, Sydney, N S W. (4)
Macdonald, Miss J. C. C., Ballintuim (12)
Macdonald, Mr and Mrs Alexander, of Erudgere, New South Wales
Macdonald, Miss Flora A., Erudgere, Mudgee. Sydney, New South Wales
Macdonald, Miss Alison N., Erudgere, Mudgee, New South Wales
Macdonald, Ronald A. L., Erudgere, Mudgee, New South Wales
Macdonald, The Rev F. R., Parish Church, Coupar Angus.
Macdonald, Miss, 31 Marketgate, Arbroath (2)
M'Dougall, James, Provost, Forfar
M'Dougall, Rev J E, of Springfield, Arbroath (2)
McGavin, Robert, Ballumbie. Dundee (2)
McGaw, Miss, Mickleham, Downs Dorking (2)
McGrady, Henry, Arnhall Dundee (6)
Macgregor, Mrs H , Bookseller, 86 High Street, Dundee (3)
Macgregor, Miss, of Abbethune (2)
Macgregor, Rev. J. Robertson, 11 Hill Terrace, Arbroath
Macgregor, Mrs Walter A., 84 Cromwell Road, London. S.W. (2)
MacHardy, A.. of Newbarns. Town Clerk, Forfar
M'Innes, Mrs George, 1 Nairne Place, Dundee
MacIntosh. A. B., 8 York Terrace, Kensal Rise. London, W.
M'Intosh, James, 41 Kinnaird Street, Arbroath
M'Intyre. Archibald, Stanley Cottage, Broughty Ferry
Mackay, Mrs. 32 Addison Place, Arbroath
Mackay, John, S.S.C.. 37 York Place, Edinburgh

Mackay, Alexander, C.A., Messrs Mackay & Mess, Albert Square, Dundee
Mackay, Sir James L., K.C.I.E., 7 Seamore Place, Mayfair, London, W. (2)
Mackay, W. S , Lorneville, Tay Street, Newport, Fife
Mackie, David, St Katherines, West Ferry (2)
Mackenzie, J R , 145 High Street, Arbroath
Mackenzie, Rev. Kenneth, 23 Magdalen Yard Road, Dundee
Mackenzie, Thomas A , 49 Queen Victoria Street, London, E.C.
Mackenzie, William, Harecraig. Broughty Ferry (2)
McKinlay, J. G., Bell Rock Brewery, Arbroath
Mackintosh, James, Solicitor, Arbroath
Mackintosh, R M. C., 29 Marketgate, Arbroath
Mackintosh, Major, Maulesbank House, Arbroath
Mackintosh, Mrs W. F., do., do.
McLaren, Lawrence, M R.C.V.S , 50 City Road, Brechin
McLean, Misses, Duncarse, Dundee (2)
McLean. James, Builder, 56 North Street, Forfar
MacLean, General, C B , C.I E., Palmerston Shanklin, Isle of Wight
MacLean, Lieut. C. K , R N., H.M.S. "Prince George." Channel Squadron
MacLean, J. A , Union Bank House, Forfar
McLean, William L., 62 North Street, Forfar
McLeish, Miss C. R., Westfield Place, Dundee (2)
McLellan. R . Garnock House. Brechin
M'Leod. Fred W., 15 Cairnie Street, Arbroath
Macmaster, Rev Hugh, The Manse Dunnichen
M'Neill, D., Chief-Constable, Arbroath
M'Phee, Mrs. 15 Queen Street, Broughty Ferry
M'Pherson John R , *Dispatch* Office, Forfar (2)
M'Wattie, James, Commerce Street Arbroath
Malcolm, Mrs, The Oaks, Lochgelly
Mann, Robert M., 21 Glassford Street, Glasgow (2)
Manning, John William, Free Library, Brechin (2)
Marchant, Charles, senr , 218 Broomielaw Street, Glasgow
Marchant, Charles, jun., 377 Argyle Street, Glasgow
Marshall, Mrs. 11 Peep o' Day Lane, Dundee
Martin, Isobel A. C , 32 Mount Road, Montrose
Martin, James, 183 West George Street, Glasgow
Mason, Ed., Mus Bac., Hill Place, Arbroath (2)
Mason, T , 115 St Martin's Lane, London, W.C. (3)
Masson, John, Hedderwick Cottage, Montrose
Mather, Joseph, 3 Cheyne Street, Edinburgh
Mathewson, Maggie A. C., Tuttie's Nook, Arbroath
Mathewson, Lizzie C., do do.
Mathewson, David, 2 North Fort Street, Leith
Mathewson, E. W., Brothock Bridge, Arbroath
Mathewson, James L., Tuttie's Nook, Arbroath
Maule, The Hon. Mrs, 53 Lancaster Gate, London (4)
Meigle, Thomas, Boghead
Melville, Mrs Swinton S., Starmead, Workingham, Berks
Melville, Walker, S , Douglas Bank, Dundee
Melvin, Alexander, 4 Savile Terrace, Edinburgh
Melvin, John, Craigrowan, Forfar

Melvin, Robert, Kinloch Terrace, Arbroath
Melvin, W. F, Dilkûsha, Montrose
Merry, George R., M.A., LL.D., 14 Dudhope Terrace, Dundee
Metcalfe, Lady Dempster, of Dunnichen
Middleton, Rev. Al., B.D., Gardner Memorial Church, Brechin
Middleton, Alexander, High Street, Montrose
Middleton, William, 13 Millgate, Arbroath
Middleton, William, jun., 54 High Street, Arbroath
Mill, Dr A. King, Kirriemuir
Mill, George, 19 Eyre Crescent, Edinburgh
Mill, George, 9 West Claremont Street, Edinburgh
Mill, George Symers, M.D., Ossett, Yorks
Mill, Miss Helen Bremner, Hill House, Arbroath
Millar, Major R. Hoyer, The Links, Montrose (2)
Millar, R. C. Hoyer, Mall Park, Montrose
Miller, Miss, Earle House, Broughty Ferry
Miller, William, 20 Thirlestane Road, Edinburgh
Milligan, Robert, 7 Keptie Street, Arbroath (2)
Mills, W. B., publisher, Kirriemuir
Miln, George, 4 Springfield Terrace, Arbroath
Miln R., of Woodhill United Service Club, 14 Queen Street, Edinburgh
Milne, Miss, Cherrybank, Forfar (2)
Milne, Miss, 18 Guthrie Port, Arbroath
Milne Mrs, Roods Street, Kirriemuir
Milne, Charles, 164 High Street, Arbroath (2)
Milne, C. H., Rector, High School, Arbroath
Milne, D., Captain 3rd V.B.R.H., Eadie Bank, Wellington Street, Dundee
Milne, Mrs D. E, Denfield Cottage, Logie by Montrose
Milne, George G., 56 High Street, Montrose
Milne, James, 4 Hamilton Green, Arbroath
Milne, John Gardyne, Green Park, Montrose
Milne, W. L., Lindsay Lodge, Hampton Hill, Middlesex (4)
Minto, The Earl of, G.C.M.G., Government House, Ottawa, Canada
Minto, Farquharson, 1 Hillend Road, Arbroath
Mitchell, Mrs, Douglasleigh, Carnoustie (4)
Mitchell, Honourable Mrs, Llanfrechfa Grange, Caerleon
Mitchell, Mrs, 7 Arrott Street, Arbroath
Mitchell, Mrs, Junction Cottage, Broughty Ferry
Mitchell, Miss, 50 High Street, Arbroath
Mitchell, Miss, Arbroath
Mitchell, Miss, Newbigging, Lethnot, Brechin
Mitchell, Miss, Nether Nigvie, Kirriemuir
Mitchell, Miss Agnes, Waverley House, Brechin
Mitchell, Rev. Alex., Ferndene, Brechin
Mitchell, Ben, Swan Street, Brechin
Mitchell, Charles, Airliesacl0, Brechin
Mitchell, J., editor, *Dundee Courier*
Mitchell, John, 13 Brandon Street, Edinburgh
Mitchell, John, Boysack, Arbroath
Mitchell, Miss, 30A High Street, Brechin
Mitford, The Lady Clementine, Batsford Park, Moreton-in-Marsh
Moffat, Lieutenant, Mount Fredith, Forfar

Moir, Jas, bank agent, St. George's Cross, Glasgow
Moir, Sergt. W., 2nd Gordon Highlanders, 8 North Street, Forfar
Moir, William, Panmure Cottage, Montrose
Moir, William, junr., The Retreat, Montrose (2)
Mollison, James Lloyd's Register, Glasgow
Moncur, John W., burgh engineer, Sunderland
Monro, T. K, M. D., 10 Clairmont Gardens, Glasgow
Moon, Dr Steele, 15, King Street, Dundee
Morgan, The Lady Katharine, Ashford Court, Ludlow
Morgan, Mrs, City Road U.P. Manse, Brechin
Morgan, David, South Mains of Ethie, Arbroath (2)
Morgan, Trooper J. W., 1st F L H., Grange of Conon, Arbroath (2)
Morison J. P., banker, Carnoustie
Morley, Right Hon. John, M.P., 57 Elm Park Gardens, South Kensington, S.W.
Morrison, John, Summerwood, West Albany Terrace, Dundee
Morison, Miss, The College Hall, Byng Place, London (2)
Morton, John, 12 Robert Street, Forfar
Muckart, D., St Vigeans
Mudie, Mrs D., 11 Watt Street, Dundee
Mudie, John, Tintagel, Clepington Road, Dundee
Mudie, Mrs, Craigowan, Broughty Ferry
Mudie, Captain R. A., Craigowan, Broughty Ferry
Mudie, Robert, Corona, Broughty Ferry
Muir, Mr and Mrs Jas., Abbey Bank, Arbroath (2)
Munro, H. T., Lindertis, Kirriemuir
Murdoch, James A., Capt. Tay Div. Royal Engineers S.M., Foxmount Broughty Ferry
Murison, Miss 6 Buckingham Terrace, Glasgow (4)
Murray, Alexander, The Elms, Montrose
Murray, A. R McLean, Grove House, Brechin
Murray, A. S., LL.D., F.S.A., British Museum, London (4)
Murray, George R. N, F.R.S., F.L.S, British Museum (Natural History), London, S W.
Murray, Rev. James, U P. Manse, Arbroath
Murray, William, 61 Hawkhill, Dundee (2)
Myles, Dr, Brechin
Myles, A W., County Clerk of Forfarshire, Forfar
Myles, R. Freer, Solicitor, Forfar
Myles, Chas. Y., Wellbank, Arbroath
Napier, Charles, Pendleton, Manchester
Napier, John, East Abbey Street, Arbroath
Naysmith, A., Chemist, Arbroath
Neish, William, of The Laws (4)
Neish, Colin G., of Tannadyce (4)
Neish, E. W., of Tannadyce (2)
Neish, Mrs Charles, 11 Hereford Square, London, S W. (3)
Neish, Mrs, 24 St Mary Street, Dundee
Newill, Misses A. and H., 20 Charles Road, S. Leonards-on-Sea
Nicol, James, Fern Dene, Brechin
Nicoll, Mrs, Broombank, Forfar (2)
Nicoll, P. S., 10 Windsor Street, Dundee

Nimmo, Misses, 4 Thornbank. Newport
Northesk, The Countess of
Northesk, The Dowager-Countess of (8)
Ochterlony, Sir David F., Bart., of Ochterlony (2)
Ogg, Sir William Anderson Dulwich, London, S.E (2)
Ogg, Donald, Kinblethmont, by Arbroath
Ogg, Mrs John 4 Brechin Road, Arbroath
Ogg, William A., manufacturer, Arbroath (2)
Ogg Wm. S., 23 Hayswell Road, Arbroath (2)
Ogilvie, Mrs G., Westlands, Broughty Ferry
Ogilvie, Mrs W., Airlie Lodge, Broughty Ferry
Ogilvie, W. M., Royal Bank House, Lochee
Ogilvy, Sir Reginald, Bart., of Inverquharity House, Strathmartine
Ogilvy, Mrs. of Clova, Balnaboth, Kirriemuir
Ogilvy, Miss A., 5 St Alban's Mansions, Kensington Court, London, W
Ogilvy, Mrs Charles, Kilnbank, Kirriemuir
Ogilvy, H. Nisbet Hamilton, Biel, Prestonkirk, East Lothian
Ogilvy, Mrs James Wedderburn, Rannagulzion, Blairgowrie (4)
Ogilvy, John, Inshewan
Ogilvy, John, Lisden, Kirriemuir
Ogilvy, Robert F., manufacturer, Kirriemuir
Ogilvy, Lieut. Wm., Kirriemuir
Ogilvy, Wm., manufacturer, Kirriemuir
Ogilvy, Major Wedderburn, Ruthven, Meigle
Oliver, Adam, S.S.C., Arbroath (2)
Ouchterlony, Colonel J. H., of The Guynd
Panton, D. S., Schoolhouse, Glamis
Parker, Charles, Cuba Cottage, Broughty Ferry
Parkinson, Dr T. W., Westwood, Brechin
Parsons, T. W., Addison Place, Arbroath
Paton, Mrs, Sunnyside House, Montrose (2)
Paton, David, M.D., Villa Rosa, Carnoustie
Paton, G. D., Barford, Warwick
Paton, James, chemist, 5 Merchiston Park, Edinburgh
Paton, John, S.S.C., D.C.S., 101 Marchmont Road, Edinburgh
Paton, John, 9 Meadow Place Buildings, Dundee (2)
Paterson, Charles S., South Milwaukee, U.S.A.
Paterson, James A., Ponderlaw. Arbroath
Paterson, Wm., W.S., 32 Charlotte Square, Edinburgh
Paul, Sir J. Balfour, Lyon King of Arms
Peareth, W. G., Princethorpe, Rugby (6)
Peddie, Bailie, Broughty Ferry
Perry, Mrs E. M. Warren, Perryville, Kinsale (4)
Peterkin, Dr., Forfar
Peters, James, 239 High Street, Arbroath
Peters, L., 27 Springfield, Dundee
Petrie, James Archibald, Clydeville, Bowling, Dumbartonshire
Philip, Alex., Panmure Street, Brechin
Phin, Mrs J., Cluny Place, Dundee
Pirie, Mrs, St Andrews House, Brechin
Pirie, Mrs Logie, Tottingworth Park, Heathfield, Sussex (3)

Playfair, The Lord, Lieut.-Colonel R.A., Fintray House, Aberdeenshire
Powell, Mrs Eyre, 19 Mellfont Avenue, Kingstown, Co. Dublin (2)
Powrie, Mrs, Reswallie, Forfar
Prain, Martin M. M., 32 Dundas Street, Edinburgh (2)
Primrose, James, Dunmore Village, Stirlingshire
Rae, James, jr., Panmure Place, Carnoustie
Rae, Robert, 9 St Vigeans Road, Arbroath
Rait, Colonel, C.B., of Anniston, Arbroath (2)
Rait, Miss, 3 Murray Park, St Andrews
Rait, Henry M., 1 Ulster Terrace, London, N.W.
Ralston, Andrew, Glamis (2)
Ramsay, Mrs, Howletts, Canterbury
Ramsay, Miss, do. do.
Ramsay, Miss E., do. do.
Ramsay, Miss N., do. do.
Ramsay, Provost, Hope Bank, Carnoustie (2)
Ramsay, Hon. Charles M., and Mrs Ramsay, Brechin Castle (2)
Ramsay, J. D., 87 St Vincent Street, Glasgow
Ramsay, Sir James, Bart., of Bamff, Alyth
Ramsay, Mrs, 27 Kyd Street, Arbroath
Rankin, Colonel J., V.D., Commanding 1st (City of Dundee) V.B.R.H., Drill Hall, Dundee
Raymond, Mrs George, Corfu, Greece
Reid, George, Royal Bank House, Arbroath
Reid, Minnie, 39 Hannah Street, Arbroath
Reid, William, The Gardens, Cortachy
Renny, General, C.S.I., 34 Evelyn Gardens, London, S.W.
Renny, Mrs, 8 Douglas Terrace, Broughty Ferry
Renny, Samuel, Jock's Lodge, Arbroath (2)
Rennie, John, Crudie, Arbroath
Rew, Mrs, 73 Keptie Street, Arbroath
Richardson, Major E. Hantonville (late 45th Regiment), Panbride House, Carnoustie (2)
Richardson, Mrs Hantonville, Panbride House, Carnoustie (2)
Riley, Thomas, 15 St Vigeans Road, Arbroath
Ritchie, Miss, 50 High Street, Arbroath
Ritchie, David, Hopeville, Dowanhill Gardens, Glasgow (4)
Ritchie, David, Anerley, Newport, Fife
Ritchie, Edward J., Cliffburn, Arbroath
Ritchie, P. J., Rio de Janeiro
Ritchie, Rev. T. L, St James' Free Church, Airlie House, Arboretum Road, Edinburgh (2)
Robberds, Rev. W. J. F., M.A., Redcliffe Vicarage, Bristol
Roberts, A. M., Town Clerk, Dumbarton
Robertson, Miss Agnes Brown, Dudhope House, Dundee (2)
Robertson, Alex., West Beach Cottage, Broughty Ferry
Robertson, Alex., of Burnside, Forfar (2)
Robertson, Mrs, do. do. (2)
Robertson, E. H., 36 Melville Street, Edinburgh
Robertson, W. Hope, 24 Coates Gardens, Edinburgh

Robertson, James, 24 Millgate, Arbroath
Robertson, James, Crawford Lodge, Carnoustie
Robertson, John, solicitor, 63 York Place, Edinburgh
Robertson, John Chas., Dudhope House, Dundee (2)
Robertson, John Earl, Invercarse
Robertson, J. M. (Captain of Port Elizabeth Town Guard)
Robertson, Miss Mary, Leysmill, Arbroath
Robertson, R. Archd., Dudhope House, Dundee
Robertson, Thos., Farnell, Trinity Road, Wandsworth Common, London, S.W.
Robertson, Wm., slater, Carnoustie
Robertson, Wm., jr., Glasgow
Robertson, Wm., Town Clerk's Office, Arbroath
Robertson, W. Brown, Dudhope House, Dundee (3)
Robertson, W. G., Warslap, Arbroath
Robinson, Miss, 4 Addison Crescent, Kensington, London, W.
Rodakowski, The Lady Dora, 72 Lancaster Gate, London, W.
Rollo, W. J., Commercial Bank, Arbroath
Romilly, The Lady Arabella, 56 Eccleston Square, London, S.W.
Rorison, The Very Rev. Vincent L., D.D., Dean of St Andrews, The Deanery, Perth
Ross, Andrew, S.S.C., Edinburgh
Ross, Miss Kate, 3 Upper Craigo Street, Montrose
Ross, James D., 35 Park Road, Brechin
Ross, John, Coul Farm, Fife
Ross, W., solicitor, Montrose
Royal Highlanders, 3rd V.B., per Colonel Smith, Dundee
Russell, John, M.D., 9 Hill Terrace, Arbroath
Rust, Robert, Cemetery Lodge, Arbroath
Rutherford, James, 18 Springfield, Dundee
Ruxton, James, chemist, 63 Keptie Street, Arbroath
Ruxton, James, 20 Brunton Place, London Road, Edinburgh
St Andrews, Bishop of, Pitfour, Glencarse, Perthshire
Salmond, Alex H., 201 High Street, Arbroath
Salmond, The Rev. Charles A., 9 Cluny Drive, Edinburgh
Salmond, D., Eldermere, Ilkley in Wharfdale, Yorkshire
Salmond, D. S., 137 West George Street, Glasgow
Salmond, Mrs George, 201 High Street, Arbroath
Salmond, Geo. B., Perth Road, Dundee
Salmond, John M., 201 High Street, Arbroath
Salmond, Joseph, Alexandra Place, Arbroath
Salmond, J. B., Springbank, Hillend Road, Arbroath
Salmond, James, Jr , do. do. do.
Salmond, Georgia Jean, do. do.
Salmond, Joseph M., 20 W. Abbey Street, Arbroath
Salmond, Major P. N., Easby Drive, Ilkley in Wharfdale, Yorkshire
Salmond, Robert, 7 St Margaret's Road, Edinburgh
Salmond, Wm. M., W. Abbey Street, Arbroath
Sandeman, D. T., 32 Buckingham Terrace, Glasgow
Sandeman, Mrs Stewart, Stanley, Perthshire

Sanderson, A., 25 Learmonth Terrace, Edinburgh
Sands, Miss, 12 Lowndes Street, London, S.W.
Sangster, Richard G., 109 Ferry Road, Dundee
Scott, Mrs, 2 Rockfield Terrace, Dundee (2)
Scott, Mrs, 9 Victoria Street, Arbroath
Scott, Miss, 26 Millgate Loan, do.
Scott, Miss, of Brotherton (2)
Scott, Alexander Keptie Angle, Arbroath
Scott, Ernest, 6 Millgate Loan, do.
Scott, Geo. A , Park House, Brechin
Scott, James, solicitor, do.
Scott, James, 9 Victoria Street, Arbroath (3)
Scott, James Addison, Newton of Arbirlot
Scott, James B., Keptie Angle, Arbroath
Scott, Rev. J. Moffat, Free Ladyloan Manse, Arbroath
Scott, Rev. Robert, Craig Manse, Montrose (2)
Scott, Thomas, Keptie Angle, Arbroath
Scott, William, do , do.
Scott, Wm. Erskine, Balhall, Brechin (2)
Scrimgeour, Wm., 32 High Street, Dundee
Scrymgeour, Charles, Margaret Bank, Newport-on-Tay
Scullen, Mrs, 130 Scouringburn, Dundee
Seaton, Mrs Lavinia, 33 Haywell Road, Arbroath
Selby, Forbes, High Street, Arbroath
Selby, James, Forrest House, Hillside, Montrose (2)
Selby, John, High Street, Arbroath
Service, Rev. W. J. Nichol, B.D., The Manse, Arbroath (2)
Shanks, Alex., 25 Ebury Street, London, S.W. (2)
Sharp, R. B., Fernhall, Dundee (2)
Shaw, David, 1 Thistle Court, Edinburgh
Shaw, W., Town House, Arbroath (2)
Shepherd, W., 39 Castle Street, Forfar (2)
Shepherd, W. L., 9 Carnegie Street, Arbroath
Sheriffs, George, Nolt Loan Road, Arbroath
Shiell, David G., Oatlea, Brechin (2)
Shiell, Jack, Brechin (2)
Shiell, Mrs, Brechin (2)
Shiell, John, Brechin
Shiell, Mrs John, Cairney, Cupar Fife
Sim, Miss, Victoria Café, Arbroath
Sim, Robert M., Arbroath
Sime, G., Crawford Lodge, Dundee (2)
Sinclair, Mrs, 104 Caldrum Street, Dundee
Sinclair, Captain John, M.P., 101 Mount Street, London, W.
Sinclair, Robert, M.D., Dundee
Sinclair, R. L., bookseller, Montrose
Small, James, of Dirnavean, Perthshire (2)
Small, David, seedsman, Brechin (2)
Smart, David, 14 Grantham Road, Clapham, London, S.W.
Smart, James, 25 Church Street, Brechin
Smieton, Jas., Panmure Villa, Broughty Ferry (2)
Smith, The Lady Esther, Greenlands
Smith, Col. W., V.D., Binn Cottage, Dundee (6)
Smith, Isabella B., do., do.
Smith, Susan, do., do.
Smith, Alex. Duncan, advocate, Edinburgh

Smith, Mrs, 4 Garland Place, Dundee
Smith, Mrs A , 22 Guthrie Port, Arbroath (2)
Smith, Adam, High Street, Arbroath
Smith, Alex., White Hart Hotel, Arbroath (2)
Smith, Alex S., Hillside, Arbroath (2)
Smith, Mrs David, 172 Montrose Street, Brechin (2)
Smith, David, 7 Craigie Terrace, Dundee
Smith, Henry. 13 Ann Street, Arbroath
Smith, Sheriff J. Campbell, The Rosaire, Dundee
Smith, Miss J., Woodlands, Arbroath
Smith, James, 41 Millgate Loan, Arbroath
Smith, James, 16 West Mary Street, Arbroath
Smith, John, jr., Chapel Park, Forfar
Smith, John Rae, bookseller, 57 Union Street, Aberdeen
Smith, Joseph C., 73 Keptie Street, Arbroath
Smith, Robert, solicitor, Dundee
Smith, Wm. C , Leabank, West Ferry
Smythe, Mrs Armstrong, of Dunninald, Montrose (4)
Sola, Madame, c/o Miss Macdonald, Windmill House, Arbroath
Soote, The Misses, Reres House, Broughty Ferry (4)
Soutar, J. S., junr., 106 High Street, Arbroath
Soutar, Robert, M.D., Castelsteel, Montrose
Soutar, W. F., Annfield, Carnoustie (4)
Soutter, J. B., Fairfield, Hamilton
Southesk, The Earl of, K T., Kinnaird Castle (4)
Southesk, The Countess of,   do.   (4)
Speid, Miss, of Forneth, Dunkeld
Spence, A. G., Wickham Court Farm, Beckenham, Kent
Spence, Stuart, Abertay, Bothwell
Spiers, Fulton, East Rockfield, Dundee (2)
Stanley, The Hon. Maude, 32 Smith Sq., Westminster
Stansfeld, Capt., of Dunninald, Montrose (5)
Steel, Mrs Flora Annie, 29 Palace Gate. London (2)
Steele, David, Royal Bank, Forfar
Steven, Thomas, Newton Place, Blairgowrie
Stevenson, Rev. John, LL.D., Glamis
Stevenson. Mrs, 116 Inverness Terrace, London, W.
Stewart, Mrs, 13 Peter Street, Dublin
Stewart, Rev. A. Morris, M.A., Free High Manse, Arbroath
Stewart, Rev. Charles, B.D., The Manse, Tannadice, Forfar
Stewart, David, Fern Villa, Perth Road, Dundee
Stewart, Donald, depute sheriff clerk, Forfar
Stewart, Rev. D. Melville, St Margaret's Manse, Arbroath
Stewart, William, burgh surveyor, Arbroath
Stewart, W. W., 5 Bow Church Yard, London, E.C.
Stone, Dr V., Montrose
Storrer, Andrew P., 116 High Street, Arbroath
Stow, Mrs, 12 Maresfield Gardens, Hampstead, London, N.W.
Stracey, Mrs Eustace, Dunninald, Montrose
Strachan, Miss, High Street, Arbroath
Strachan, Alexander D., wood and coal merchant, Forfar (2)
Strachan, Alex. N., Towernook, Arbroath
Strachan, Fred, Alexandra Place, Arbroath

Strachan, James M., 16 High Street, Brechin
Strachan, Rev. John, The Manse, Cortachy
Strachan, W. B., bookseller, Arbroath
Strathmore, The Earl of, Glamis Castle (6)
Strathmore, The Countess of,   do.
Strong, J., The Academy, Montrose
Stuart, C. Lindsay, Montrose
Stuart, John, 29 Strawberry Bank, Dundee (2)
Stuart, Rev J. and Mrs Niblock-Stuart, The Manse, Montrose (3)
Stuart, Robert, 19 Dalhousie Place, Arbroath
Sturrock, W. C., 63 Craiglea Drive, Edinburgh
Sutherland, Rev. George S., Free St Paul's Manse, Montrose
Sutherland, J. T., 260 High Street, Arbroath
Suttie, Mrs, Union Villa, Arbroath (3)
Swain, John & Son, Ltd., per A. Dargavel, managing director, 58 Farringdon Street, E.C.
Swan, Mrs W. R., Ogilvy Place, Arbroath
Swinburne, Miss, of Marcus
Symon, A. A., Lochland Cottage, Arbroath
Tarbet, James, 9 Albert Street, Forfar
Tayler, Mrs, 19 Rubislaw Terrace, Aberdeen
Taylor, Mrs J. B., Affleck, Monikie, near Dundee (2)
Taylor, John, Newbank Cottage, Letham, Forfar
Taylor, John Adam, 34 Helen Street, Arbroath
Taylor, R. M., Towerbank, Arbroath
Taylor, Thomas, Balmullie Mill, Inverkeilor
Taylor, James,   do.,   do.
Taylor, Rev. W., M.A., Montrose
Tailyour, Miss Renny, Balmedie, Aberdeenshire
Tailyour, Colonel H. W. Renny, Shrewsbury House, Mirrion, Co. Dublin
Tailyour, W. Stewart, Ormesby, near Middlesbro'-on-Tees
Tait, W. A., 32 Charlotte Square, Edinburgh
Tennant, A., Bank of Scotland, Montrose
Thom, Wm., Auchterforfar, Forfar
Thomson. Mrs, Deuchar, Brechin (8)
Thomson, Alex., 4 Osborne Place, Dundee (2)
Thomson, A. M., Abbey Lodge, Arbroath
Thomson, G., Lochview, Hillend Road, Arbroath
Thomson, George Rutherford, Hill Place, Arbroath
Thomson, Lt.-Col. J. E., 44 South Street, St Andrews
Thomson, Robert, Station Road, Carnoustie
Thomson, Mrs Sinclair, 9 Devonshire Terrace, Hyde Park, London, W. (6)
Thomson, Wm., 13 Marchmont Crescent, Edinburgh
Thomson, W. M. Gordon, Red Court, Broughty Ferry
Thackeray, Capt. Fred. R. (late 74th Highlanders), Yarrow Road, 4 East Dereham, Norfolk
Tosh, Alexander, C.A., Reform Street, Dundee
Tosh, David, 31 West Port, Arbroath
Tosh, James, Shandford, Fern, Brechin (2)
Tough, James, Exchange Inn, Arbroath
Traill, Mrs, Viewfield, Arbroath (4)
Troup, Rev. G. E., M.A., West Free Church, Broughty Ferry
Tullibardine, The Marchioness of, Blair Castle, Blair Atholl

Tullis, David, Glencairn, Burnside, Rutherglen
Tullis, James T., The Anchorage, Burnside, Rutherglen
Tullis, John, Inchcape, Dennistoun, Glasgow (2)
Turnbull, Thomas, Harestanes, Jedburgh
Tyrie, Mrs, Woodmyre, Edzell
Varé, Madame, Rome
Vallentine, W. M'Inroy, Brechin
Vallentine, Ex-Provost, Brechin (2)
Walker, Alexander, 12 River Street, Brechin (2)
Walker, Bailie A. B., Carnoustie
Walker, Mrs Fountaine, 87 Cadogan Gardens, London (S.W.)
Walker, Fred., 62 Commercial Street, Dundee
Walker, Harry, 7 Clarendon Terrace, Dundee
Walker, H. Giles, Balgersho, Coupar Angus
Walker, Jane H., M.D., 62 Gower Street, London
Walker, Thos. H. H., 8 Melville Terrace, Dundee
Wallace, Mrs, 6 Kirkwood Street, Ibrox
Wallace, A. S., V.S., Millgate, Arbroath
Wallace, Geo. R., Towernook, Arbroath
Wallace, T. R., Victoria Street, Arbroath
Wannan, Dr W. A., 51 Marketgate, Arbroath
Watt, Alex., Inchcape, Paisley
Watson, Miss, Woodmuir Villa, West Newport, Fife
Watson, Charles H., West Park Road, Dundee
Watson, Edwin A., Norwood Cottage, West Newport, Fife
Watson, Forbes, 6 Greenmarket, Dundee
Watson, James, 5 Clarendon Terrace, Dundee
Watson, Robert F., of Hassendeanburn, Hawick (2)
Watt, George, Sheriff Court Buildings, Dundee
Watt, Rev. Hugh Geo., D.D., 14 Clarendon Terrace, Dundee
Watters, Douglas B., Nolt Loan Road, Arbroath
Webster, Francis, Ashbrook, Arbroath
Webster, G. K., 32 Milner Street, Lennox Gardens, London
Webster, Mrs H. Wedderburn, Beaulieu Villa, Gladstone Terrace, Carnoustie
Webster, Jas., 103 Magdalene Green, Dundee
Webster, Johnston, 11 Mansionhouse Road, Edinburgh
Webster, Miss M'Callum, Easton House, Elgin (2)
Webster, W. W., Denley, Arbroath
Wedderburn, Miss, Haines Hill, Twyford, Berks (2)
Wedderburn, Henry Scrymgeour, of Birkhill, Cupar Fife
Wedderburn, Dr Maclagan, 71 East High Street, Forfar (2)
Weinberg, Miss, Fernbrae, Dundee
Westwater, Henry, 3 Elgin Place, Arbroath (4)
Whamond, J. Robbie, 3 Crown Court, Old Broad Street, London, E.C.

Wharncliffe, The Earl of, Wortley Hall, Sheffield
Whimster, James, Rosehill, Montrose (2)
Whitehead, J. L., Elmbank, Broughty Ferry
Whiteman, F., Montrose
Whitton, Andrew, of Couston, Newtyle (2)
Whitton, D. P., 26 Exchange Street, Dundee (2)
Whyte, Mrs, 12 Market Street, Brechin (2)
Whyte, James S., 57 Guthrie Port, Arbroath
Wilkie, David, Ardmore, Kirriemuir (2)
Wilkie, James, Aberbrothock, Cavendish Road, Clapham, London, S.W.
Wilkie, James, solicitor, Kirriemuir (4)
Wilkie, James, 55 Kinnaird Street, Arbroath
Wilkie, John, Mount Florida, Glasgow
Will, John Shiress, Q.C., Ardovie, Brechin
Will, W. Watson, 1 St Agnes Place, Kennington Park, London, S.E.
Williamson, S., Coplay Neston, Cheshire
Williamson, William, 1 Carnegie Street, Arbroath (2)
Williamson, W. G., 22 Dishland Street, Arbroath
Willis, Mrs, The Rectory, Warrington
Wills, D. C., Town-Clerk, Montrose
Wills, George M., 1 Drapers' Gardens, London
Willsher, George, Pitpointie, Auchterhouse, Dundee
Wilson, Charles, Tayview, Arbroath
Wilson, David L., Holmlea, Arbroath
Wilson, D. T., 99 High Street, Arbroath (2)
Wilson, J. R., Helenbank, Carnoustie
Wilson, Thomas, Glamis Castle Gardens, Glamis
Wilson, William, Hill Road Factory, Arbroath
Windram, D., 181 Monument Road, Edgbaston, Birmingham (2)
Wishart, Mrs, 22 Barrack Street, Dundee
Wishart, George, Market Street, Forfar
Wright, Mrs E. W., Westby House, Forfar
Wyllie, David, 27 Hayswell Road, Arbroath
Wynton, J. F., 1 Cairnie Place, Arbroath
Wyse, H., sr., Royal Bank, Dundee
Wyse, Henry T., High School, Arbroath (2)
Wyse, R. C., 33 Lombard Street, London, E.C.
Yeaman, A., W.S., Edinburgh (2)
Y.M.C.A., Arbroath, per Mr A. Mather
Young, Mrs, of Lincluden, Villa Jeanne, Dinau, Côtes du Nord, France (5)
Young, Miss, Hospitalfield, Arbroath (2)
Young, C. S., 8 South Tay Street, Dundee
Young, James, Fordhouse, Montrose
Young, John, Montrose Academy, Montrose
Young, K. O. B., of Ascreavie, Kirriemuir (2)
Young, P., Scottscroft, 52 Avenue Road, Highgate, London, N.
Young, Peter, Mar's Hill, Wormit, Fife
Yule, Mrs, 20 Victoria Street, Arbroath

www.ingramcontent.com/pod-product-compliance
Lightning Source LLC
Chambersburg PA
CBHW080224170426
43192CB00015B/2739